Also by Virginia Postrel

THE FUTURE AND ITS ENEMIES

THE SUBSTANCE OF STYLE

THE POWER OF GLAMOUR

LONGING AND THE ART OF VISUAL PERSUASION

VIRGINIA POSTREL

Simon & Schuster

New York   London   Toronto   Sydney   New Delhi

Simon & Schuster
1230 Avenue of the Americas
New York, NY 10020

First Simon & Schuster hardcover edition November 2013

SIMON & SCHUSTER and colophon are registered trademarks of Simon & Schuster, Inc.

For information about special discounts for bulk purchases, please contact Simon & Schuster Special Sales at 1-866-506-1949 or business@simonandschuster.com.

The Simon & Schuster Speakers Bureau can bring authors to your live event. For more information or to book an event, contact the Simon & Schuster Speakers Bureau at 1-866-248-3049 or visit our website at www.simonspeakers.com.

Designed by Nancy Singer

Manufactured in the United States of America

10 9 8 7 6 5 4 3 2 1

Library of Congress Cataloging-in-Publication Data

Postrel, Virginia I., 1960-
   The power of glamour : longing and the art of visual persuasion / Virginia Postrel.—First [edition].
       pages cm
1. Aesthetics. 2. Glamour. I. Title.
   BH39.P66925 2013
   111'.85—dc23
                                         2013026988

ISBN 978-1-4165-6111-8
ISBN 978-1-4767-1887-3 (ebook)

TO STEVEN

CONTENTS

I.

THE NATURE OF GLAMOUR 1

ONE
THE MAGIC OF GLAMOUR 3

Icon The Aviator 24

Icon Smoking 28

TWO
INARTICULATE LONGINGS 31

Icon The Princess 49

Icon Wind Turbines 52

II.

THE ELEMENTS OF GLAMOUR 55

THREE
DREAMS OF FLIGHT AND TRANSFORMATION AND ESCAPE 57

Icon The Golden State 71

Icon The Makeover 75

FOUR

THE ART THAT CONCEALS ART   79

Icon Wirelessness   102

Icon The Superhero   105

FIVE

LEAVE SOMETHING TO THE IMAGINATION   109

Icon The Window   128

Icon Shanghai   131

III.

THE EVOLUTION OF GLAMOUR   135

SIX

FROM A MUSE OF FIRE TO THE GLEAM OF A THOUSAND LIGHTS   137

Icon The Horseman   162

Icon The Gibson Girl   166

SEVEN

THE WORLD OF TOMORROW   171

Icon The Suntan   200

Icon The Striding Woman   203

EIGHT

THE USES OF ENCHANTMENT   209

Acknowledgments   225

Notes   231

Index   257

THE POWER OF
GLAMOUR

I.

THE NATURE OF GLAMOUR

Toni Frissell Collection, Library of Congress

ONE

THE MAGIC OF
GLAMOUR

When she was four years old, Michaela DePrince saw a picture that changed her life. Then known as Mabinty Bangura, she was living in an orphanage in Sierra Leone; her father had been murdered during the country's civil war, and her mother had starved to death. Even among the orphans the little girl was an outcast, deemed an unadoptable "devil child" because of her rebellious personality and the vitiligo that left white patches on her dark skin.

One day, a discarded Western magazine blew against the orphanage's fence, carrying with it an image from a mysterious and distant world. "There was a lady on it, she was on her tippy-toes, in this pink, beautiful tutu," DePrince recalls. "I had never seen anything like this—a costume that stuck out with glitter on it. . . . I could just see the beauty in that person and the hope and the love and just everything that I didn't have." She thought, "This is what I want to be." Entranced by the photo, the little girl ripped off the magazine's cover and hid it in her underwear. Every night she would gaze at it and dream. The image of the graceful, smiling ballerina "represented freedom, it represented hope, it represented trying to live a little longer. . . . Seeing it completely saved me," she says. She yearned "to become this exact person."

DePrince was lucky. Adopted by an American couple not long after she found the magazine, she showed her new mother the tattered clipping and began studying ballet when she settled in New Jersey. By age seven she was already dancing en pointe, and in 2012, at seventeen, she joined the Dance Theatre of Harlem as a professional ballerina. "I just moved along fast," she says, "because I was so determined to be like that person on the magazine."[1]

DePrince's story is not just a heartwarming tale. It's an illustration of a common and powerful phenomenon. The same imaginative process that led an orphaned child to see her ideal self in a photo of a ballerina has sent nations to war and put men on the moon, transformed the landscape and built business empires. It made California the Golden State and Paris the City of Light. Cinema and fashion traffic in it; so do tourism and construction. It sells penthouses and cruises, sports cars and high-heeled shoes, college educations and presidential candidates. It inspires religious vocations and scientific research, suicidal terrorism and show-business dreams. It gives form to desire and substance to hope.

Glamour. The word itself has mystique, spelled even in American English with that exotic *u*. When we hear "glamour," we envision beautiful movie stars in designer gowns or imagine sleek sports cars and the dashing men who drive them. For a moment, we project ourselves into the world they represent, a place in which we, too, are beautiful, admired, graceful, courageous, accomplished, desired, powerful, wealthy, or at ease. Glamour, the fashion writer Alicia Drake observes, offers "the implicit promise of a life devoid of mediocrity."[2] It lifts us out of everyday experience and makes our desires seem attainable. Glamour, writes the fashion critic Robin Givhan, "makes us feel good about ourselves by making us believe that life can sparkle."[3]

Consider two glamorous images. The first, from a 2008 ad for the Riviera Palm Springs hotel, employs the stereotypical elements of what many people think of as glamour. With their glistening luxury, the black limousine, white satin, and pearl necklaces hark back to the black-and-white films of the 1930s, evoking the styles we now call "old Hollywood

glamour." Glowing against the desert twilight in her strapless gown and elegant updo, the model contrasts with the dimly lit photographers in their jeans, distancing herself from their workaday world. She is special—the center of attention and the embodiment of luxury, admiration, and fame. Even as she smiles for the cameras, she remains inaccessible; her cool self-possession is cordoned off from the eager camera flashes by a velvet rope. She doesn't look us in the eye, preserving her mystery and allowing us to enter the photo and imagine ourselves in her place: transformed into stars, living a life of excitement and acclaim in the Palm Springs of legend.

If the Riviera scene represents popular stereotypes of "glamour," Toni Frissell's evocative 1947 photograph of a lithe young woman in tennis clothes, at the beginning of this chapter, reminds us that glamour's essential elements have nothing to do with red carpets, limousines, or satin gowns. Here we see a more tranquil picture of a desert getaway. Perched gracefully on a curving stucco wall, the model looks not at the viewer but at the hills beyond. Like the Riviera's star, she appears poised and self-contained; this woman, however, appears to be alone. We follow her gaze, trace the light along the top of her extended arm, and imagine the sun on our own skin. We do not know who or where she is, nor do we need to. The mystery again encourages us to project ourselves into the scene, filling

By not looking us in the eye, the model allows us to enter the photo and imagine ourselves in her place: transformed into stars, living a life of excitement and acclaim in the Palm Springs of legend. Riviera Palm Springs

in the details with our own desires. Rather than documenting a particular place or fashion moment, the portrait evokes timeless ideals. It embodies youth, beauty, athleticism, self-possession, wealth, leisure, and—published in a February issue of *Harper's Bazaar*—escape to a benign eternal summer. (No sweat, sunburn, or dehydration here.) This image, too, heightens the viewer's yearning for the life it represents: not of fame and excitement in this case but of tranquility and ease. It, too, is glamorous.

Although people often equate them, glamour is not the same as beauty, stylishness, luxury, celebrity, or sex appeal. It is not limited to fashion or film, nor is it intrinsically feminine. It is not a collection of aesthetic markers—a style, as fashion and design use the word.[4] Glamour is, rather, a form of *nonverbal rhetoric*, which moves and persuades not through words but through images, concepts, and totems. (Even when conjured as word-pictures, glamorous images are perceived and remembered as emotionally resonant snapshots, not verbal descriptions.) By binding image and desire, glamour gives us pleasure, even as it heightens our yearning. It leads us to feel that the life we dream of exists, and to desire it even more.

Though usually a transitory pleasure, this sensation can also inspire life-changing action. From the cub reporters imagining themselves as the Woodward and Bernstein of *All the President's Men* to the forensic-science

Photo by Grey Crawford, interior design by Darryl Wilson

Courtesy of Aston Martin

students inspired by *CSI: Crime Scene Investigation*, young people flock to careers made suddenly glamorous by dramas that highlight professions' importance and downplay their tedium.[5] For the novelist Yiyun Li, then a child in 1970s China, the glamour of American life emanated from a Western candy wrapper, the prize of her collection: "It was made of cellophane with transparent gold and silver stripes, and if you looked through it, you would see a gilded world, much fancier than our everyday, dull life." The wrapper, she writes, "was the seed of a dream that came true: I left China for an American graduate school in 1996 and have lived here since."[6]

Glamour is powerfully persuasive. Yet because it relies on imagery and channels desire, it is often dismissed as trivial, frivolous, and superficial. Photographers use *glamour* euphemistically to refer to soft-core erotica; interior design magazines apply the word to anything shiny or luxurious; and many self-styled "glamour addicts" assume *glamour* refers only to fashion, makeup, or hairstyling. Those who do take the phenomenon seriously tend to be critics, who condemn glamour as a base, manipulative fraud. "We are bewitched by the false god of glamour and the fake promise of advertising," writes the British clergyman and journalist Martin Wroe.[7] But there is much more to glamour than either "addicts" or critics imagine. Even in its most seemingly frivolous forms, glamour shapes our most fundamental choices and illuminates our deepest yearnings. Although often perilous and always selective, it is not intrinsically malign. Glamour, as we shall see throughout this book, is a pervasive, complex, and often life-enhancing force.

Glamour is, as David Hume said of *luxury,* "a word of an uncertain signification."[8] In recent years, cultural-studies scholars have attempted to limn histories of glamour.[9] But without addressing the underlying psychology or adequately developing a theory of exactly how glamour works, such research tends to devolve into catchall chronicles of fashion and celebrity. The results can be ludicrous, as when the historian Stephen Gundle declares Paris Hilton "indisputably glamorous."[10] At the height of her celebrity, Hilton was many things: rich, famous, photogenic, sexy, pretty, and stylishly dressed. But few adults found her glamorous. She was the anti–Grace Kelly, the touchstone people cited when trying to explain what is *not* glamorous.[11]

To avoid such pitfalls, this book begins by building a definition of glamour that allows us to distinguish glamour from style, celebrity, or fame; to establish the relationship between glamour and such associated phenomena as charisma, romance, spectacle, elegance, and sex appeal; and to identify the common elements uniting disparate versions of glamour across audiences and cultural contexts.

In this chapter, we begin to understand *what kind of phenomenon glamour is*: like humor, a form of communication that elicits a distinctive emotional response. In the next chapter, we'll identify and investigate that response—a sense of projection and longing—and explore why so many different objects can produce it: *what glamour does*. We will discover that, like the gilded world seen through a candy wrapper, glamour is an illusion "known to be false but felt to be true," which focuses and intensifies a preexisting but previously inchoate yearning. The following three chapters then extract and examine the essential elements—*a promise of escape and transformation; grace; and mystery*—that appear in all versions of glamour and distinguish it from other forms of nonverbal rhetoric, thus explaining *how glamour works.*

As we develop this theory, we'll also learn how to detect glamour's less-obvious manifestations and, potentially, how to construct or dispel it. The theory allows us to understand why such diverse and sometimes contradictory things can seem glamorous: how Jackie Kennedy is like the Chrysler Building or a sports car like a Moleskine notebook, or why some audiences might find glamour in nuns, wind turbines, or *Star Trek.* We'll also resolve certain smaller puzzles. Why, for instance, is glamour so easily lost? How can it be associated so strongly with both elegance and sex appeal? What is its connection to androgyny? Why are certain aesthetic tropes, such as glittering light, silhouettes, or black-and-white imagery, so often associated with it?

Having built a specific definition for glamour, we can then examine its history without fear of going astray. Beginning with chapter six, we'll trace the growth and evolution of glamour as both a spontaneous phenomenon and a calculated tool of persuasion. We'll first examine how, and under what conditions, glamour manifested itself in premodern times and how it changed and proliferated with the growth of large, commercial cities. Then, in chapter seven, we'll look at the forms and influence of glamour in the twentieth century, focusing on its importance in exploring and defining modernity. Finally, we'll consider how glamour has evolved in today's media-savvy and fragmented culture.

In addition to the book's primary text, which uses examples to identify and illustrate theoretical and historical patterns, the "Icon" sidebars offer detailed examinations of glamorous archetypes. Instead of focusing on one specific feature of glamour, each icon allows us to see glamour's many different aspects at work simultaneously. Together, the icons also demonstrate the wide variety of glamour's manifestations, from the fashionable femininity of the Gibson Girl to the high-tech freedom of wirelessness. Like most of the book's images, the icons are placed in chapters where they have particular resonance or complement the argument, but they are not addressed in the main text. Holographically drawing on the book's ideas, the content of each "Icon" sidebar is not limited to the subject of a single chapter, and the sidebars need not be read in a particular order.

———

We begin not with the phenomenon but with the word, whose history offers valuable clues to the nature of glamour. Popularized in English by Sir Walter Scott at the turn of the nineteenth century, the old Scots word *glamour* described a literal magic spell. Glamour (or a glamour) made its subject see things that weren't there. A 1721 glossary of poetry explained: "When devils, wizards or jugglers deceive the sight, they are said to cast *glamour* o'er the eyes of the spectator."[12] Glamour could, Scott wrote in 1805, "make a ladye seem a knight; / The cobwebs on a dungeon wall / Seem tapestry in lordly hall." That power was believed to stretch into the real world. In his diary, Scott worried that "a kind of glamour about me" was making him overlook errors in his page proofs; he wondered whether the right herbal concoction "would dispel this fascination."[13] (As both magic and metaphor, *glamour* and *fascination* are closely related.)

During the nineteenth century, *glamour* expanded to include less literal charms, while maintaining the sense of making things look better than they really were. "The glamour of inexperience is over your eyes," Mr. Rochester tells Jane Eyre when she calls his mansion splendid, "and you see it through a charmed medium: you cannot discern that the gilding is slime and the silk draperies cobwebs; that the marble is sordid slate, and the polished woods mere refuse chips and scaly bark."[14] In his 1898 novella *Youth*, Joseph Conrad wrote, "Oh, the glamour of youth! Oh, the fire of it, more dazzling than the flames of the burning ship, throwing a magic light on the wide earth, leaping audaciously to the sky." He wistfully recalled "the deceitful feeling that lures us on to joys, to perils, to love, to vain effort."[15]

Note that Conrad is not saying that it is glamorous to be young—a judgment from the outside. Rather, his "glamour of youth" is an internal, psychological state. Young people, he suggests, are particularly susceptible to glamour. Like a veil, a distorted lens, or a mind-altering drug,

the "charmed medium" of glamour affects not the object perceived but the person perceiving. Reflecting this sense of the word, by 1902 *Webster's* included two new definitions: "a kind of haze in the air, causing things to appear different from what they really are" and "any artificial interest in, or association with, an object, through which it appears delusively magnified or glorified."[16]

As useful as this history is, however, we shouldn't confuse the word *glamour* with the phenomenon, since the lack of a specific word to describe an experience does not mean that the experience does not exist. Max Weber did not invent charisma. Umami, the hearty fifth taste, is not unique to Japanese palates. While some scholars maintain that glamour is inherently modern, this book argues that the experience is not unique to the modern cultures that use the word, only more widespread and more likely to be deliberately constructed and consciously recognized.[17]

Nonetheless, the history of the word *glamour* does highlight two important aspects of the phenomenon. First, glamour is an illusion, a "deceitful feeling" or "magic light" that distorts perceptions. The illusion usually begins with a stylized image—visual or mental—of a person, an object, an event, or a setting. The image is not entirely false, but it is deceptive. Its allure is created by obscuring or ignoring some details while heightening others. That selection may reflect deliberate craft. Or it may happen unconsciously, when an audience notices appealing characteristics and ignores discordant elements. In either case, glamour requires the audience's innocence or, more often, willing suspension of disbelief.

To glamorize is to fantasize. It is also, in some sense, to lie. "The best photographers are the best liars," said the twentieth-century fashion photographer Norman Parkinson, who was known for the glamour of his work.[18] Even when it arises unintentionally, glamour presents an edited version of reality. There are no bills on the new granite countertops, no blisters rubbed by the elegant shoes, no cumbersome cords on the stylish lamps, no bruises on the action hero, no traffic on the open road, no sacrifices in the path of progress.

Second, glamour does not exist independently in the glamorous object—it is not a style, personal quality, or aesthetic feature—but emerges through the *interaction between object and audience*. Glamour is not something you possess but something you perceive, not something you have but something you feel. It is a subjective response to a stimulus. One may strive to construct a glamorous effect, but success depends on the perceiver's receptive imagination. Young men must imagine seafaring as a series of adventures and triumphs. Jane Eyre must want to see the mansion as splendid, not to look for cobwebs and slime, or for the moral rot of a madwoman in the attic. Consider, by contrast, a passage from *Peter Pan*, in which the glamour of the pirate life, presumably derived from boys' adventure tales, fails to work its magic on Wendy:

> No words of mine can tell you how Wendy despised those pirates. To the boys there was at least some glamour in the pirate calling; but all that she saw was that the ship had not been tidied for years. There was not a porthole on the grimy glass of which you might not have written with your finger "Dirty pig"; and she had already written it on several.[19]

Unsusceptible to pirate glamour, Wendy sees the grime that the boys, like Jane Eyre, overlook. A "glamorous" person, setting, or style will not produce glamour unless that object resonates with the audience's aspirations, and unless the audience is willing to entertain the illusion. Conversely, one audience may find glamorous something another audience deems ordinary or even repulsive.

We see these two characteristics—illusion and subjective response—playing out in one of the phenomenon's oldest forms: martial glamour. From Achilles, David, and Alexander through knights, samurai, admirals, and airmen, warriors have been icons of masculine glamour, exemplifying courage, prowess, and patriotic significance. Beginning in the nineteenth century, warfare was one of the first contexts in which English speakers used the term *glamour* in its modern metaphorical sense. "Military heroes who give up their lives in the flush and excitement and glamour of battle," opined a US congressman in 1885, "are sustained in the discharge of duty by the rush and conflict of physical forces, the hope of earthly glory and renown."[20] A 1917 handbook on army paperwork was "dedicated to the man behind the desk, the man who, being away from the din and glamor of battle, is usually denied popular favor, yet who clothes, feeds, pays, shelters, transports, and otherwise looks after the man behind the gun."[21] (Whether in warfare or business, logistics is the quintessential "unglamorous" but critical support activity.)

European nations began World War I with a glamorous vision of war, only to be psychologically shattered by the realities of the trenches. The experience changed the way people referred to the glamour of battle, treating it no longer as a positive quality but as a dangerous illusion. In 1919, the British painter Paul Nash wrote that the purpose of *The Menin Road*, his bleak portrait of a desolate and blasted landscape, was "to rob war of the last shred of glory[,] the last shine of glamour."[22] Briefly conscripted in 1916, D. H. Lawrence lamented "this terrible glamour of camaraderie, which is the glamour of Homer and of all militarism."[23] An American writing in 1921 asked fellow veterans of the Great War, "Are you going to tell your children the truth about what you endured, or gild your reminis-

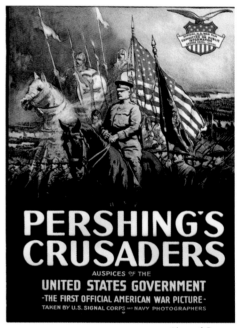

Library of Congress

cences with glamour that will make them want to have a merry war experience of their own?"[24] In the 1920s, pacifism, not battle, became glamorous.

For some audiences martial glamour endures. Today's military recruitment videos are full of imagery uniting the contemporary glamour of technology with the ancient glamour of battle: a paratrooper leaping from a confined plane into the open sky; a commander issuing silent hand signals as troops move stealthily through a forest; a jet rising gracefully from a carrier deck or swiftly crossing bare terrain; silhouetted soldiers rappelling from a helicopter or down a mountainside; screens glowing in a darkened command center. Like classic Hollywood glamour photographs, these images often use sharp contrasts between light and darkness to heighten drama and veil individuals in mystery, encouraging viewers to project themselves into the picture. These scenes bespeak a world of swift, decisive action, enduring camaraderie, perfect coordination, and meaningful exertion. They glamorize military life.

———

Glamour is not limited to celebrity, wealth, or theatrical performance. It is a powerful form of rhetoric that can sell just about anything. As such, it is a far more common experience and more widely used sales tool than the short list of "glamour industries"—film, music, fashion—suggests. We can find obvious glamour in sports, technology, tourism, the job market, and the stock market. *Glamour stock* is even a term of art, the opposite of *value stock*. It refers to a stock whose price represents an especially high multiple of the company's earnings, reflecting either rational prospects for future growth or delusionary fads. These securities, the term suggests, may derive their allure from wishful thinking. "Glamour and excitement are not the same as a sound investment," warned a 2010 *Wall Street Journal* report on the initial public offering of electric-car maker Tesla Motors. "Indeed the reverse is more often the case."[25]

With their evocations of a new life in a new home, real-estate promotions often traffic in a sort of off-the-shelf glamour, recycling visual tropes. Consider two strikingly similar 2007 ads for high-rise condominiums. In the first, promoting the Metropolitan in Dallas, an attractive young woman

in a short dress and high heels sits on her windowsill, her bare arms draped around one bent knee. Her head is turned to look out at the nearby skyscrapers of downtown. In the second, for Rector Square in Lower Manhattan's Battery Park, a black-clad young man assumes almost exactly the same pose. From his window, he gazes across the water toward the Statue of Liberty.

Each ad offers multilayered glamour. Glimpsing only their partial profiles, we project ourselves into the role of the young condo dwellers. They invite us to imagine sharing their new life, being them or being with them. And they in turn contemplate the scene beyond their windows and feel the pull of its glamour—the promise of a skyline's mysteriously glistening windows or a river's passage toward unknown destinations.

Although the two images are almost identical in composition, they are actually selling two different ideals. The Metropolitan promises "the future of the city," a bustling alternative to the suburban life typical of Dallas. Rector Square, by contrast, offers tranquility, an escape from the noise, garbage cans, and graffiti of other Manhattan neighborhoods.[26] The two ads evoke the different yearnings of different audiences.

Like any form of rhetoric, glamour depends for its success on a receptive audience. But even when recognized as an illusion, it can be quite convincing. Enticed by a travel brochure promising "winter sun" amidst the London gloom, the author Alain de Botton considers the ad's manipulative allure.

Those responsible for the brochure had darkly intuited how easily their readers might be turned into prey by photographs whose power insulted the intelligence and contravened any notions of free will: over-exposed photographs of palm trees, clear skies, and white beaches. Readers who would have been capable of skepticism and prudence in other areas of their lives reverted in contact with these elements to a primordial innocence and optimism. . . . I resolved to travel to the island of Barbados.[27]

The brochure's images turn a vague dissatisfaction with gray skies and damp days into a yearning for happiness, for rebirth, for a sustained version of the innocence and optimism the photos momentarily evoke. An escape to Barbados, the brochure suggests enticingly, is the means by which those emotions can be achieved. By focusing imaginative yearnings, glamour motivates not just momentary fantasies but real-world action: buying vacations and dresses, sports cars and condos; moving to new cities and pursuing new careers; even electing presidents.

The most striking recent exemplar of glamour was not, in fact, a movie star or fashion plate but a political candidate: Barack Obama in 2008.[28] With its stylized portraits of the candidate gazing upward and its logo featuring a road stretching toward the horizon, the iconography of Obama's first presidential campaign was classically glamorous. (*The Onion* satirized the candidate's many glamorous photographs in a story headlined "Obama Practices Looking-Off-into-Future Pose."[29])

The source of the candidate's glamour was not merely his campaign's graphic design, however, but the persona those images signified. Like John Kennedy in 1960, Obama combined youth, vigor, and good looks with the promise of political change. Like Kennedy (and Ronald Reagan, another glamorous president), the candidate was both charming and self-contained. While Kennedy's wealth set him apart, Obama's mystery stemmed from his exotic background—an international upbringing and biracial ethnicity that defied conventional categories and distanced him from hum-

The most striking recent exemplar of glamour was not a movie star or a fashion plate but a presidential candidate: Barack Obama in 2008.

Getty Images/Congressional Quarterly

drum American life. He was glamorous because he was
different, and his differences mirrored his audience's aspirations for the country.

The candidate also had little national record, allowing supporters to project diverse political yearnings
onto him. Even well-informed observers couldn't agree
on whether Obama was a full-blown leftist or a market-
oriented centrist. "Barack has become a kind of human
Rorschach test," said his friend Cassandra Butts during the 2008 race. "People see in him what they want
to see."[30] The press corps, wrote *Washington Post* media
critic Howard Kurtz early in the campaign, "sees the
man as an empty vessel into which its fondest hopes can
be projected."[31] Obama's call for "a broad majority of
Americans—Democrats, Republicans, and independents

Jessica Sample

of goodwill—who are re-engaged in the project of national renewal" invited the audience to entertain their own fantasies of what national renewal
would look like.[32] Obama's promise of hope and change meant different
things to different people.

An asset in a campaign, glamour can make it difficult to govern. A
president must make decisions, and any specific action will disappoint—
and potentially alienate—supporters who disagree. Nor is governing ever
as easy and conflict-free as the campaign dream. Disillusionment is inevitable. In his 2012 reelection campaign, Obama rallied his base more with
fear of his opponents than hope for his second term. "The 2004 version
of Barack Obama, who captured the nation with a dazzling speech about
unity and went on to win the presidency on a message of hope, died on
Monday. He was 8 years old," wrote ABC News reporter Matt Negrin in
May 2012.[33] As his mystery and grace dissipated, so did Obama's glamour.

As a psychological phenomenon and rhetorical tool, glamour is like
humor. It is an imaginative experience in which communication and association create a recognizably consistent emotional response. With glamour

the response is an enjoyable pang of projection, admiration, and longing. Glamour, writes the essayist Jim Lewis, "offers us a glimpse into another world, more perfect than this one, and for that moment, enchantment swirls around us. And then it is gone again."[34]

Glamour may be as universal as humor (though some people have a keener "sense of glamour" than others), but its manifestations vary from person to person, culture to culture, and era to era. In her study of glamour in mid-twentieth-century American buildings, the architectural historian Alice Friedman draws one such contrast. For one group of 1950s Americans, she suggests, "ideas about glamour"

came from Hollywood and rock 'n' roll, clustering around the iconic images of such celebrities as Marilyn Monroe, Elvis Presley, and James Dean. Others rejected those heroes, preferring to focus on—and emulate—the aura of the "classy" cosmopolitans like Grace Kelly, Audrey Hepburn, and Cary Grant, whose Americanness (or that of the characters they played in the movies) was tinged with European sophistication and upper-class charm.[35]

Grace Kelly and Cary Grant in *To Catch a Thief* (1955): For many Americans in the 1950s, their cosmopolitan polish was the epitome of glamour. *Photofest*

Reinfried Marass

Even within the same culture, different audiences have different ideals and desires, and therefore resonate to different images. Some people find glamour in elegant simplicity; others, in baroque excess. Some glamorize a whirl of parties; others, the solitude of a mountain retreat. For every military recruiting poster, there is a bumper sticker inviting viewers to "Visualize World Peace." Declaring "That's not glamorous" is akin to saying, "That's not funny." Glamour is subjective. It must be defined not by the critic's taste but by the audience's reaction, using as clues the elements that generate the response.

Some versions of glamour, emphasizing wealth, beauty, and sex appeal, are especially widespread and enduring. But they are neither necessary nor sufficient to the experience, any more than plays on words or scatological jokes are essential to humor. As for styles, to equate beaded gowns or mirrored furniture with glamour is like treating a pratfall or a Monty Python routine as the definition of humor.

Its subjective nature can make detecting glamour tricky. Like an old joke, an image a previous generation found glamorous may fall flat, or even become incomprehensible, to a new audience. The decline of one kind of glamour, whether of nineteenth-century Parisian grandes dames or of the mid-twentieth-century Rat Pack, often presages the rise of another kind, representing different values or aspirations: the glamour of bohemian cafés or of rock stars. A geisha's glamour meant one thing in the nineteenth century, when geisha were chic style setters, and another after the 1920s, when they became custodians of tradition. In mid-twentieth-century America, a mink coat was the glamorous representation of feminine indulgence. A half century later, it has been replaced by ubiquitous photos of hot-stone massages.

Through much of the twentieth century, middle Americans felt a lack of cosmopolitanism, sophistication, and style. They dreamed of Paris.

"Model in Silverblue Mink," 1956, copyright Virginia Thoren, courtesy of June Bateman Fine Art and the Virginia Thoren Collection at the Pratt Institute Libraries

Today, their counterparts yearn instead for pleasure and simplicity: good, fresh food in a beautiful place without too much bustle. So now they dream of Italy, minus the inefficiencies and frustrations of real Italian life and, of course, without all the other tourists. Witness the popularity of Tuscan architecture and décor and of *Under the Tuscan Sun* and *Eat, Pray, Love*, both of which were on the *New York Times* best-seller list for years.[36] Once, studying abroad meant a semester or two in Paris. Today Italy is the second-most-popular destination for American college students, after the United Kingdom, having passed Spain in 2002–03. France is a distant fourth and if current trends continue will soon be replaced by China.[37]

Glamour is like humor in another way: examine its object too closely and you're likely to spoil the effect. Just as humor relies on surprise, glamour requires distance. A glamorous image appeals to our desires without becoming explicit, lest too much information break the spell. In its blend of accessibility and distance, glamour is neither transparent nor opaque. It is *translucent*. It invites just enough familiarity to engage the imagination, allowing scope for the viewer's own fantasies.

But "inquiring minds want to know," as the old tabloid slogan put it, so the audience itself often destroys the very glamour it loves. The more we're drawn to a glamorous person, place, or thing, the more we seek to fill in the details or to experience the thing itself. We discover the sports hero's temper and steroid use, the politician's spin machine and unsavory allies, the "fairy-tale" princess's bulimia and troubled marriage, the movie star's plastic surgeries and brainless enthusiasms. When young fan Jane Wilkie toured RKO Studios in 1940, she was disillusioned to see Ginger Rogers "chewing gum—at least two sticks, very possibly a five pack—with considerable gusto. . . . For me, Wrigley struck down an idol," she recalled decades later. "It hadn't occurred to me that movie stars chewed gum, wheezed with head colds, or used the john."[38]

Experience also turns the inspiring into the ordinary. Skyscrapers become nothing more than buildings, jets merely a way to get places, your dream job just your job. Only two years after challenging the country to land a man on the moon, President Kennedy was already worrying that the space program had "lost its glamour."[39] At best, familiarity replaces glamour with enjoyment, affection, or sympathy. At worst, knowledge leads to cynicism and disappointment. We discover the flaws obscured in the idealized images. "Venice is glamorous, until the breeze off the Adriatic brings in the smell of rotting fish and raw sewage, at which point it is like Hoboken with better architecture," says a disillusioned visitor.[40]

This process produces one of glamour's most puzzling qualities: its fragility. Excited fashion headlines often proclaim "Glamour is back!" without explaining why it vanished in the first place. Someone is always trying to restore glamour to something or some place: to New York, Monte Carlo, Palm Springs, Shanghai, Miami Beach, or Budapest; to engineering, the space program, or high-energy particle physics; to resorts, cruises, department stores, or air travel.[41] Yet those efforts often fail. If we enjoy glamour so much, why can't we have it, like candlelight or satin dresses, whenever we want? Why isn't glamour, like luxury, something money can buy?

The reason lies in the nature of glamour. It is not a product or style but a form of communication and persuasion. It depends on maintaining exactly the right relationship between object and audience, imagination and desire. Glamour is fragile because perceptions change.

———

Glamour creates a "reality distortion field"—Silicon Valley's capsule description of Steve Jobs's persuasive magic—and because of its artifice, it is always

Dorothy Jordan, photographed by George Hurrell: "All of us glamorize everything," because art demands selection. *Courtesy of Pancho Barnes Trust Estate Archive, © Estate of George Hurrell*

suspect. The real puzzle is not why glamour keeps disappearing but why it survives at all. Its mystery and grace violate our self-proclaimed commitment to honesty, transparency, comfort, realism, practicality, even overt sexuality. Reviewers praise filmmakers and authors for not glamorizing their subjects. Social critics denounce movies that glamorize violence or cigarette smoking. Whether selling refrigerators or revolution, glamour is an alluring form of propaganda and not entirely to be trusted. We may have lost our faith in literal enchantments, but we still know glamour can be perilous.

When Catholic liturgy asks the faithful to reject the "glamour of evil," worshippers are vowing to see evil for what it is and not, like Eve contemplating the forbidden fruit, to let themselves fall for an attractive appearance and the promise of desire fulfilled. But we can abjure the glamour of evil without declaring the evil of glamour. Simply to condemn glamour as a lie is to damn imagination. Every innovation requires perceiving a world different from the one that exists, and all art demands selection. "All of us glamorize everything, including the documentaries [sic] who glamorize filth and squalor," said the Hollywood photographer George Hurrell, defending the glamour of his studio-era portraits. "It's a question of emphasizing . . . the dirt or the beauty—the viewpoint you assume when you start out."[42] Emphasizing the squalor and hiding the beauty may be regarded as more "serious" than creating a glamorous image, but it is equally deceptive.

There is something civilized, and distinctly human, about glamour. It is, like any form of rhetoric, a humane art of persuasion. "If glamour is magic, if it's really about casting a spell, one should happily confront the manipulation of it all," advises the fashion designer Isaac Mizrahi. "It's adult to manipulate and only human."[43]

A scene in the classic film *Queen Christina* (1933) captures the eternal dilemma. Disguised as a young man, the queen (Greta Garbo) encounters the Spanish ambassador Antonio (John Gilbert) in a rural tavern. Discussing their countrymen's different approaches to courtship, Christina pronounces the elaborate Spanish rituals "glamorous, and yet somewhat mechanical."

Christina: Evidently you Spaniards make too much fuss about a simple, elemental thing like love. We Swedes are more *direct*.

Antonio: Why, that's civilization—to disguise the elemental with the glamorous.

By using the word *disguise*, Antonio acknowledges that glamour is a falsehood, an illusion. But, he declares, civilization itself is defined by such illusions—by art and artifice, customs and manners. To Antonio, disguising the elemental is a great achievement, not a base fraud. Glamour makes desire more than an animal impulse. Its purpose is not simply to camouflage sexual passion but, by bestowing meaning upon it, to transform it into something more enduring and significant.

Antonio: A great love has to be nourished, has to be . . .

Christina: A great love . . .

Antonio: Don't you believe in its possibility?

Christina: In its possibility, yes, but not in its existence. A great love, a perfect love, is an illusion. It is the golden fable of which we all dream. But in ordinary life, it doesn't happen. In ordinary life, one must be content with less.

Glamour versus realism, civilization versus directness, golden fables versus ordinary life, the pursuit of love versus contentment with less—which should we choose? That neither is obviously wrong only makes the question more difficult. Yet even in our wised-up age, we do not want a world bereft of glamour's magic. For all its dangers, glamour is a special art. We value not only its transient pleasures but also the inspiration and insight it provides. Glamour may be an illusion, but it reveals the truth about what we desire and, sometimes, what we can become.

Icon
THE AVIATOR

From the days of biplanes and silk scarves, the aviator has been an archetype of masculine glamour, combining youth, daring, grace, bravery, technical mastery, sexual allure, and forward-looking modernity. Even the practical costume of flight suit, helmet, goggles, or—that touchstone of glamour—sunglasses seems calculated to heighten aviators' glamour, holding viewers at an intriguing distance.[1]

World War I aces, writes the historian Robert Wohl, "exemplified more purely than any other figure of their time what it meant to be a man."[2] That most aces died young only added to their ageless allure. After World War I, British fighter pilots were called "glamour boys." The term was both admiring and pejorative, particularly among other military men. It drew a contrast between the celebrated knights of the air and the anonymous foot soldiers and support crews below.[3]

Charles Lindbergh: "You are that dream-self we all long to be," wrote a fan.

Library of Congress

The twentieth century's most glamorous aviator, however, was a civilian: Charles Lindbergh, whose allure after his 1927 solo flight from New York to Paris was as potent as any movie star's. "You are that dream-self we all long to be," declared a fan.[4]

What audiences saw in the young flier depended on their own ideals. To his American public, the clean-cut young man with a pioneering spirit embodied the best of their country's heritage. His discipline and midwestern modesty combined youth with the values of an earlier time, redeeming the disillusioned and decadent Jazz Age. "You symbolize our splendid, secret dreams / Ideals of manhood, virtues we hold dear," another devotee versified.[5]

In France, where Lindbergh's grace and deference charmed the public, the praise took on local coloration. Air force officer and poet Pierre Weiss praised the aviator's "moral elegance" and "intellectual refinement," contrasting him with "a second-class hero, with a cigarette hanging from his mouth"—the stereotypical American, in other words. Lindbergh's achievement, Weiss wrote, had inspired "the French masses to re-discover themselves . . . a people who bear in their hearts a desire for the infinite."[6]

Although Lindbergh's feat clearly resonated with his audience's preexisting yearnings, his profile also benefited from deliberate media craftsmanship. The flier's image sold newspapers and magazines, children's books and sheet music, decorative textiles and souvenir spoons. He was *Time* magazine's first Man of the Year. When Lindbergh published his account of his flight, *We*, only two months after landing in Paris, the book became an immediate best seller. That success led publisher G. P. Putnam to look for another opportunity to capitalize on aviator glamour.

Putnam found his new icon in Amelia Earhart, who in early photos was deliberately styled to look like Lindbergh. "Lady Lindy" gave aviation a feminine face, providing an alluring yet similarly wholesome image of the modern woman. Although not the best female flier, nor even the most beautiful, Earhart, who later married Putnam, was surely the most glamorous. The mystery of her 1937 disappearance only added to her mystique.[7]

The Tuskegee Airmen, here photographed by Toni Frissell in a classic skyward-looking pose, claimed the aviator's glamour for African Americans. Of the many black units in World War II, they are the most famous. Although their story was largely unknown to white Americans before a star-filled 1995 HBO movie, they were a source of pride for other blacks during the war. The airmen, the historian J. Todd Moye suggests, "were among the first Americans to imagine the kind of racially integrated society that most Americans now take for granted."[8] Any black military unit might have played that role, but the aura of aviation gave the airmen's assertion of competent equality a particular punch.

Given the power of aviator glamour in the early twentieth century, it inevitably became a tool for despotic political purposes as well. Benito Mussolini

Col. Benjamin O. Davis, the commanding officer of the 332nd Fighter Group, better known as the Tuskegee Airmen, and Edward C. Gleed, group operations officer, at their base in Ramitelli, Italy, March 1945.

Toni Frissell Collection, Library of Congress

learned to fly after World War I, and throughout his career he linked aviation with the future of Italy—and with his personal image. A celebratory 1936 biography styled him *Mussolini Aviatore*, and in 1938 the Futurist painter Alfredo Gauro Ambrosi created an "aeroportrait" of the dictator's helmeted head superimposed on a stylized vision of Rome from the air. "All good citizens, all devoted citizens must follow with profound feeling the development of Italian wings," Mussolini declared in 1923.[9]

A decade later, Italo Balbo, the Fascist government's marshal of the air force, led a squadron of twenty-five seaplanes on a transatlantic flight, landing to enormous acclaim in Chicago for the Century of Progress World's Fair. A monument marking the occasion still stands near the shores of Lake Michigan, and Balbo Drive still runs through the South Loop.[10] "For Italians," writes Wohl, "fascism was synonymous with flying."[11]

While Italian images drew on the abstractions of Futurism, the modernist movement emphasizing newness, technology, and speed, Soviet propaganda posters appropriated the conventions of Russia's traditional religious art— transforming aviators into literal icons. Instead of Christ ringed by an almond-shaped halo, or *mandorla*, posters would show a flight-suited pilot against a similarly angled Soviet star. These iconic Soviet aviators were neither reckless aces nor individualistic Lindberghs. "What Soviet authorities offered up is a vision of the glamorous aviator in which the aviator is disciplined," explains the historian Scott W. Palmer, "and his work is undertaken in service of a larger, collective mission, which is to construct socialism."[12]

Contemporary politicians still occasionally try to tap into aviator glamour— a flight-suited George W. Bush on an aircraft carrier declaring "mission accomplished" in Iraq, for instance, or John McCain's presidential campaigns using portraits of the candidate as a handsome young flier. But these ill-fated examples notwithstanding, for the past several decades aviator glamour has mostly been confined to the movies. The laconic ease of Sam Shepard's Chuck Yeager in *The Right Stuff* (1983), the cocky bravado of Tom Cruise's Maverick in *Top Gun* (1986), and the wisecracking aplomb of Will Smith's Steve Hiller in *Independence Day* (1996) all partake of the same essential grace. So does Denzel Washington's alcoholic Whip Whitaker in *Flight* (2012), as he executes an impossible maneuver to save his plane and later struts down the hall to face a board of inquiry, with his aviator shades—and aviator's aura—hiding the signs of his late-night binge. These unflappable men are masters of their fates, of their machines, of the air itself. They are the knights of the sky, *Les chevaliers du ciel*, the title of a 2005 French action film.[13]

As Whip Whitaker's secret vices suggest, however, even in the movies, the aviator's glamour has become suspect. In *Catch Me If You Can* (2002) and *The Aviator* (2004), Leonardo DiCaprio portrays two cautionary versions of the archetype: the con man and the perfectionist. Pretending to be a pilot in *Catch Me If You Can*, his Frank Abagnale Jr. uses aviation's glamorous aura to distract his marks. Dressed in a pilot's uniform, he seduces women and scores free plane rides, cons bank clerks into cashing fake payroll checks, and, in one of the film's most memorable scenes, walks through an airport surrounded by women he's recruited to take glamorous, but phony, jobs as Pan Am stewardesses. Distracted by the pretty women, the cops miss the man they've come to arrest.

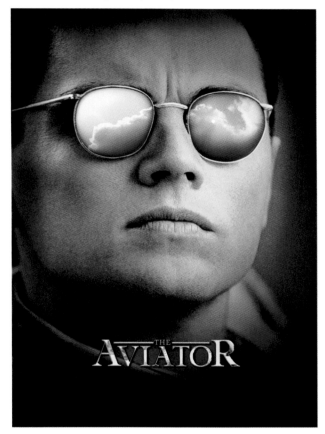

In *The Aviator*, DiCaprio's Howard Hughes demands aircraft with bodies so smooth he cannot feel a single rivet. The obsession that makes Hughes a great engineer proves his fatal flaw, however. He goes mad because he cannot abide the real world's imperfections. Perhaps, the film hints, movie stars understand the limits of glamour's illusions better than engineering geniuses. "Nothing's clean, Howard," Ava Gardner (Kate Beckinsale) tells him, "but we do our best."

Even in the movies, the aviator's glamour has become suspect. *Photofest*

Icon
SMOKING

Smoking used to be glamorous, the cigarette an icon of sophistication, power, sex, art, and, to the young, all the grand and mysterious privileges of adulthood. "It was a time when brilliant, brooding professors lectured while holding unfiltered cigarettes in stained fingers, when girls wearing cashmere sweater sets gestured gracefully with extra-longs, when handsome fraternity boys clutched a can of beer in one hand and a cigarette in the other. I wanted to know what they all knew, and for sure, I wanted one of those boys," recalls an unapologetic smoker. "So I practiced smoking."[1]

Smoking gave the awkward something to do with their hands and the graceful an extension of their grace. Like a folding fan, a plume of cigarette smoke simultaneously concealed and called attention to the smoker. A cigarette

Humphrey Bogart lights Lauren Bacall's cigarette in *To Have and Have Not* (1944): a sign of intimacy, suggesting both sex and solicitude.

Photofest

amplified gestures and emphasized the mouth. Depending on the smoker and the audience, it could represent any number of ideals and aspirations. For nineteenth-century bohemians, the historian Elizabeth Wilson writes, "Smoking orchestrated time, gave it a rhythm, punctuated talk, theatrically mimed both masculinity and femininity, was the intellectuals' essential accessory, was also an erotic gesture, enhancing the mystery of some unknown drinker seated at her table, veiled in a bluish haze."[2]

In Franklin Roosevelt's upturned holder, a cigarette spoke of optimism and progress. In the Marlboro Man's rugged hands, it represented masculine independence. James Dean's cigarette symbolized rebellion, Marlene Dietrich's was all about seduction, and a Shanghai calendar girl's epitomized modern femininity. Ayn Rand romanticized smoking as an emblem of creative thought and technological dominance: "I like to think of fire held in a man's hand. Fire, a dangerous force, tamed at his fingertips. . . . When a man thinks, there is a spot of fire alive in his mind—and it is proper that he should have the burning point of a cigarette as his one expression."[3] Lighting a lover's cigarette was a sign of intimacy, suggesting both sex and solicitude.

Five decades of scientific evidence and antismoking propaganda have largely punctured the glamour of smoking. It has become that dirty habit that kills people. "I miss my lung," says the cowboy on a Marlboroesque antismoking billboard. Smokers are those poor addicts huddling next to their office buildings on cold, wet days—the antithesis of grace.

But a trace of glamour remains. As more and more places forbid smoking, observes the British journalist Simon Mills, lit cigarettes have become the markers of "heroic, sexy social outlaws." The interior designer and socialite Nicky Haslam, who lights but doesn't inhale, calls the practice "deliciously illicit."[4] Perhaps, suggests the essayist Katie Roiphe, the TV show *Mad Men* owes some of its cult appeal to the characters' conspicuous smoking, which provides an alluring contrast to the health-conscious discipline of today's young professionals. The show, she writes, offers "the glamour of spectacularly messy, self-destructive behavior to our relatively staid and enlightened times."[5]

Femme fatale Sharon Stone lights up in *Basic Instinct* (1992): "What are you gonna do? Arrest me for smoking?" *Photofest*

In the movies, smoking has come to symbolize a cool contempt for social conventions and bourgeois rules. Mob moll Uma Thurman smokes in *Pulp Fiction* (1994), as does femme fatale Sharon Stone in her infamous scene in *Basic Instinct* (1992). "There's no smoking in here," a policeman tells her as she sits down to face interrogation. Uninhibited, unintimidated, and undeterred, she replies, "What are you gonna do? Arrest me for smoking?"

Playing up the bad-girl theme, in 2011 the fashion designer Nicola Formichetti sent the pop star Lady Gaga down his runway smoking, in a typical bit of Gaga spectacle.[6] The real rebel glamour came a few days later, however, when the supermodel Kate Moss, absent from the runway for seven years, strutted down the Louis Vuitton catwalk on the UK's National No Smoking Day: "The moment Kate Moss sashayed across the room in hotpants and high heels, puffing on a cigarette," Jess Cartner-Morley, the *Guardian*'s fashion editor declared, "there was no longer any doubt who the star of this show was."[7]

© Annie Leibovitz/Contact Press Images

TWO

INARTICULATE LONGINGS

Before we can understand how glamour works, we have to further define what it does. If, like humor, glamour elicits an identifiable emotional response, what are those emotions? If glamour is a form of nonverbal rhetoric, of what does it persuade us?

One influential theory, advanced by the Marxist critic John Berger in his 1972 BBC series and book *Ways of Seeing*, is that glamour elicits *social envy* in order to sell commercial goods. Berger defines glamour as "the state of being envied." He argues that advertising images generate glamour by "showing us people who have apparently been transformed" by whatever is being advertised "and are, as a result, enviable." Glamour is, in this view, a byproduct of capitalism's vicious game, in which only a few winners enjoy privileged status. The many losers are jealous and, thus, susceptible to glamour. "Glamour," Berger declares, "cannot exist without personal social envy being a common and widespread emotion."[1]

Although Berger's description does capture glamour's transformational promise, his desiccated view misses many of its most potent appeals. He is blinded by envy, conflating it with *desire*. Envy is, of course, one form of desire—the wish to have what someone else has—and the social status Berger emphasizes in his analysis is indeed one desirable good. But it is hardly the only one. Most important, the resentment and hostility essential to true envy are missing from most forms of glamour. Glamour may be an illusion, but it is rarely a mean or vicious one, nor do audiences commonly dream of being resented for achieving a glamorous state. Glamour is not about separating winners from losers. Rather, the glamorous object—whether person, place, or thing—is a kind of alter ego. As Jay Z raps, "When you see me, see you!"[2] Someone or something glamorous represents "that dream-self we all long to be," a magic mirror in which we see ourselves transformed.[3] We aspire to be like, or be with, those we find glamorous, not to rob them of the attributes we admire.

Take Angelina Jolie, the subject of one of the most psychologically telling, because personally revealing, contemporary descriptions of movie-star glamour: a 2009 *Harper's Bazaar* essay, "The Power of Angelina," by the feminist writer Naomi Wolf. The article is not a conventional celebrity profile—Jolie and Wolf did not meet—but, rather, a discussion of the "life narrative" Jolie has "crafted." Though framed explicitly as a story about artifice, it is pervaded by Wolf's yearning to believe. Over the course of the essay, Jolie's life functions as proof that the longings that inform Wolf's own oeuvre are attainable: to be effortlessly thin and beautiful (*The Beauty Myth*), to participate in high-level public debates *(Fire with Fire)*, to indulge sexual desire without condemnation or consequence (*Promiscuities*), and to become a mother without

Printed by permission of the Norman Rockwell Family Agency. Copyright © 1954 The Norman Rockwell Family Entities

hassle or pain (*Misconceptions*). "The magic of Jolie's self-presentation?" writes Wolf. "She makes the claim, with her life and actions, that, indeed, you can get away with it. All of it."

This is not social envy. It is more akin to a schoolgirl crush. In one passage, Wolf projects her longings as the divorced mother of two onto Jolie's own brief period as a single mother, in the process reworking a classic glamorous icon:

Then there is the plane. Women are so used to being dependent on others (certainly on men) for where they go, metaphorically, and how they get there. Flying a private plane is the classic metaphor for choosing your own direction; usually, that is a guy thing to do, yet there was Jolie, with her aviator glasses on, taking flying lessons so she could blow the mind of her four-year-old son. That is the ultimate in single-mom chic.

Airplanes and aviators are touchstones of modern glamour, and here Wolf alters their meaning. She transforms the plane from a universal symbol of freedom, mastery, and escape into a child-centered accessory demonstrating "single-mom chic." In the process, she domesticates Jolie's considerable appeal as a motorcycle-riding action star—a "man's woman"—and also implicitly replaces the married-and-childless Amelia Earhart with a more personally satisfying aviatrix archetype.

Contrary to Berger's definition, however, Wolf does not begrudge Jolie her glamorous life, nor does she covet Jolie's social status. Rather, she admires the actress and longs to share the world she represents and, indeed, to bring other women along. "Jolie's image is not just a mirror of one woman," she concludes, "but also a looking glass for female fantasy life writ large."[4] That one fan can project so many different yearnings onto the actress, without exhausting her possible meanings, demonstrates why Jolie is such an icon. Glamour is most powerful when its object encompasses multiple desires.

In an early analysis of Hollywood glamour, the 1939 book *America at the Movies*, the researcher Margaret Farrand Thorp defined movie glamour as "sex appeal . . . plus luxury, plus elegance, plus romance," suggesting that this elusive quality emerged from the mixture of all these elements.[5] Like a complex perfume, glamour is enriched by layered notes, each with a different emotional resonance. Yet even astute analysts often try to reduce glamour to a narrow appeal. "'Elegance' seems dubious and 'romance' a euphemism," writes the fashion historian Valerie Steele, responding to Thorp. Conflating glamour and its ironic impersonator "glam," Steele declares that glamour is "never discreet or ladylike."[6] In this view, glamour has nothing to do with elegance. It is all about sex and luxury—the more conspicuous, the better. But equating glamour with flashy sexuality and over-the-top bling is as limiting as equating it with envy.

After all, Grace Kelly, who has been called "the most frequently referenced glamour icon in the history of fashion," was polished and elegant, her sex appeal both unmistakable and discreet.[7] Jackie Kennedy, another icon, wore suits like armor, designed to hide her body. "PROTECT ME," she wrote to the designer Oleg Cassini.[8] Greta Garbo's sex appeal emerged from mystery and worldly nonchalance, not flash. Any reasonable definition of glamour must include these icons, as well as such masculine touchstones as James Bond, Steve McQueen, and Cary Grant.

As subjects and sources of desire, luxury and sex appeal can be potent elements in creating glamour. But not every form of luxury or sex appeal is glamorous. Mystery is required, and the most glamorous objects often contain a tantalizing element of denial, as the film critic Manohla Dargis recognizes when she lauds contemporary Chinese films, "cinemas of longing," for creating "an extraordinary glamour born from the tension between release and repression."[9] Glamour leaves us wanting more.

More important, sex and luxury are not the only possible desires, or

Maggie Cheung and Tony Leung Chiu Wai in *In the Mood for Love* (2000), one of the Chinese films the critic Manohla Dargis describes as "cinemas of longing." *Photofest*

even the only common ones. Contrary to Steele's suggestion, Thorp did not use the word *romance* as a euphemism for sex—she already had *sex appeal*—but as a reference to something equally alluring to the predominantly female audiences she analyzed: the idealization of romantic love. The movies let viewers imagine being lavished with attention and devotion, minus the humdrum negotiations and daily routines of real relationships.

"What the typical adult American female chiefly asks of the movies is the opportunity to escape by reverie from an existence which she finds insufficiently interesting," Thorp wrote. These moviegoers wanted something more precious than luxury, she said: "to be appreciated, not just by implication but right out loud."

> Their ideal is still the ideal husband of the Victorian era who told his wife at breakfast every morning how much she meant to him, but that husband is not a type which the postwar [World War I] American man has any interest in emulating. He prefers to conceal his deeper emotions at breakfast, and during the rest of the day as well. His wife, consequently, has to spend her afternoons at the movies.
>
> In the movies a wife finds it quite worth while to get into a new evening frock for a *tête-à-tête* dinner at home because her husband is sure, by dessert time at least, to take her hand across the intimately small and inconvenient table and say, "Darling, you get lovelier every day."[10]

In today's more demonstrative age, we still recognize the allure of luxury and leisure in old movies but overlook the glamour of their portraits of married love, whether expressed in intimate endearments or rapid-fire affectionate banter.

Note, too, that these are *portraits*—still images of life transformed—not narratives. As we'll explore in chapter four, Hollywood glamour emanates not from the details of any given plot but from the evocative images and ideas that carry over from movie to movie, lingering in memory to stir the viewer's own fantasies even when story lines are forgotten.

So here is one answer to the question of what glamour does. It offers a lucid glimpse of desire fulfilled—if only life could be like *that*, if only we could be *there*, if only we could be like *them*. For all its associations with material goods, the fundamental and insatiable desires glamour taps are emotional.

Critics like Berger often assume that glamour creates those desires. They imagine that if glamour disappeared, so would dissatisfaction—that, for example, women would not long to be young and beautiful if there were no cosmetic ads or movie stars.[11] But glamour only works when it can tap preexisting discontent, giving otherwise inchoate longings an object of focus. Analyzing British moviegoers' recollections of 1930s movies, the film scholar Annette Kuhn captures the phenomenon well when she ar-

U.S. Marine Corps

gues that "there is an armature of desire, or wanting, onto which cinema hangs itself, so that the armature is clad with cinematic content." The desire precedes the glamour, but the glamour gives it a specific form. In the case of 1930s films, "the abstract notion of better things, or a better life," Kuhn continues, quoting her interviews, "is given content in the shape of the 'way of living,' the 'lovely' singing and dancing, and the 'easy life' enjoyed by people in films. At last, though, the underlying wish—both more and less than a desire for lovely things and an easy life—is baldly stated: 'perhaps one day life will be like that.'"[12]

By turning diffuse yearnings into specific but selective images, glamour concentrates what the Japanese call *akogare*: "unfulfilled longings," aspiration, and idealization, with a suggestion of the distant, foreign, or unattainable.[13] It gives form to what the advertising pioneer Lois Ardery, writing in 1924, described as "inarticulate longings."

We all know the woman who went to buy a practical blue ging-ham dress and came home with an impractical pink silk negligée.

We all *are* that woman now and then. . . . Our known want and recognized need is for a blue gingham dress. But the sight of a pink silk negligée somehow sets aflame a desire which, until this unrestrained moment, we have not known existed! Dormant desires, unknown even to ourselves; but how full of possibilities![14]

Beholding the pink silk, the shopper realizes she yearns to be not merely a practical housewife but an enticingly feminine seductress. She achieves that identity, if only in her imagination, by buying the negligee. It provides the cladding to the armature of her unspoken desire.

Glamour takes many forms because both the objects that embody such longings and the longings themselves—the cladding and the armature—vary from person to person. If the yearning to belong to an elite is the armature, for one person the cladding may be the image of US Marines as "the few, the proud"; for another it's getting past the bouncer and into the city's hottest club; for another it's matriculating at Harvard; and for yet another it's joining that movie trope, the "hand-picked team" of heroes. One would-be writer finds a display of Moleskine journals irresistibly glamorous while another is drawn to a photo of a mountain retreat or "a little attic in Paris with a skylight."[15]

Different audiences may also have different underlying desires, meaning that both armature and cladding vary. For some, nothing is more glamorous than a red-carpet entrance lit by camera flashes; others project themselves into the peaceful solitude of a lone kayaker or a Zen garden. Bollywood films offer one set of fantasies for the rural villager imagining urban wealth and another for the overseas urbanite longing for an idealized homeland.[16] An adult fan of superhero comics contrasts himself with other subscribers to an e-mail list called Glamour, whose predominantly gay members include many in the entertainment industry. "Their idea of glamour would be to get invited to the right party," he says. "To me growing up, the idea of glamour was to be the guy who could save the right party from a meteor."[17] Their vision expresses the desire for exclusivity and social recognition, his for power, adventure, and significance.

Regardless of the form it takes, glamour reveals emotional truths. It shows us what we find lacking in real life and who we want to be. The glamour of celebrity arises from the desire for admiration, adulation, and love: the yearning to be recognized as important. The glamour of fashion appeals to our desire for transformation, promising a makeover of our lives or our selves as well as our appearance. The glamour of luxury comes not only from the lure of material pleasures but also from the suggestion that we could gracefully fit into the setting to which they belong. However illusory its particulars, glamour is always emotionally authentic.

By figuring out how glamour answers a particular audience's longings, we can see how it operates and why it can arise in such seemingly unlikely places as superhero comic books—or convents. If you think glamour is all about diamonds and sex appeal, there are few less likely exemplars than a nun sworn to poverty and chastity. Yet so common is (or was) the glamorization of nuns that it has caused problems for real-life sisters. "It was the icon of veiled, virtuous virginity that audiences flocked to" in movies about nuns, "not the complicated women behind them," writes Rebecca Sullivan, a scholar who has studied portrayals of nuns in American popular culture. In the mid-twentieth century, she notes, nuns had an "aura of sacrificial glamour."[18]

At least that's how the young Mary Gordon saw them: as the most glamorous of women. As much as she enjoyed her Grace Kelly paper dolls and her cowgirl costume, the author writes of her childhood in the 1950s, her "nun doll and the nun book had a special shimmer. They made me feel exalted and apart." Her father would brag, "My daughter will either be a nun or a lady of the night."

> I didn't know what a lady of the night was. It sounded glamorous, but no more glamorous than the image of a nun. He and I had a party piece about nuns. He would say, "Honey, what do you want to be when you grow up?" And I would say, without skipping a beat, "A contemplative." . . .
>
> I had had a glimpse of a real contemplative, a glimpse that would press itself into the hot wax of my imagination. . . . I went

into the chapel with my parents. From the back I could see one of the nuns kneeling in prayer. Her form was impeccable: back straight, hands folded, head bowed for the inspiration of the Holy Ghost. A beam of light fell on her. And I knew that saturation in pure light was the most desirable state in the world.

As a teenager, Gordon tangled with the real nuns who were her teachers, but maintained her glamorous vision of the religious life thanks to movie images. Although a Jewish friend was appalled by the restrictive convent portrayed in *The Nun's Story* (1959), starring Audrey Hepburn as the brilliant Sister Luke, Gordon "found it enchanting—the silences, the gliding walk, above all the belief in perfection. . . . Whatever Sister Luke's life is, it is not trivial. Whether she succeeds or fails, the stakes involved are the highest."[19] To feel "exalted and apart," to be saturated in pure light, to believe in perfection, and above all, *to matter*. These are desires utterly at odds with the social envy portrayed by Berger. Like advertising images, the glamour of nuns unquestionably sold something to its audience, but that something was not the promise of social status.

Audrey Hepburn in *The Nun's Story* (1959): Like advertising images, the glamour of nuns unquestionably sold something to its audience, but that something was not the promise of social status.

Courtesy of Everett Collection

The yearning to matter—the desire for significance—is as common and deeply felt as any material craving. It informs the glamour of military service, sports, the art world, the intellectual life, and, in some cases, celebrity. It often accompanies another longing. Contrary to Berger's obsession with envy, which he calls "a solitary form of reassurance," many forms of glamour tap a desire for fellowship and belonging.[20] The "glamour of camaraderie" that D. H. Lawrence condemned as "the glamour of Homer and of all militarism" takes peaceful forms as well. When Gil Pender (Owen Wilson), the protagonist of *Midnight in Paris* (2011), finds himself suddenly transported to the Paris of the 1920s, he not only meets his literary idols but is instantly accepted and encouraged by them. Unlike Gil's dismissive fiancée, these important, accomplished people understand his longings and cherish his talents. It's a deeply appealing fantasy.

In it we see not only the allure of the Paris of *A Moveable Feast* but also of Camelot, Hogwarts, the Galt's Gulch of *Atlas Shrugged*, the Algonquin Roundtable, or the *Star Trek* universe—any setting where audience members who normally feel alienated from everyday reality can imagine themselves honored and at home. *Star Trek*'s allure may be lost on fashionistas but for the right audience, the show's distant and idealized universe offers its own glamour, arising from the graceful, mysterious setting: a future where today's conflicts and frustrations have disappeared. In the *Star Trek* universe, people no longer have to worry about distance, disease, money, energy supplies, racial conflict, stupid bosses, or disrespectful and bullying peers. "I never really fantasized about being the captain of the Enterprise," writes Kevin Curran, a Chicago lawyer who runs a *Star Trek* blog. "I just fantasized about living on the Enterprise, surround[ed] by these people who treated each other the way I wanted to be treated."[21]

Like studio-era movies, this fictional setting addresses not one but many different kinds of desire. It offers the obvious allure of adventure and exploration, along with *Star Trek*'s famously inclusive vision of "infinite diversity in infinite combinations." But many fans cite another, less remarked-upon appeal, analogous to the glamorous portrayal of married affection in old movies: the idea of a highly functional, meritocratic workplace where "everyone has a role, and is important."[22] *Star Trek*, says a female fan, offers a way "to escape and do it by being on a ship where there is a place for me, where I have a useful skill and can contribute to the mission." Its appeal lies in "both belonging and escape."[23]

Like studio-era movies, the *Star Trek* universe addresses not one but many different kinds of desire. It offers "both belonging and escape."

The Light Works/Tobias Richter

"You've always had a hard time finding a place in this world, haven't you? Never knowing your true worth," Captain Pike (Bruce Greenwood) tells the young Jim Kirk (Chris Pine) in the 2009 *Star Trek* reboot, encouraging him to enlist in Starfleet. "You can settle for something less, an ordinary life. Or do you feel like you were meant for something better? Something special."

Something special. That longing links *Star Trek* to fashionable party-goers, faithful Marines, and contemplative nuns. It is the promise of at once standing out as special and fitting into a group that shares your values and recognizes your worth. The glamour of this promise is often strong enough to sustain subcultures of devotees who create real-world fellow-ships around it. The *Star Trek* conventions, costumes, and collectibles that seem eccentric to outsiders (and to self-aware fans) serve the same emotional purposes for that audience that car shows, couture gowns, or postcards of Paris serve for theirs. Such activities and artifacts transform projection into participation, giving utopia a tactile presence.

———

This, then, is what glamour does as rhetoric. It focuses preexisting, largely unarticulated desires on a specific object, intensifying longing. It thus allows us to imaginatively inhabit the ideal and, as a result, to believe—at least for a moment—that we can achieve it in real life. It persuades us that the life we long for is almost within our grasp. Glamour is defined not by the specific desires it promotes but by the process of projection and sense of yearning it creates and, as we'll explore in subsequent chapters, by the recurring elements that generate that projection and yearning: the promise of escape and transformation; grace; and mystery. Many different glamorous objects can spark similar emotions, because they appeal to different personalities and different ideals.

In embodying the ideal, glamorous objects represent a special case of what the cultural anthropologist Grant McCracken calls "displaced meaning." Every culture, he observes, maintains ideals that can never be fully realized in everyday life, from Christian charity to economic equality. These ideals may uphold incompatible principles, deny the relation of cause and effect, require impossible knowledge, or demand more consistent or emotionally contradictory behavior than human beings can sustain. Yet for all their empirical failings, such cultural ideals supply essential purpose and meaning, offering identity and hope. To preserve and transmit them, cultures develop images and stories that portray a world in which their ideals are realized—a paradise, a utopia, a golden age, a promised land, a world to come (whether after death, the Messiah, the Second Coming, the Revolution, or the Singularity). McCracken writes:

When they are transported to a distant cultural domain, ideals are made to seem practicable realities. What is otherwise unsubstantiated and potentially improbable in the present world is now validated, somehow "proven," by its existence in another, distant one.[24]

The mythmaking of displaced meaning gives cultures the characters, artifacts, geography, and emotions that make their cherished abstractions seem attainable and true, while keeping those ideals safely removed from the constraints and compromises of real life. Through common myths, legends, rituals, and spectacles, a culture's members feel connected to these distant realms and the ideals they represent.

Glamour represents a way through which individuals access *personal* versions of displaced meaning. Angelina Jolie's "life narrative" embodies Naomi Wolf's picture of ideal womanhood. To its fans, *Star Trek* portrays the ideal workplace. Your dream house represents not just a dwelling but your concept of the ideal family life, the ideal job, the ideal self—of happiness, significance, tranquility, love, and fulfillment. Hence the glamour of home-interiors magazines and the ads that fill them. These images

Photofest

lead the viewer to think, *Life Would Be Perfect If I Lived in That House*, as Meghan Daum titled her humorous memoir of a life obsessed with moving and remodeling in a search for "domestic integrity."[25]

Like rituals and myths, glamour, too, makes the ideal seem available and real. But rather than striking awe, providing didactic lessons, or simply demonstrating the plausibility of cultural values, glamour sparks imaginative projection. It intensifies individual yearning. That emotional effect distinguishes it from other ways of accessing displaced meaning. So, too, does its individualistic nature. Whether the ideals it evokes are idiosyncratic or widely shared, glamour always arises from an individual's subjective reaction. New types of glamour may catalyze new subcultures—or, as we'll see in chapter seven, even reshape the dominant culture—by representing previously undefined versions of displaced meaning. But their power depends on the individual's response.

Since owning a component of the dream makes the entire ideal seem like something we can someday claim, McCracken argues, commercial goods often serve as "bridges to these hopes and ideals."[26] Such bridges are thus likely objects of glamour. The perfect house may be out of reach, but you can buy the perfect stove; the writer's retreat may be only a dream, but you can still have a great notebook. Like Viking ranges and Moleskine notebooks, such tangible, commercial "bridges" may themselves be glamorous. Or they may remind us of some form of glamour. In the 1930s, middle-class families in New York would hire specialty businesses to install elaborate padded satin headboards and matching quilted satin comforters in their bedrooms. "The headboard was the most glamorous thing you could have. It came right out of the movies," says Joan Kron, who later became a prominent style journalist, recalling her childhood apartment. "When you had that you thought you were Joan Crawford or Ginger Rogers."[27]

By its nature, however, displaced meaning is always out of reach. We can hold only the representative, not the ideal itself. Remembering the "amazing dresses" a former ballroom-dancing partner made for her, the competitive dancer and dance scholar Juliet McMains writes, "It was never as much fun being in the dress as it was imagining being in the dress, touching it from afar. The dress was a symbol of Glamour, but it was not

Glamour itself. Glamour cannot be caught inside a dress. It is elusive, always slipping away just when it seems within grasp."[28] The otherwise practical housewife who splurges on a negligee may feel beautiful in it, but she will also find that a new garment is not a new life. The inarticulate longings remain, waiting to be reawakened by the next glamorous object. Offering foreplay, not fulfillment, glamour heightens desire.

One reason glamour constantly reemerges in new forms is that the process of projection, yearning, and pursuit is itself pleasurable. That experience represents a version of what the sociologist Colin Campbell calls "modern, self-illusory hedonism." Unlike the sensation-seeking hedonism of food, drink, and sex, Campbell argues, the insatiability of modern consumption comes from the pursuit of *emotional* pleasure. Rather than a hedonism that repeats familiar sensations, this modern version is a process in which people first enjoy *anticipating new experiences* and the goods that convey them. In this kind of hedonism, Campbell writes, "the individual is much more an artist of the imagination," turning images from the real world into daydreams in which flaws have been edited out and "happy coincidences" become routine. The result is *"an illusion which is known to be false but felt to be true"*—an important characteristic of glamour as well (emphasis added). This imaginative illusion creates "a longing to experience in reality those pleasures created and enjoyed in imagination, a longing which results in the ceaseless consumption of novelty."[29]

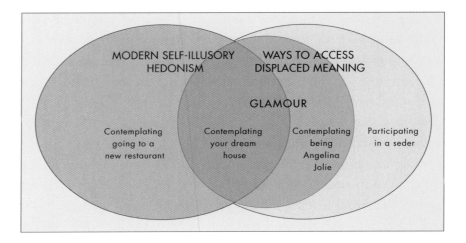

As Campbell describes it, modern, self-illusory hedonism sounds the same as glamour. But as the Venn diagram illustrates, the overlap isn't perfect. Glamour always implies reaching for displaced meaning; it promises not just pleasure but an experience of the ideal. It's possible to enjoy imagining a new experience that would fit easily into your existing life and doesn't represent anything greater than itself: eating in a new restaurant, for instance, or upgrading your iPhone to the latest model. Such pleasurable contemplation represents modern, self-illusory hedonism but not glamour. It suggests no real change from current circumstances, let alone a connection to displaced meaning.

Photo by Grey Crawford, interior design by Darryl Wilson

Conversely, as a way of accessing displaced meaning, glamour encompasses experiences that, while imaginable, aren't even theoretically possible and so fall outside Campbell's concept. Audiences may project themselves into becoming Angelina Jolie, living in 1920s Paris, or joining the *Starship Enterprise*'s crew. Like glamour, Campbell's "modern self-illusory hedonism" fosters projection and longing, and it, too, relies on mystery and grace. But it's too connected to the real world to encompass every form of glamour.

Still, the pleasures of modern, self-illusory hedonism do include contemplating experiences that are theoretically possible but practically out of reach. Belying Berger's crabbed notion of social envy, Campbell notes that "people regularly enjoy looking at pictures of products which they cannot—nor are ever likely to be able to—afford." Such contemplation offers pleasures of its own, many of which derive from the momentary experience of glamour. We see glamorous clothes, cars, or homes and imagine how good it would feel to inhabit them.

The problem comes when people can act on their longings and the details of reality collide with the edited fantasy. "I fall for the awesome four-inch heels every time, hoping to strut around like an archetypal fashion girl," says the London retailing executive Joanna Jeffreys. The sight of the shoes lifts her out of everyday reality and into a more exciting world, promising to transform her into a head-turning icon with limousines on call and the grace to maneuver in footwear designed for show. "But then morning comes," she continues, "and the idea of running for the number 10 bus in my Alaïa stingray-skin platforms doesn't seem so appealing."[30] If she couldn't afford the shoes, she'd never fully grasp how impractical they are. But since she does buy them, she has to face their limitations.

Campbell argues that such disillusionment is inevitable. As a result, he says, "the modern hedonist is continually withdrawing from reality as fast as he encounters it, ever-casting his day-dreams forward in time, attaching them to objects of desire, and then subsequently 'unhooking' them from these objects as and when they are attained and experienced."[31]

Since the audience isn't actually fooled, however, sometimes the symbol is enough. "The value of the good is *not purely illusory*," argues the sociologist Jens Beckert, taking issue with Campbell. "Indeed, when goods become material representations of otherwise abstract or distant events, values and ideals, they offer a mental realization of the desired. The symbolically charged good evokes sensations that virtually embody the realization of the desired state." The absurdly impractical shoes may never be worn, but they still offer a bridge to an ideal self and thus, their beauty aside, a source of ongoing pleasure. Besides, Beckert argues, merely striving to achieve the ideal can, in itself, be rewarding: "Striving and attaining are not strictly separate from each other."[32]

Glamour not only inspires consumer purchases or pleasurable daydreams. It can also move people to life-changing positive action. As flamboyant boys alienated from their "gritty, violent hometown" of Reading, England, Simon Doonan (now creative ambassador-at-large at Barneys) and his friend Biddie (now a successful drag performer) "saw glamour and modish excitement in the faraway and only boredom and dreariness in the here and now." They imagined, Doonan writes, an ideal life among the Beautiful People celebrated in glossy magazines.

These effortlessly stylish trendsetters owned sprawling palazzos in Rome and ultragroovy pied-à-terres in Chelsea. They slept in six-

Reinfried Marass

foot circular beds covered with black satin sheets and white Persian cats. The Beautiful People were thin and gorgeous, and they had lots and lots and lots of thick hair, and their lives seemed to be about a hundred million times more screechingly fabulous than Biddie's life and mine combined. They did not work much, but they had buckets and buckets of money, which they spent on things like champagne and caftans and trips to Morocco to buy caftans.

Inspired by these images, the two friends left for London in the early 1970s, strapping to the top of the car the object that best represented the glamorous new life they sought: a "massive, rhubarb-colored floor pillow."

The Beautiful People all had floor pillows. We knew they did. We had seen the Beautiful People lolling on their squishy floor pillows in trendy Sunday magazine spreads. Even if a Beautiful Person was photographed sitting on a couch or a tuffet or a poof, there was inevitably a floor pillow in the background. If we had any hope of being accepted by the Beautiful People, we needed that floor pillow. It was a calling card of sorts.[33]

However absurd it came to seem in retrospect, back home in Reading, the floor pillow had provided tangible proof that the life of the Beautiful People really existed and that the two friends might claim it. The floor pillow was a bridge to otherwise distant ideals.

When Doonan finally met the Beautiful People, they turned out to be boring and unimpressive. But by inspiring his and Biddie's move to London, their glamorous images led the two friends to find new and satisfying lives that would have been impossible in Reading. Glamour is an illusion and, according to its critics, a dangerous snare. But because it recognizes and concentrates real desires, the mirage can also prove a valuable, life-enhancing inspiration.

Elizabeth Taylor in *X, Y, and Zee* (1972): The "Beautiful People" all had caftans and floor pillows. *Courtesy of Everett Collection*

Glamour, we can now say, is a form of nonverbal rhetoric, an illusion "known to be false but felt to be true." It focuses inchoate desires and embodies them in the image or idea of a person, a setting, an artifact, or occasionally a concept. By inviting projection and making the ideal feel attainable, the glamorous image intensifies longing and, in some cases, moves the audience to action. Glamour can take many forms, because there are many kinds of desire and because the same desire can be expressed in multiple ways.

This describes what glamour *does* but only begins to say what it *is*. It does not tell us how to construct glamour and only begins to suggest how glamour, with its connection to displaced meaning, differs from other types of nonverbal persuasion: a photo of a frosty glass of beer on a hot summer's day, for instance. We now turn to the defining elements of glamour, beginning with how it answers a multiplicity of desires with the same essential promise.

Icon
THE PRINCESS

"Dress Up in Dreams" says the sign adorning the Disney Store's display of princess costumes. It's a persuasive invitation. In 2011 alone, the company sold $3 billion in Disney Princess merchandise, from dolls and dresses to backpacks and beds.[1] It got into the business almost by accident. In 2000, the new head of the company's consumer products division noticed that many of the girls attending a *Disney on Ice* show had cobbled together their own princess costumes. The next day he gave his team a mandate: to churn out products that would allow "girls to do what they're doing anyway: projecting themselves into the characters from the classic movies."[2] The glamour came first, the merchandising later.

It's a truism: *Every little girl dreams of being a princess*. (A Google search for that exact phrase turns up more than 821,000 instances.[3]) The power of the archetype predates Disney's marketing machine and will no doubt outlive it, because to play princess is to embrace two eternally alluring promises: *You are special* and *Life can be wonderful*. Those promises are princess glamour's stable emotional core. But what exactly they mean changes with audience and circumstances.

Long before Disney reimagined Snow White and Cinderella, the fairy tales on which those movies were based portrayed princesses as special creatures, blessed (and sometimes cursed) beyond the experiences of regular folk. A princess was beautiful, honored, and, by dint of birth or marriage, rich. In a world far less affluent than our own, to be a princess meant escaping poverty and hardship—an association that persisted well into the twentieth century. "I'll live like a princess in a house that runs like magic," declares the excited housewife depicted in a World War II–era American Gas Association ad, describing her "post-war dream."[4]

Playing on these associations, mass marketers in the 1920s used obscure European princesses to lend an aristocratic aura to their products, infusing everyday experiences with glamour. A Pond's cold cream ad featuring Princesse Marie de Bourbon of Spain described her "patrician-white" skin as having "the delicacy of the

Courtesy of Everett Collection

jasmine flower that blooms in the tangled depths of old, neglected Catalonian gardens."[5] Princess Giambattista Rospigliosi (née Ethel Bronson of Manhattan) declared that only Lux soap was good enough for laundering the precious lace of her great-grandmother's wedding veil.[6]

While the wealth and status of real-world royalty once gave the archetype much of its allure, by the late twentieth century the archetype had glamorized actual royalty, with all the illusion that implies. Having grown up on Barbara Cartland romance novels, the young Diana Spencer fantasized to a friend that marrying Prince Charles "could be quite fun. It would be like Anne Boleyn or Guinevere!" (The fates of these two legendary ladies prompted the response, "I bloody hope not!") When she did marry the prince, Diana reified her princess fantasies in her famous wedding dress. "She would be a fairy bride for her father and her Prince," writes Tina Brown in her biography of the princess. "Those creamy ruffles and ivory frills would float her away from the agonies of the present to a future of certain love."[7]

In the years since Diana, the princess archetype has become even more detached from the privileges of real-life royalty. When supermodel Kate Moss's daughter, Lila, then four years old, met actual princesses Beatrice and Eugenie, the little girl was not impressed. "How come if you are princesses you don't have tiaras *and* a pink dress?" she demanded.[8] As for the public's new favorite

The 1981 wedding of Prince Charles and Diana Spencer, whose own glamorous vision of life as a princess was drawn from Barbara Cartland romance novels. *Rex Features/ Courtesy of Everett Collection*

princess, the limited glamour of Kate Middleton, now the duchess of Cambridge, lies in her poise, wholesome attractiveness, and impeccable personal style. Her marriage to Prince William is just the way she became famous, not a fantasy in itself. Fans crave her great hair more than her royal status. She could just as well be the latest ingenue actress.

As the unimpressed young Lila demonstrates, princess glamour has largely become a childhood fantasy. It represents a feminine version of the appeal Michael Chabon, in his novel *The Amazing Adventures of Kavalier & Clay*, ascribes to superheroes. Princesses, too, express the "lust for power and the gaudy sartorial taste of a race of powerless people with no leave to dress themselves."[9] For some young girls, playing princess is, in fact, merely the stage before playing superhero.[10] Like the superhero, the princess has a special identity, destiny, and costume. She is more than an ordinary girl.

Among today's educated urbanites, however, princess glamour is suspect. The postfeminist mothers of princess-besotted little girls worry that the archetype teaches their daughters to be pretty and helpless, waiting for a prince to rescue them instead of acting on their own behalf. "I don't want my daughter to be a princess; I don't want her to be girly or silly, or anything that is attributed to princess idolatry," declares the feminist blogger Marina DelVecchio, the mother of a princess-loving three-year-old. "I want her to be strong and intelligent, fiery and confident."[11]

A more sanguine contemporary mother, blogger Sasha Brown-Worsham, observes, "'Princess culture' is what you make it."[12] The princess archetype comes in many versions—one reason for its power and persistence. Iconic princesses range from the domestic Cinderella to the warrior Xena, from the cleverly faithful Penelope to the dangerously beautiful Helen, from feisty Princess Leia to the many cinematic reinventions of Elizabeth Tudor. The 2012 movie *Snow White and the Huntsman* reimagines its heroine as a good-hearted, relatively plain rebel leader.[13] Wonder Woman is both superhero and princess.

Beyond feeling special, what it means to dream of being a princess depends largely on the dreamer. "When I was a kid, my best friend and I dressed up as princesses," recalls a blog commenter. "In our play we were always kidnapped by the bad guys and had to use our kickass martial arts and fencing skills to escape. While wearing pretty dresses."[14]

Icon
WIND TURBINES

In the mid-twentieth century, jet airplanes and rocket ships were the glamorous visual symbols of technological optimism. Their images lent excitement to car ads and diner décor, children's pajamas and packages of sewing needles. Jets and rockets were everywhere, promising a bright future. Then in the pessimistic 1970s, these once-iconic forms disappeared from common view. "The future" no longer seemed so glamorous. We were doomed, it seemed, to ecological catastrophe if not nuclear war. "Natural" was in; hard, mechanical forms were out. Besides, jets and rockets were old news.

Three decades later, their successor emerged. Wind turbine images are the new evocative symbols of technological hope. Their graceful forms adorn ads for everything from Volkswagen to Aveda, Skyy vodka to Goldman Sachs. On Shutterstock, the world's largest subscription-based stock-photo agency, turbines are nearly as popular as the long-iconic lightbulb.[1]

For the people who create them, the images represent grace and beauty. "They're among my favorite things to photograph," says Sandra Santos, who sells cards with dreamy photos of California windmills against a purpling sky. But like the stylized rockets of the mid-twentieth century, turbines have meanings that go beyond their immediate aesthetic pleasure. For Santos, as for many others, they "are iconic images of a world moving forward."[2] When Spike Lee directed a 2010 TV commercial for the left-leaning news network MSNBC, a shot of windmills appeared as the voiceover affirmed "the freedom to believe that our best days are still ahead."[3]

Policy wonks assume the current rage for wind farms has something to do with efficiently reducing carbon emissions. So they spend their time debating load mismatches and transmission losses. These practical discussions miss the emotional point. To their most ardent advocates, and increasingly to the public at large, wind turbines aren't just about generating electricity. They're symbols of an ideal world—longing disguised as problem solving.

Like rockets and jets, wind turbines combine sleek, graceful lines with the mystery of newness and distance. Few of us have direct experience with them,

iStockphoto

and fewer still understand exactly how they work. But we know what they mean. Turbines, in the words of singer Thomas Dolby, tell us to "dream big, imagining a beautiful future for our children, despite all the evidence that says they're doomed."[4]

As emblems of technological progress, today's wind turbines embody a different dream from those midcentury jets and rockets. While the old icons zoomed forward toward some unseen but surely wonderful destination, the new ones move yet remain stationary. Turbine images promise progress without change, simultaneously appealing to the original idea of sustainability—a steady-state world without economic growth—and to the popular desire for prosperity and abundance. These new icons of eco-consciousness cater to what Al Gore denounced in *Earth in the Balance* as "the public's desire to believe that sacrifice, struggle, and a wrenching transformation of society will not be necessary" to avoid catastrophic climate change.[5] They promise that a green future will be just as pleasant as today, only cleaner and more elegant.

Like other forms of glamour, turbine images represent the world not as it is but as we would like it to be. In stock-photo glamour shots, wind power seems clean, free, and infinitely abundant. Turbines spin silently, while the wind blows constantly and in exactly the right amount. The sky is unfailingly photogenic, a backdrop of either puffy clouds or a brilliant sunset; the landscape is both empty and beautiful; and there are no transmission lines anywhere.

In the real world, wind farms face growing resistance. Some critics consider them the equivalent of the supersonic Concorde jet: an inspiring technology, perhaps, but an economically inefficient way of getting the job done and, thus, a subsidy-dependent boondoggle. Other opposition comes from people who live near potential sites. Some neighbors object to the noise, while others find wind turbines ugly.[6]

While the fashion for wind-turbine images feeds positive public feelings about actual turbines, image is not reality. The question is whether, having become glamorous icons, wind turbines will eventually become as common (and hence unglamorous) as jets—or whether they'll prove the latest incarnation of flying cars and electricity too cheap to meter.

II.

THE ELEMENTS OF GLAMOUR

THREE

DREAMS OF FLIGHT AND TRANSFORMATION AND ESCAPE

Even in an era when air travel is both commonplace and fairly unpleasant, few images are more glamorous than a jet ascending into a sunset or silhouetted against a full moon. Seen at a distance, the sleek craft rises toward a horizon full of possibilities. No matter how many times we've flown, we can still feel the glamour of the image, because this feeling isn't about the actual experience of travel. It's about soaring toward something new. Looking at the rising plane, we do not imagine ourselves as the pilot or passengers; we project ourselves into the aircraft itself. Momentarily leaving behind the constraints and disappointments of ordinary existence, we fly toward our hopes and dreams.

All glamour appeals to and intensifies what the novelist Michael Chabon, in *The Amazing Adventures of Kavalier & Clay*, calls "dreams of flight and transformation and escape."[1] Glamour is not just illusory but escapist—and the escapism it offers is emotionally specific. It does not stir adrenaline, astonishment, or laughter, distracting us from current circumstances. Rather, glamour provides an emotionally compelling alternative, focusing inarticulate longings on totems that imply change and connect us with the ideal. In the image of a rising jet or a speeding convertible, a runway model or a martial-arts hero, a beachside vista or a big-city skyline, we experience the same dream: that we might soar beyond present constraints, cast off our worries, become better, freer, more accomplished, admired, respected, and desired versions of ourselves.

"The best and most enduring fashion is inspired by our longings for transcendence," writes Manolo the Shoeblogger, commenting on a particularly glamorous fashion collection. "We wish to move beyond ourselves, to leave behind the mundanity of our lives and be carried aloft to the higher plane, to the place where we are more beautiful, more charming, more alluring, and where we are dressed only and forever in Christian Dior, 2011 Spring Couture Collection."[2] Or, for those with different aspirations, to the place where we are shod in a constant rotation of vintage Air Jordan sneakers, cherished more than a decade after their namesake's retirement as a player, because they still embody their original promise: "I felt they could make me fly," writes collector Art Eddy, "just like MJ."[3]

The runway show of the Christian Dior 2011 Spring Couture Collection: "The best and most enduring fashion is inspired by our longings for transcendence." *GoRunway.com*

The promise of escape and transformation defines what kinds of totems can be objects of glamour. It explains, for instance, why glamorous artifacts are usually items we can literally inhabit or wear (clothes, cars, jewelry); items that contribute to and symbolize a particular environment and lifestyle (a crystal decanter, a writer's notebook, a cook's kitchen, an aviator's chronograph); or items that extend the owner's capabilities and powers (an iPad, a Leica). Ralph Lauren, a master of glamour as a designer and businessman, collects classic cars, primarily Ferraris, that do all three. These vehicles are not only beautiful but evocative. They represent, he suggests, "an escape, or an entry into wonderful worlds."[4]

Glamour's promise of escape and transcendence distinguishes it from forms of nonverbal rhetoric that evoke more immediate desires. Glamour does not offer simple utility or sensation. It doesn't promise a more reliable car, a thirst-quenching beverage, or an orgasm. It is not that literal. Even the stereotypical glamour of a male rap star surrounded by beautiful, scantily clad women lies not in sex per se—a rap video is not pornography—but in the enticing depiction of a world and persona in which the viewer can imagine being doted on and desired, with sexual favors available for the asking. Like Marlene Dietrich or James Bond, the video sells sex *appeal*: a state of being, not a specific sensory pleasure. Similarly, the glamour of champagne lies not in the taste of the drink but in the lifestyle it signifies. The glamour of art collecting comes not from the aesthetic pleasure of a specific painting but from imagining the collector's life of excitement, status, and fellowship—of doing something special and belonging to a special world. The desires glamour serves and intensifies are never purely physical. They are emotional.

Those desires—for love, wealth, power, beauty, sex appeal, adulation, friendship, fame, freedom, dignity, adventure, discovery, self-expression, or enlightenment—vary from person to person and culture to culture. But glamour suggests they can all be attained through personal transformation or escape from current circumstances. Glam-

our leads us to imagine ourselves in the other: another person, another place, another life. It doesn't depict familiar pleasures in an appealing way but implies change and new experiences, allowing us to mentally experiment with new settings and identities. Glamour's promise of escape and transformation can create an enjoyable but transient experience, provide a source of solace in difficult circumstances, or offer direction toward real-world action.

A scene in the 1931 movie *Possessed* encapsulates the way glamour works to focus inchoate desires through the lens of escape and transformation. Heading home after a dull day's work at a paper-box factory, a young woman named Marian (Joan Crawford) parts company with her boring small-town boyfriend and comes upon a train slowly pulling toward the local station. She gazes up as one illuminated window after another goes by, each providing a glamorous glimpse of a richer, more interesting life: a bartender mixes a cocktail in a gleaming shaker while a chef puts the finishing touches on an elegant meal; a waiter lays out silverware on a white linen tablecloth; a maid irons silken lingerie; a young woman prepares to don a fine stocking; a couple in a tuxedo and satin gown dance from window to window, then dip to a kiss. It's a self-referential scene, mirroring the moviegoing experience. And Marian's longing is palpable.

As the train slows to a stop, she is startled out of her reverie when a man seated on the caboose offers her a cocktail. "Looking in?" he says. "Wrong way—get in and look out." The rest of the movie is about what happens when she does. She leaves her small town for New York City and reinvents herself as the cultured mistress of a wealthy man (Clark Gable). With a fake name and phony background, Marian's new identity is an illusion. But it contains the truth about who she wants to be. By becoming a new person in a new place, she achieves not only luxury, excitement, and sophistication but true love and, by the movie's end, a proposal of marriage.[5]

Unlike escapist entertainment that simply provides emotional distraction, glamour is escapist in the profound sense identified by the geographer Yi-Fu Tuan. Echoing *Queen Christina*'s Antonio, Tuan argues that escapism is the essence of culture, which he defines as "the totality of means by which I escape from my animal state of being." This uniquely human escapism allows us to shape the world, and ourselves, through deliberate action.

> A human is an animal who is congenitally indisposed to accept reality as it is. Humans not only submit and adapt, as all animals do; they transform in accordance with a preconceived plan. That is, before transforming, they do something extraordinary, namely, "see" what is not there. Seeing what is not there lies at the foundation of all human culture.[6]

Seeing what is not there is, of course, exactly what glamour makes us do. It leads us to imagine tapestries on a dungeon wall, a gilded world in a candy wrapper, or happiness on a tropical beach. Escapism has a bad reputation, but as we'll explore in the next chapter, the promise of escape and transformation is not where glamour's fundamental illusion lies. The dream may omit important details, from the discomfort of new shoes to the loneliness of a new city. The transformation may be a long shot, or in some cases literally impossible. But the mere idea of escape and transformation is not inherently false. It is, as Tuan says, at the heart of human culture. For individuals and for societies, the chance to imagine a different life in different circumstances is essential to progress. Thus the science-fiction author Gregory Benford defends his genre against a critic's claim that "science fiction is to technology as romance novels are to marriage: a form of propaganda." True enough, Benford admits, "but no one can accomplish anything without first imagining it."[7]

With its promise of escape and transformation, glamour can inspire life-sustaining hope and sometimes spark real-world change, offering both solace and direction. The feminist historian Sally Alexander argues that the escapist films and glamorous ads of the 1930s played an important role in liberating working-class British women, first psychologically and eventually materially, from the constrained world of their birth. With their images of "streamlined kitchens, effective cleaning equipment, cheap and pretty clothes and make-up," Alexander writes, advertisements and movies "enabled women to *imagine* an end to domestic drudgery and chronic want." These images cloaked the armature of discontent with specific goods representing a better life. "Few women replaced the copper with the washing-machine or the outside lavatory with the bathroom during the 1930s," she writes. "But the dream was there and houses were built with these amenities, and by the end of the decade families were moving into them."[8]

Jazz pianist and singer Hazel Scott and her husband, Congressman Adam Clayton Powell Jr., in a *Life* photograph taken at the opening night of the New York club Bop City in April 1949. *Getty Images/Martha Holmes*

Similarly, *Ebony* founder John H. Johnson built his fortune on understanding what postwar African Americans found glamorous and why. He knew, declared a typical tribute after his death in 2005, that "black readers wanted to dream a little, perhaps to copy a table setting of Marian Anderson, to read about the achievements of black people all over the world."[9] *Ebony* affirmed the right of readers to identify with such pleasures and accomplishments. The seemingly frivolous glamour of beauty, wealth, and celebrity gave readers what they yearned for: entertainment, yes, but also a publicly affirmed sense of dignity, worth, and fully rounded humanity.

In his influential 1957 book *Black Bourgeoisie,* the sociologist E. Franklin Frazier excoriated the black press, led by Johnson's publications, for this escapism. "Its exaggerations concerning the economic well-being and cultural achievements of Negroes," he wrote, "its emphasis upon Negro 'society' all tend to create a world of make-believe into which the black bourgeoisie can escape from its inferiority and inconsequence in American society."[10] As a matter of empirical reality, Frazier was absolutely correct. The world portrayed by *Ebony* was largely an illusion, pieced together from evidence that was scattered and often strained. In the 1950s, not even the wealthiest and most culturally influential black Americans escaped the racial caste system.

But to its audience, the magazine's hopeful glamour provided psychological sustenance and a political message. Even the most trivial celebrity feature declared that white supremacy was a false ideology and that Jim Crow was not the inevitable and permanent state of the world. "We're trying to inspire people," Johnson said.[11] *Ebony*'s make-believe allowed readers to see a world that was not there and, over time, to bring it closer to reality.

In November 2005, the cover of the magazine's sixtieth anniversary issue featured three Oscar-winning Hollywood stars: Denzel Washington, Halle Berry, and Jamie Foxx, each with a history of varied leading roles worthy of a studio-era icon. Moviegoers, Margaret Ferrand Thorp had explained in her 1939 study, "are primarily white and no white American, the industry maintains, would ever make his escape personality black."[12] By 2005, that was no longer so true. "Seeing a black lead actor just isn't an issue for people anymore. It would have been just 10 years ago," Ed Guerrero, a scholar of African-American cinema, told the *New York Daily News* earlier that year, after movies starring Ice Cube and Samuel L. Jackson took the week's top two box-office slots.[13] Black actors might still struggle to win roles, but white moviegoers had again and again proved willing to identify with them. Three years later, the country elected its first black president, the most glamorous in decades.[14]

———

Glamour fuels dissatisfaction with the here and now, even as it makes present difficulties easier to endure by suggesting the existence of better alternatives. This paradox means that one writer can observe that glamour contains "a moral element" that has "something to do with optimism, cheer and celebration, glamour being a language that denotes great faith in life," while another suggests that glamour's appeal originates in despair: "If you're trying to escape through a fantasy you have to be pretty desperate, right? That's the sense of 'despair' that I mean—a feeling of being trapped and having no options left."[15]

Both are correct. By tendering the promise of escape and transformation, glamour feeds on both hope and hardship. This ambiguity was captured poignantly in the 1991 documentary *Paris Is Burning*, which portrayed the competitive drag balls among poor black and Latino men in New York City. "A ball is to us, is as close to reality as we're going to get, to all that fame and fortune and stardom and spotlights," a ball participant explains on camera. "It's like crossing into the looking glass, into Wonderland," says a fan. Along with stereotypical drag-queen personas, featuring over-the-top gold lamé gowns and contemptuously regal strutting, the film shows contestants competing in categories that ache with the longing of the poor and excluded. Men in suits and eyeglasses, carrying cheap briefcases that betray the illusion, enact "Executive Realness" as the emcee announces "the well-dressed man of the eighties."

"In a ballroom you can be anything you want. You're not really an executive, but you're looking like an executive," says ball veteran Dorian Corey. "And therefore you're showing the straight world that I can be an executive. If I had the opportunity I can be one, because I can look like one. And that is like a fulfillment. Your peers, your friends, are telling you, 'Oh, you'd make a wonderful executive.'" The glamour of the balls includes not only fame, acclaim, and beauty but also fellowship and acceptance. "You go in there and you feel 100 percent right, being gay," says the unnamed fan. "That's not what it's like in the world—it's not what it's like in the world. It should be like that in the world."

Madonna's hit 1990 song "Vogue" took its inspiration from a club dance that evolved in the Harlem ball competitions. The lyrics explicitly relate escape from the troubles of the outside world to transformation

Horst/Vogue © Condé Nast

into a "superstar" on the dance floor. To lyrics referring to such iconic stars as Marlene Dietrich, Fred Astaire, and Greta Garbo, the song's video adds visual references to Hollywood and fashion glamour. It uses the high-contrast black-and-white style of studio-era films for its sets and costumes and includes direct allusions to photos by George Hurrell, Horst P. Horst, and other photographers. "Vogue" is a celebration of the joys of glamour. Yet outside the cinema, the dance club, the balls, and the video screen, the real world is always there. Most of the performers in *Paris Is Burning* died within a few years of the film's release, some from AIDS or violence, others from chronic diseases like diabetes. Just because you want escape and transformation doesn't mean you can have them.

The tension between hope and despair, and between escapist illusion and inner truth, plays out sympathetically in Nella Larsen's tragic 1928 novella *Quicksand*. Again and again, the book's protagonist Helga Crane relocates, always in the belief that in the next place she will find a life that affirms her identity and satisfies her longings. As Helga contemplates each of her many moves, Larsen repeatedly articulates the glamour of new settings. Envisioning a move from New York to Copenhagen, Helga began to make plans and to dream delightful dreams of change, of life somewhere else. Someplace where at last she would be permanently satisfied. Her anticipatory thoughts waltzed and eddied about to the sweet silent music of change. With rapture almost, she let herself drop into the blissful sensation of visualizing herself in different, strange places, among approving and admiring people, where she would be appreciated and understood.[16]

The daughter of a Danish immigrant mother and a black American father, Helga fits uneasily into a segregated society. But her more fundamental problem is one of intellect and temperament. She craves leisure, beauty, and understanding yet is too introverted, bookish, and uncompromising to achieve satisfaction. Helga ends the book trapped in rural Alabama and pregnant with her fifth child, able to dream no longer of a hopeful future but only of a lost and desirable past. The wistfulness of nostalgia replaces the hopefulness of glamour.

Unlike many social critics, however, Larsen excoriates neither glamour nor escapism. The author's attitude is more complex. Glamour, she suggests, can be life-sustaining and psychologically essential even when it is delusive and misleading. The rare periods of happiness Helga does experience come about because of her flights into glamour. The literary critic Judith Brown observes,

> The novel understands the price Helga pays for her commitment to those objects that reflect and refract her ideal image yet withholds its judgment, neither condemning nor condoning the choices she makes. . . . Glamour has a price, according to Larsen . . . but is, perhaps, worth it, offering as it does the pleasures powerful enough to enchant the everyday, to provide a different, and better, if only transitory, sense of uplift.[17]

Only in those elusive, illusory moments of enchantment does Helga find contentment.

Glamour entails vulnerability less because it is illusory than because it is revealing. It reminds us what we find lacking in real life and who we want to be. It stokes discontent. If the gap between reality and desire is too great, that knowledge may be painful. "People's fantasies are what give them problems," said Andy Warhol. "If you didn't have fantasies you wouldn't have problems because you'd just take whatever was there."[18] Warhol, who was obsessed with glamour, did not actually reject fantasy. To the contrary, he admired and encouraged it. But he himself felt the pangs of unfulfilled longing. For all his fame, wealth, and artistic accomplishment, he was always troubled by the one thing he couldn't achieve: beauty. "I always found it touching when Andy called somebody a beauty who obviously was not. . . . He wasn't blind or being kind," remembers Bob Colacello, the long-time editor of Warhol's magazine *Interview*. "It was just that by stretching the definition of beauty to the limit, he thought that—with his bad skin, bad teeth, bad hair—he might fit in too."[19] But he knew he never did.

Writing of Ayn Rand's depression after the publication of her monumental novel *Atlas Shrugged*, biographer Anne Heller recalls one of the author's early works:

> In her play *Ideal*, the Garboesque screen idol Kay Gonda can believe in her fans' devotion only if they are willing to risk their lives for her; the heroine cries out, "If all of you who look at me on the screen hear the things I say and worship me for them—where do I hear them? . . . I want to see, real, living, and in the hours of my own days, that glory I create as an illusion! I want it real!" Rand wrote those lines in 1934. Kay Gonda spoke for her creator then, and spoke for her in 1959.[20]

Rand had no more hope of meeting in real life the idealized, emotionally simplified characters she conjured as an author than she did of personally inhabiting the tall, blond body of her dreams. Like Helga Crane, she was temperamentally unable to make peace with the limitations and compromises of the real world. As unhappy as it made her, however, her longing for the ideal drove her achievement and defined who she was.

Taken as a guide rather than the literal truth, however, glamour need not entail disappointment. By pointing toward real avenues of escape and transformation, even its most improbable sources can channel inchoate desire into personal fulfillment. Growing up impoverished and abused in the still largely segregated South, Oprah Winfrey glimpsed a distant, more perfect world on TV: a beautifully gowned Diana Ross singing on *The Ed Sullivan Show*, Sidney Poitier arriving at the Academy Awards, and, oddly but most influentially, the TV newsroom of *The Mary Tyler Moore Show*. A series whose comedy was largely based on embarrassing situations, the show wasn't intended to be glamorous. But the right audience can always edit away the flaws. For Winfrey, the sitcom provided an intensely alluring portrait of friendship, collegiality, meaningful work, personal safety, and economic independence. Its protagonist was smart, pretty, stylish, and respected by her colleagues. For all their quirks, the characters lived interesting, fun-filled lives without significant hardship. The setting—the idea and ideal of the characters' lives—was far more important than the details of any particular plot.

"I wanted to be Mary Tyler Moore," Winfrey recalls, equating the actress with her character. "I wanted to be Mary. I wanted to live where Mary lived. I wanted Mr. Grant in my life. I wanted my boss to be like that." Following Mary's example, she pursued a career in television news, eventually finding her niche as a talk-show host. One of the highlights of Winfrey's triumph as a TV star in her own right was re-creating *The Mary Tyler Moore Show*'s opening credit sequence, with herself in the leading role. Instead of showing the character Mary Richards driving into Minneapolis to find a new life, this version showed Winfrey coming to Chicago and, like Mary, ending a sequence of joyful scenes by exu-

A scene from the opening sequence of *The Mary Tyler Moore Show*. Although not intended to be glamorous, for a young Oprah Winfrey the sitcom provided an alluring vision of friendship and meaningful work. "I wanted to be Mary," she says.

Photofest

With its portrait of lively conversation among Frederick the Great and his friends, including Voltaire (left in this detail), Adolph von Menzel's *Die Tafelrunde* represented to the young Karl Lagerfeld "the life that was worth living."

berantly tossing her hat in the air. "Whenever I'm having a down day," she told her audience in 1997, "I just pop that [recording] in. I love that!" Winfrey had projected herself into a glamorous fiction and, with a few adjustments, made it come true.[21]

A glamorous vision need not produce such literal fulfillment to prove a valuable inspiration. Consider the fashion designer Karl Lagerfeld. As a little boy, he saw a picture that enchanted him and focused his aspirations. It was a glamorous image not of an athlete, a movie star, or a fashion model but of an eighteenth-century luncheon, Adolph von Menzel's *Die Tafelrunde*. The painting shows Frederick the Great and nine friends, including Voltaire, gathered around an elegantly appointed table in an ornate round room. To one side, French doors open onto a sunny garden. With its crystal chandelier, marble statues, velvet coats, and attentive servants, the scene is unquestionably luxurious. But most striking are the lively faces of the men as they engage in spirited conversation—a conversation that we, of course, cannot hear. Young Karl yearned to join the party. At the age of seven, said Lagerfeld in 2000, "I decided that this elegant and refined scene represented the life that was worth living, a sort of ideal that I have since endeavoured to achieve." As an adult, he worked tirelessly as a designer to attain the lifestyle Menzel's scene represented, a dream Lagerfeld's biographer Alicia Drake describes as "a world of wit and erudite conversation, a world of light and luxury, choreographed manners and costume, a world of curiosity and a possibility of the superlative."[22]

Here is the paradox. The glamour that inspired Lagerfeld was an illusion. The painting naturally omits the unpleasant aspects of eighteenth-century existence (even for aristocrats), from the terrors of smallpox to the lack of indoor plumbing. More important, the manners and customs of eighteenth-century aristocrats are long gone, as Lagerfeld himself acknowledges. "All that has followed is petit bourgeois," he said in 1979.[23] For good or ill, the life of that party cannot be reclaimed by re-creating the scene with antiques and a contemporary group of fashionably attired men. We are different now. As a literal prescription, Lagerfeld's endeavors were bound to fail. His story about the painting appeared in the catalogue for an auction disposing of his eighteenth-century furnishings, the tangible bridges to his youthful dream. "Suddenly you are confronted with a past that can no longer be your present or become your future," he wrote, explaining why he had decided to relinquish his treasures.[24] Lagerfeld never got exactly what he envisioned, and he never could have. But his pursuit of that dream inspired a successful career and a huge body of creative work.

Even when futile, the pursuit of an ideal can have benefits. In a famous passage in *The Theory of Moral Sentiments*, Adam Smith depicts a "poor man's son, whom heaven in its anger has visited with ambition." The young man is enchanted by an unexamined image of happiness, in this case the glamour of wealth and leisure.

> He finds the cottage of his father too small for his accommodation, and fancies he should be lodged more at his ease in a palace. He is displeased with being obliged to walk a-foot, or to endure the fatigue of riding on horseback. He sees his superiors carried about in machines, and imagines that in one of these he could travel with less inconveniency. He feels himself naturally indolent, and willing to serve himself with his own hands as little as possible; and judges, that a numerous retinue of servants would save him from a great deal of trouble. He thinks if he had attained all these, he would sit still contentedly, and be quiet, enjoying himself in the thought of the happiness and tranquillity of his situation. He is enchanted with the distant idea of this felicity. It appears in his fancy like the life of some superior rank of beings.

That distant and glamorous idea sends the ambitious young man on a journey far more arduous than Alain de Botton's trip to Barbados. He spends his life striving to reach the station he imagined, only to achieve material success without the felicity of his dreams. "Through the whole of his life," writes Smith, "he pursues the idea of a certain artificial and elegant repose which he may never arrive at, for which he sacrifices a real tranquillity that is at all times in his power." He is deluded by glamour, tricked by an illusion. Yet his achievement is not only real but socially beneficial: "It is this deception which rouses and keeps in continual motion the industry of mankind."[25]

Note the nature of the deception. It is not that wealth is out of reach. Smith is writing in an era in which a poor man can in fact rise beyond the status of his birth, and his hypothetical young man does succeed financially. This is not a story of failure and broken dreams. Rather, the young man's lucid picture of the good life—the glamorous vision that inspires his quest—omits important details. It leaves out years of laborious effort, showing only the results of all that hard work, and forgets that new circumstances bring new sources of discontent.

This omission suggests the second element essential to all forms of glamour. Whether inspiring life-altering action or momentary reverie, glamour always obscures the difficulties and distracting details of life as it is really lived. Vacation posters say nothing about jet lag; movie stars' portraits remove blemishes. Glamour promises not only flight and transformation and escape but impossible grace.

Icon
THE GOLDEN STATE

A rose festival in the depths of winter. Palm trees and sunshine. Beautiful bodies on beautiful beaches. Test pilots and hot rods. Brilliant inventors turned billionaires. Movie stars turned statesmen. The Golden Mountain. A Magic Kingdom. Across continent or ocean, the farthest frontier. In song and story and, of course, on screen, California has long represented the promise, fulfilled or broken, of escape and transformation.

Beginning in the late nineteenth century, boosters selling transportation and real estate portrayed the state as a distant yet accessible paradise, with gentle weather, bountiful land, and endless opportunities— a place as desirable for farmers and families as for would-be movie stars. Certain symbols recurred again and again: beaches and palm trees, of course, but also open hillsides and white-walled mission architecture, golden poppies and orange trees heavy with fruit. To tourists and transplants alike, California appeared exotic but friendly, an El Dorado safe for women and children.

It was "the *golden state*, the land of *golden dreams*," write KD and Gary F. Kurutz in *California Calls You: The Art of Promoting the Golden State 1870 to 1940*. Those dreams began with a literal gold rush, but "the golden nugget that initially symbolized California gave way to the golden grain, golden orange, golden poppy, 'black gold,' and the Golden Gate. All became symbols that expanded the imagination and the dreams of opportunity."[1]

In the fall of 1919, California's booster glamour worked its magic on a young architect who dreamed of escape from the "psychological collapse" of Europe's demoralized interwar culture. "I wish I could get out of Europe," he wrote in his diary, "and get to an idyllic tropical island where one does not have to fear the winter, where one does not have to slave but finds time to think, or even more important, can have a free spirit." A travel poster obsessed him: "California Calls You," it read.[2]

He was Richard Neutra, and in 1925 he and his family settled in Los Angeles. Over the next half century, the houses Neutra designed created new visual symbols of the California good life: modern homes in which outdoors and indoors, leisure and ambition, nature and artifice, mind and body could happily coexist. Although disillusioned migrants are as central to the California myth as palm trees and surfboards, Neutra was not disappointed. "I found what I had hoped for," he wrote, "a people who were more 'mentally footloose' than those elsewhere, who did not mind deviating opinions . . . [a place] where one can do almost anything that comes to mind and is good fun."[3]

Crowded, plagued by fiscal crises, and no longer so exotic, California in recent years has lost some of its glamour. But the aura still lingers. "You could travel the world / But nothing comes close to the Golden Coast," sings Katy Perry in "California Gurls," the summer pop hit of 2010.[4]

Julius Shulman's photograph of the Kaufmann House in Palm Springs, designed by Richard Neutra, became a visual symbol of the California good life.

iStockphoto

Many a young, recession-weary professional now looks westward toward Silicon Valley, with dreams fueled by media portrayals of easy riches. "They ask me if it's as glamorous as they've heard it made out to be," writes Samihah Azim, a bemused product manager at a startup. "My first reaction is, 'lolwut?! Working in tech is . . . glamorous? Ya'll [sic] need to stop watching so much *The Social Network.'*" But for all the long hours and risks of failure, she admits "working in technology is 'glamorous' in that there are vast opportunities out there to do something you truly enjoy."[5] Neutra would understand. The gold rush aside, the California dream has never really been about money. The state's glamour radiates from the promise that here is where you can reinvent your life and find the better, happier, truer you.

Drawing on that glamour, Apple prominently labels its products "designed in California." The slogan, notes a technology blogger, makes you "think of *California*, not the *actual* state, with its endless dismal boulevards full of muffler shops and donut stores, but the California of memory: the Beach Boys, the Summer of Love, and the beatniks, a utopian land of opportunity, an escape, where you go when you leave behind the cold winters and your conservative parents back in Cleveland."[6]

When Ferrari introduced a much-anticipated new grand-touring convertible in 2008, it called the car the California.[7] Although the car, which is aimed particularly at customers in Russia, China, and the Middle East, shares its name with a midcentury Ferrari classic, the company clearly thinks California still maintains its glamour. So does electric car maker Tesla, playing up its California connection to portray its products as the vehicles of the future. Tesla, notes a business commentator, "isn't selling cars. It's in the West Coast Cool business. . . . Most of the press shots of Tesla's first car, the Roadster, look as if they were taken on the Pacific Coast Highway."[8]

In a 2010 commercial, K-Swiss advertises its shoes—also "designed in California"—with an updated portrayal of the state as a place of free spirits who need not fear the winter. As a choir of young voices sings "California Sun" in the background, the ad mixes shots of triathletes with quirkier versions of people having fun outdoors: hitting a tennis ball that's been set on fire, turning an aerial backflip at shuffleboard, racing on tiny tricycles. The ad ends with a skateboarder headed toward a sunset over the ocean; his dog runs ahead of him on a leash, propelling the board forward. "Have an Awesome Day," says the screen. The ad, writes a fan who posted it on YouTube, "makes me want to go to California!"[9]

California is still calling.

Icon
THE MAKEOVER

In the twentieth century, the ancient idea of metamorphosis got a distinctly modern update. Female audiences thrilled to stories of transformation accomplished not through wizardry or divine power but through the adept application of know-how and technology. In movies and magazines, and eventually on television, the magic of Cinderella became the glamour of the makeover.

Anyone could be a beauty, it suggested. You needed only the right attitude and a little skill. "An 'overnight transformation' may be effected . . . using methods that are perfectly simple and available," declared *Mademoiselle* in January 1937, a few months after introducing the "before and after" feature as a beauty-magazine staple. In a recurring column, the magazine's consultant promised to solve beauty problems "scientifically," allowing readers to copy his prescriptions at home.[1]

At least that was the theory. But the makeover's allure has never been about laboriously following do-it-yourself advice. It's about having the attention of specialists who see your unique potential, know all the right tricks, and devote their esoteric knowledge to revealing—or creating—the new you. Clients, says Diane Gardner, a Southern California hairstylist and makeup artist who specializes in makeovers, "don't know how they could look their best, but they want to trust me to give them what looks best."[2] That expertise makes the transformation seem effortless, and the subject feel special. "It's exciting to have important people do stuff for you," said Karen, a nurse from rural Arkansas in a 2003 episode of the reality show *Extreme Makeover*.[3]

For its pioneering 1936 makeover, *Mademoiselle* enlisted a squadron of specialists—a Hollywood makeup artist, dress designer, wig maker, dentist, and speech coach—to transform a nurse and aspiring actress who described

Mary Evans/WALT DISNEY PICTURES/Ronald Grant/Everett Collection

Anne Hathaway reenacts one of her many movie makeovers on a poster for *The Princess Diaries* (2001)

herself as "homely as a hedgehog." Twenty-one-year-old Barbara Phillips emerged looking less like a gawky farm girl and more like an elegant star. Her glasses were gone, her flat chest disguised by a custom evening gown, her teeth capped, and the planes of her long, narrow face resculpted with cosmetics.

"A stranger was gazing at me out of the mirror," she wrote. "Her face was full and rounded, her lips full and wide, her even, straight teeth gleamed. . . . I didn't feel like Barbara Phillips and certainly I didn't look like her."[4]

Yet it really was her. The team of experts knew how to find her previously hidden beauty, making conceivable her dream career. To an audience gazing at before and after pictures or the "reveal" scene in a movie or reality show, the glamour of the makeover taps two longings: to be beautiful, certainly, but also to be truer to your inner ideal. The outward transformation signifies, and enables, movement toward a better life.

After one of the most famous movie makeovers, Julia Roberts's Vivian in *Pretty Woman* (1990) leaves behind her life as a street prostitute, winning the love of the rich, handsome Edward (Richard Gere). He sees that Vivian really is a classy, funny, honest, pretty woman, not a sleazy, untrustworthy whore, and he gives her the outward trappings that befit her inner self. "Herein lies the real appeal of this film for female audiences—the transformation, or makeover itself," write the film scholars Elizabeth A. Ford and Deborah C. Mitchell. "The idea that a woman can change her appearance, acquire some etiquette, fly up the social scale virtually overnight, and end up with a guy oozing with money, power, and good looks is mighty seductive."[5] Vivian's good heart—the real identity masked by the hooker outfit—also transforms Edward, making him a more compassionate person.

In the movies, a physical makeover often gives the subject the confidence or opportunity to assert her true, formerly hidden self. Bette Davis's Charlotte in *Now, Voyager* (1942) stands up to her domineering mother. Tess (Melanie Griffith), the aspiring executive in *Working Girl* (1988), tells her hairdresser friend to chop her big, blue-collar hair into a neat bob. "You want to be taken seriously, you need serious hair," she says.

But not every fictional transformation is so voluntary. *"She's turning me into someone else,"* complains the angry protagonist Mia in the novel *The*

Princess Diaries, as her grandmother forces her previously bohemian style into royal polish.[6] Here's the trade-off disguised by the glamour of instant beauty. The transformation requires turning over your appearance—your public self—to other people. Even well-intended prescriptions can feel dictatorial, and change may require giving up important parts of your identity.

In George Bernard Shaw's *Pygmalion* and in *My Fair Lady* (1964), the quintessential makeover movie, Henry Higgins (Rex Harrison) is an insensitive bully. He calls Eliza (Audrey Hepburn) names ("bilious pigeon," "heartless guttersnipe," "presumptuous insect") and threatens not to feed her unless she masters her language lessons. He treats her like a tool or a toy—a "live doll," says his mother—rather than a full-fledged person.

A *Twilight Zone* episode, "Number 12 Looks Just Like You" (1964), turns an extreme makeover into a subject of horror. It portrays a society in which each person who comes of age must undergo "the Transformation," replacing the individual's unique appearance with one of a few standard models. "I don't see why you're so unhappy," the resistant protagonist's mother (supermodel Suzy Parker) tells her, "when all they want to do is make you pretty."[7]

People who do real-life makeovers recognize the potential conflicts, which reality shows sometimes exploit for dramatic interest, and clients usually get the last say. Emily Bloemker, an Episcopal priest featured on the reality show *What Not to Wear*, says she's kept "about 70 percent" of what the makeover team prescribed. But she ditched the big, fluffy brunette hair that had her shaking her tresses like a model in a shampoo commercial. She returned to her previous blond color and an attractive straight, shoulder-length style more appropriate to her professional role and her inner self.[8] In the long run, an "overnight transformation" is only appealing if it reflects who you want to be.

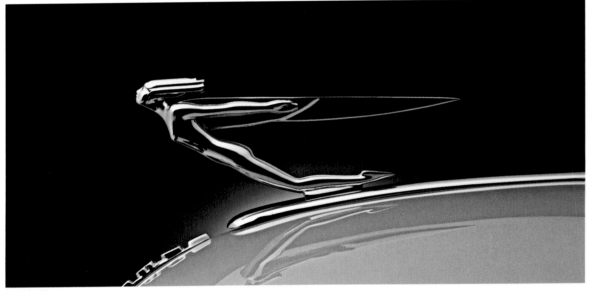

FOUR

THE ART THAT
CONCEALS ART

From transcontinental travel to witty conversation, glamour makes the difficult appear easy. The high heels never pinch; the sports car never gets stuck in traffic; the star never has a runny nose, a bad hair day, or lipstick on her teeth. Rain doesn't spoil the vacation. Electrical wires don't mar the view. Nature doesn't call, and nobody runs out of cash. Glamour appears *effortless*.

The word comes up again and again when people talk about glamour. We read of the "effortless glamour" of Blake Lively or Catherine Zeta-Jones, the "effortless way" Cary Grant wore a suit, or George Clooney's "effortless charm."[1] The fashion designer Rachel Roy praises "the effortless ease, the quiet, confident glamour" of the then–newly betrothed Kate Middleton.[2] "To look glamorous in the heat," *Lucky* magazine recommends "the effortless, jet-set style of St. Tropez."[3] *Guardian* arts and culture correspondent Vanessa Thorpe sets off for the Amalfi Coast in search of the "effortless glamour" she remembers from her grandparents' vacation slides.[4]

"Glamorous people make difficult tasks seem effortless," writes the fashion critic Robin Givhan. "They appear to cruise through life shaking off defeat with a wry comment. No matter how hard they work for what they have, the exertion never seems to show."[5] From Fred Astaire and Jet Li to James Bond and Danny Ocean, glamorous heroes are literally and figuratively sure-footed. They not only move gracefully but also always seem to know what to wear and how to behave, never fumbling for the right words or the bellman's tip. They face danger with humor and clever improvisation. Whether disguising himself as a redcap or escaping out a hospital window, quipping to his kidnappers or seducing Eva Marie Saint, Cary Grant's imperiled ad executive in *North by Northwest* (1959) is as adept as Bond, without 007's gadgets or secret-agent training.

This apparent effortlessness is what Baldassare Castiglione, writing in the early sixteenth century, called *sprezzatura*: the graceful nonchalance that "conceal[s] all art and make[s] whatever is done or said appear to be without effort and almost without any thought about it."[6] *Sprezzatura* makes its possessor seem like a superior being and the observer feel momentarily transformed, enveloped in that aura of confidence and competence. Like the glamorously streamlined surfaces of the Chrysler Building, however, *sprezzatura* is a façade—a form of artifice that demands care to create and maintain. Like streamlining, it is a manifestation of glamour's second essential element: *grace*, the actual or apparent elimination of flaws, distractions, weaknesses, costs, support structures, or frictions.

If the longing for escape and transformation is glamour's emotional core, grace is its central illusion, the quality that gives us the words *glamorize* and *glamorization*. Grace is what makes glamour so dangerous and so alluring. By hiding anything that might break the spell, it renders our desires clear and accessible. "Glamour," writes the industrial designer Diego Rodriguez, "gives us a chance to believe that there's no such thing as entropy."[7] It draws us into a world where complexions are flawless and bodies lithe; where convertibles glide along twisting roads, and pristine windows overlook blue seas; where clothes fit perfectly, planes are punctual, goblets sparkle, love is true, and youth endures. "Grace is the absence of every thing that indicates pain or difficulty, or hesitation or incongruity," wrote William Hazlitt, the early-nineteenth-century essayist.[8] Grace clarifies the perception of desire and hides the negative aspects of fulfilling our longings.

The need for grace explains why glamour is so strongly associated with theater. Even when it isn't produced for stage or screen, glamour requires a kind of theatrical performance: an exchange between object and audience in which the manipulation of reality may be understood but must be concealed. While literal magic might operate through sheer power, metaphorical glamour must persuade by moving the audience's emotions and imagination. As the ads for the 1978 movie *Superman* declared, "You'll believe a man can fly." Like Superman's aerial adventures, glamour is a special effect.

Creating it involves two distinct but complementary ways of hiding pain, difficulty, flaws, and entropy. In the first, the grace exists in the real world, if only for an instant, but the costs of achieving it are unseen. The preparation and support are hidden either offstage or before and after the graceful moment. "I participate in the creation of effortless-seeming glamour, acknowledging that the illusion of perfection doesn't come naturally to everybody," says Cameron Silver, the Los Angeles retailer famed for dressing actresses in timelessly stylish vintage couture.[9] Momentarily real but nonetheless an illusion, this form we can call *theatrical grace*.

In the second type, the grace isn't real. It's an image crafted directly through manipulation and editing, as when a photographer selects, crops, and retouches a single photo from a shoot. "Bring out the best, conceal the worst, and leave something to the imagination," advised the great studio-era photographer George Hurrell, explaining how he created his glamorous portraits of Hollywood stars.[10] Existing only in the still image or the audience's selective imagination, this type we can call *darkroom grace*. Whichever

Jean Harlow portrait by George Hurrell: The photographer sculpted faces with masterful composition and lighting and, once in the darkroom, wielded a heavy retouching pencil. *Courtesy of Pancho Barnes Trust Estate Archive, © Estate of George Hurrell*

kind of grace is at work, the result is a glamorous moment that lingers in the mind, distilling desire.

⸻

For theatrical grace, the audience must not know, or must be willing to overlook, the effort behind the effortlessness. *Sprezzatura* is an illusion. Even in the naturally gifted, it requires cultivation. "She's disciplined," said Humphrey Bogart of Audrey Hepburn, "like all those ballet dames."[11] To turn Sean Connery's natural physical grace into James Bond's social polish, director Terence Young took the young actor to fine restaurants, taught him to evaluate wines, had his suits and shirts custom-tailored, and made Connery sleep in one of the new outfits so that Bond's clothes would feel natural.[12] Grace Kelly achieved her mellifluous voice only after rigorous coaching, which mellowed her vocal tones and eliminated her nasal Philadelphia accent.[13] Cary Grant spent his youth training as an acrobat, acquiring control over his movements. He achieved his "effortless" appearance by measuring the collars of his shirts and the lapels of his custom-made suits, returning them to the tailor if they were a tiny bit off. "It takes 500 small details to add up to one favorable impression," he said.[14]

Ginger Rogers and Fred Astaire in *The Gay Divorcee* (1934): Combining theatrical and darkroom grace, they danced their well-practiced routines on floors coated with glossy Bakelite, with scratches removed between takes so that the couple's feet never seemed to touch the ground. *Ullstein/Everett Collection*

By depicting the practiced or choreographed as natural and spontaneous, glamour makes the ideal feel attainable and the observer feel transported and at ease. "Each time Fred Astaire won over the heart of a reluctant Ginger Rogers by sweeping her up in a flurry of pivots, dips, and syncopated time steps, audiences forgot (since the film never showed) how many shoes were bloodied in the studio to create the appearance of impromptu courtship," writes the dance scholar Juliet McMains.[15]

These movies don't invite us to imagine ourselves as real-world dancers, struggling through difficult rehearsals to create a great performance. Instead, we project ourselves into an effortless celebration of courtship and love. Astaire and Rogers labored mightily to create those dances, but the characters they played did not. Similarly, says Apple design chief Jonathan Ive, the designers and engineers behind some of today's most glamorous products "try to solve very complicated problems without letting people know how complicated the problem was."[16] Though laboriously crafted, the resulting graceful forms seem inevitable. The experiments and failures required to achieve them are hidden behind the scenes.

In concealing effort, glamour differs from romance, which often portrays hardship. Think of the training sequences in martial-arts movies, the battles in *Star Wars* or *Lord of the Rings*, the artist's struggling years in the garret, the entrepreneur's office cot and diet of ramen noodles. Behind-the-scenes reality shows like *Project Runway* or *The Rachel Zoe Project* are essentially romances about the creation of glamorous moments, dramatizing the effort behind the effortless appearance of a runway show or red-carpet look. Romance does idealize reality—it omits the tedious, meaningless, and boring—but it heightens the glory of success by showing

Getty Images/Walter Iooss Jr.

the struggle that produces it. Glamour is less narrative. It captures not a story but a scene: the dance, not the rehearsals; the still photo, not the film. Glamour and romance are closely related, but glamour is about being, not becoming. We experience the result, not the process.

The relationship between subject and audience is also different. In a romance, the audience feels a range of emotions along with the characters: excitement, fear, anger, love, grief, joy. Glamour, by contrast, remains an outside view, requiring mystery and distance. In the classic versions of the character, we don't inhabit James Bond's mental universe. We project ourselves into his setting and talents. He is "all façade."[17] We do not feel what he feels but, rather, what the idea of him makes us feel. This distanced identification is why anonymous models or even inanimate objects can be glamorous. We do not need to know them from the inside; we fill their images with our own emotions and desires.

Glamour also differs from spectacle, as the intimacy of Fred and Ginger differs from the kaleidoscopic showgirls of a Busby Berkeley number, Beyoncé differs from Lady Gaga, or the widely reproduced photograph of Olympic gymnast Gabrielle Douglas stretched high in the air over the balance beam differs from her entire, peril-filled routine. Both glamour and spectacle celebrate surfaces, but they do so for different purposes: glamour to let us imagine ourselves similarly transported and transformed, spectacle to overwhelm its audience with extraordinary achievement and pure form. (Although we usually think of spectacle as entertainment, in authoritarian regimes like North Korea it also constitutes a form of magnificence, the aesthetic display through which traditional monarchs and conquerors signaled their power.) Though glamour and spectacle sometimes appear together, they have different emotional effects. Glamour inspires projection and longing; spectacle produces wonder and awe.

Spectacle heightens difficulty and danger; think of the juggler tossing chainsaws or the motorcycle daredevil leaping a canyon or a long line of cars. These feats make the audience gasp with fear and astonishment. By contrast, glamour maintains *sprezzatura*. The glamour of a bullfighter or a Formula One driver arises from the way he makes death-defying maneuvers look easy, allowing the audience to share his apparently effortless calm. In other cases, spectacle showcases the costly and rare, emphasizing how unusual they are. Glamour, on the other hand, portrays luxuries as normal experiences, making them feel casually attainable and thus all the more reasonable to desire. That ease stokes the audience's yearning. All the barriers are hidden.

———

While *theatrical grace* conceals the undesirable in time and space, *darkroom grace* directly crafts the glamorous image. To create his glamorous por- traits, Hurrell sculpted faces with masterful composition and lighting and, once in the darkroom, wielded a heavy retouching pencil. He eliminated freckles, lines, and under-eye circles; extended eyelashes to impossible lengths; and enlarged the sparkles in stars' eyes. His glamorizing touch could turn the sexy but pudgy-featured and worn-looking Jean Harlow into a delicate and otherworldly goddess.[18]

By contrast, Howell Conant's 1955 photos of Grace Kelly on vacation in Jamaica portray the young actress as an exemplar of "natural glamour,"

© Howell Conant/Bob Adelman Books Inc.

a graceful, elegant sexiness without the obvi- ous artifice of Hurrell's portraits. In these pho- tos, write the critics Kay and Digby Diehl, "we feel we are seeing the candid, unguarded 'every- day' Grace, unassisted by hairdressers or makeup artists. The natural glamour of this 25-year-old woman is both timeless and seductive."[19] Delib- erately composed as an alternative to Hurrell's studio productions, the portraits are not as spon- taneous as they appear. For the famous photo of Kelly rising from the sea, Conant manipulated the light—Kelly's sister held a reflector—and, as always, disguised his subject's square jaw by not shooting her straight on. Kelly also wore water- proof makeup, which had just been invented. Her bathing suit's straps were removed to showcase her shoulders and, below the water, she stood carefully on tiptoes to avoid the spiny sea urchins covering the sea floor.

Most important, the iconic shot was not the first Conant took in this pose but, rather, the best of eight.[20] Even "natural" glamour requires selection and editing. It extracts a perfect moment from the flow of time, an evocative image from the surrounding details.

Both Hurrell's heavily retouched portraits and Conant's seemingly unmanipulated images embody darkroom grace, disguising flaws and eliminating distractions. "Always omit the blemishes—they're not part of the good picture you want," Andy Warhol advised.[21] Even such iconic candid photos as Ron Galella's "Windblown Jackie" or Alberto Korda's famous shot of Che Guevara, "Guerrillero Heroico," achieve their glamour by cropping out extraneous background. The full version of Galella's 1971 photo of a trim Jackie striding toward a Manhattan street includes an ugly pole in the foreground, a large expanse of sidewalk, and the distractingly rumpled bottoms of her trousers.

Similarly, on Korda's original 1960 contact sheet, Che is flanked by another man's profile on his right and palm fronds on his left. And in the image most people know from T-shirts, banners, and posters, Che's face is further abstracted into a Pop Art icon of positive and negative space. "This reduction of the real world provides the perfect vehicle for distancing the image from

The paparazzo image "Windblown Jackie" demonstrates darkroom grace even in a candid photo. *Getty Images/Ron Galella*

the complexities and ambiguities of actual life. . . . Che lives in these images as an ideal abstraction," says the photography curator Jonathan Green.[22]

Whether achieved through misdirection or editing, deliberate manipulation or selective imagination, darkroom grace is the deception people usually mean when they refer to "glamorizing" something or someone. It creates a seemingly accurate image distilled to its most desirable essence.

Julius Shulman, the architectural photographer who crafted the pictures by which we know many iconic modern buildings, particularly Southern California homes, referred to this artifice as "'transfiguration'— the process of idealization, glorification, and dramatization."[23] Heightening contrasts with infrared film and stark black and white, Shulman created images truer to the architects' purist visions than the structures themselves.[24] In his photographs, the buildings look more intense and vivid than in real life. The whites are whiter, the shadows darker, the surfaces cleaner, the inhabitants' lives more alluring. "Glamorized Houses," *Life* magazine headlined a 1949 article about Shulman's work.[25]

In recent years Photoshop has made such manipulation easier and more widely recognized. While inept retouching prompts ridicule, effective alterations draw much more hostile criticism and, in some places, government regulation.[26] Writing on behalf of *Jezebel*'s antiretouching crusade, the site's editor in chief Jessica Coen denounces "the fucked-up imagery that is consistently and persistently gracing newsstands as the beauty standard to which we should all aspire." (The vulgarity is itself an antigrace note; candid writers don't hide their propensity to curse.) When cover photos edit out celebrities' flyaway hair, wrinkles, freckles, and skin textures, lest "you might *see* these things preserved for posterity in a magazine," Coen argues, the public is "cruelly had." Impressionable young women in particular are "force-fed a lie," leading them to aspire to unattainable beauty.[27] Coen takes the anti-Warhol position: Always include the blemishes. Anything less is dishonest.

But we need only consider theatrical grace to see that the real deception (or artifice) lies in pulling a living human being out of time and space. Critics like Coen rarely object to the equally artificial grace of a ballet or a Beyoncé video. A single static two-dimensional portrait—a selective representation "preserved for posterity"—is, by its very nature, deceptive. Viewers perceive such a portrait differently from a real human being. If, as Coen claims, young women do not realize that "most waists don't really bend without a roll of flesh" or that "a 40-year-old woman actually does have some wrinkles," it is because they've mentally edited away those flaws in the people they see every day. In the flux and movement of life, the mind overlooks imperfections that appear glaring in a still image. Retouching may therefore produce an image truer to the mind's eye. And, of course, lighting (not to mention makeup) can manipulate perceptions as effectively as Photoshop or Hurrell's pencil.

Contrary to what many contemporary critics seem to imagine, such calculated, illusory grace didn't start with Photoshop or, for that matter, with modern media. The longing for ideal beauty is ancient, and so is the art that expresses it. Centuries before movie stills or fashion photography, painters glamorized the subjects of portraits and genre paintings. "You have depicted her better than

Julius Shulman's "transfiguration" created images truer to the architects' purist visions than the structures themselves.

© J. Paul Getty Trust. Used with Permission. Julius Shulman Photography Archive, Research Library at the Getty Research Institute (2004.R.10)

any other," the duke of Mantua wrote in the early seventeenth century, complimenting the painter of his wife's portrait, "since you have improved and embellished her looks without diminishing her likeness."[28] Distinct from the classicist perfection of mythological or religious figures, which downplayed individuality to produce archetypes, this glamorization flattered individuals. Like today's fashion photos, it also heightened the desire to look and act like the people in the paintings, whose apparently realistic images established unrealistic standards of grace. Glamorized portraits, the art and fashion historian Anne Hollander argues, help to explain the persistence of such impractical, uncomfortable styles as huge lace ruffs.

> In the superior world of the painter, noble personages in all sorts of awkward gear were created and presented in a state of ideal dignity and refinement; and so a standard was set for perfect appearance that might be followed by the living originals, who could feel beautiful in their trappings instead of trapped. Consequently, still bigger lace ruffs and even thicker silk skirts might continue in vogue, even into the next generation, because Rubens and Van Dyck and their colleagues were at work rendering them glorious to see, wonderfully becoming, and apparently effortless to wear.[29]

In an era before large, ubiquitous, well-lit mirrors (much less candid photos), such portraits might shape both aspirations and self-images. Ruff wearers could picture themselves with the personal ease and perfectly starched collars of their portraits rather than the discomforts and wrinkles of real life.

Both overzealous retouchers and their critics mistake the purpose of darkroom grace. It is not "perfection" but emotional effect. Too perfect a surface can be uncanny and disquieting, and thus distracting, or too inert and lifeless to draw in the viewer. Excessive polish can also call attention to the effort involved, destroying *sprezzatura*. "You have to find a balance of studied naturalness," says Adam Fortner, a Texas interiors stylist.[30] More alluring than perfect polish is what the literary scholar Sarah Skwire calls the "erotically-charged sweet spot" of "déshabille—careful carelessness,

Like the complex braids that bind some, but not all, of a Botticelli maiden's tresses, effective glamorization balances control with lively possibility.

artful artlessness, delicately tousled perfection," which is "all about suggestion, implication, nuance, and detail."[31] Like the complex braids that bind some, but not all, of a Botticelli maiden's tresses, effective glamorization balances control with lively possibility.

By hiding exertion, incongruities, and costs, glamorous images situate their objects not in quotidian reality but in the always out-of-reach realm of displaced meaning, where images represent more than themselves. Although such images do not reflect the mechanically factual record of uncropped candid snapshots, they nonetheless reveal a kind of truth.

In eliminating extraneous detail, their illusory grace resembles what the historians of science Lorraine Daston and Peter Galison call "truth to nature," the standard that Enlightenment naturalists used in their scientific atlases. An atlas engraving would not show an accurate rendering of a single, particular specimen. Rather, the scientist sought to portray the typical or ideal, without distracting variations. A sugar-maple leaf, for instance, would have five lobes, even though real leaves sometimes have three, and it certainly wouldn't show signs of damage from weather or insects, however common such flaws might be in real life. Similarly, the eighteenth-century anatomist Bernhard Siegfried Albinus explained how he portrayed a human skeleton:

> I made choice of one that might discover signs of both strength and agility; the whole of it elegant, and at the same time not too delicate; so as neither to shew a juvenile or feminine roundness and slenderness, nor on the contrary an unpolished roughness and clumsiness; in short, all of the parts of it beautiful and pleasing to the eye. For as I wanted to shew an example of nature [*naturae exemplum*] I chused to take it from the best pattern of nature.

Depicting botanical specimens or anatomical organs, these scientists distilled away the variation of actual plants and animals to reveal what they believed was nature's underlying truth.[32]

Whether created through theatrical or darkroom grace, or some combination of the two, the "best pattern" of glamorization reveals a different kind of truth—in this case, an emotional, psychological truth, which we can call "truth to desire." Rather than capturing the typical, truth to desire makes the *subjective* ideal feel lucid and real, intensifying the audience's longing. One reason Jean-Baptiste-Siméon Chardin's eighteenth-century scenes of everyday French life were beloved, Anne Hollander argues, is that the pictures' rosy-cheeked subjects expressed an "often unacknowledged" truth "about the satisfactions of being perfectly dressed."

Jean-Baptiste-Siméon Chardin's *The Hardworking Mother*: "The lady examining embroidery with her daughter crosses her high-heeled shod feet with the aplomb of the Marquise de Pompadour."

Superstock/Everett Collection

> Every single one of Chardin's characters has the straight, almost arched back of current fashion, a perfect figure, and a perfectly groomed head, perfectly fitting clothes (worn with stays even by humble women and girls), and extra-long legs. All are youthful and good-looking, whether they are laundry maids and cooks or ladies of the house and their children, whether well-to-do or very much less so. All deportment is graceful and becoming without exception, not just decent and circumspect: the lady examining embroidery with her daughter crosses her high-heeled shod feet with the aplomb of the Marquise de Pompadour.[33]

The techniques and pleasures of such paintings, and of the popular commercial prints made from them, Hollander argues, were similar to those of the movies. These images, like Hollywood productions, provided an emotionally inviting setting that was at once detailed and idealized.

A similar combination of the detailed and the ideal is what made the TV show *Mad Men* such a cult hit, argues the branding consultant Tom Parrette. He contrasts realistic images of early 1960s Manhattanites—"hordes of unassuming, unglamorous people" in frumpy scarves and "slouchy sports coats" who create "an awkward assemblage of imperfection"—with the "impeccably groomed, hyper-realistic outfits" of the show's characters. These figures don't just create advertising, he suggests; they exemplify it. "Don and Betty and Joan and Peggy and Pete are billboards for how we want to remember that era," he writes. Like a brand-building campaign, the show's setting presents "a version of the 60s scaled up for emotional satisfaction."[34]

As the magic that makes life's obstacles disappear, grace is both a powerful tool of seduction and a seductive end in itself. In the seemingly effortless leaps of a ballerina or a basketball star, the perfect coordination of a sculling crew or a movie heist, the luminescent polish of a model's face or a Lamborghini's paint, we experience a quality as rare and desirable as beauty or fame. We yearn to possess grace and to inhabit a graceful world—to escape friction, struggle, frustration, and decay. Always a component of glamour, grace can also be an object of it.

The yearning for grace creates two broad categories of glamour, representing two versions of escape and transformation. *Autonomy* portrays life without dependence, while *synchronization* draws on the grace of perfect coordination.

Autonomy includes the glamour of "living off the grid," hitting the open road, or sailing off into the sunset, without responsibilities, entanglements, or refueling. It spurs purchases of off-road vehicles by people who drive them to the office and supermarket. It stokes survivalist fantasies. In a long-running advertising campaign, Corona beer has used the glamour of autonomy to present an enticingly tranquil contrast to more-raucous beer promotions. Although often humorous, the ads associate Corona with the dream of escape and independence. All you need, they suggest, is a beach, a chair, and a bottle of Corona.[35] In one commercial, a vacationing businessman skips stones into the ocean, following them with his buzzing cell phone. In the real world, such disregard might well mean the loss of the job that made the vacation (and the beer) possible.

But it fits the fantasy. The glamour of autonomy includes the dream of escape from "getting and spending," from the demand not only to work but, more important, to choose among competing desires. *Sprezzatura* admits no budget constraints. "Glamour is founded upon an income," wrote Margaret Thorp in her 1939 study of the movies, "but real glamour seldom looks at the bill."[36]

Autonomy also includes the glamour of the spotlight, of being the sole focus of attention, admiration, and acclaim. One reason audiences find Academy Award acceptance speeches so tedious is that they ruin the magic of the triumphant moment. The glamour of winning an Oscar, which countless aspiring stars play out in front of bedroom mirrors, comes from being singled out as special. When James Cameron celebrated his 1997 film *Titanic*'s triumphs by exulting, "I'm the king of the world," he enacted that fantasy. "Sure, we thought he was a jerk," observes the Hollywood journalist Sharon Waxman, "but at least it was more interesting than listening to his co-producer Jon Landau reel off an endless list of names we'd never heard."[37] The polite acknowledgment of backstage players destroys the illusion of autonomy, forcing the audience to contemplate the mundane, even bureaucratic, processes behind the star.

If autonomy represents the glamour of standing out, synchronization offers the glamour of fitting in. It's the ideal of the well-oiled machine and the hand-picked team: of the dance pair rather than the soloist, the sculling crew rather than the lone kayaker, the team of ninjas rather than the kung-fu master. Here, actions, goals, and personalities mesh smoothly. Synchronization encompasses the social glamour of witty repartee—saying the right thing at the right moment, not an hour later—and of camaraderie in a common cause. It intensifies the glamour of fellowship, making the connections between people seem intuitive or telepathic. Such perfect co-ordination allows even a glamorously autonomous hero like James Bond to know that a beautiful accomplice will arrive to pick him up at exactly the right moment.

Bond, however, not his accomplice, is clearly in charge. While for some audiences synchronization offers the glamour of belonging, for others it expresses the power fantasy of effortless command: the glamour embodied in the "push button" images of 1950s gadgets, in every kind of remote control, and in the command to "Make it so," as *Star Trek*'s Captain Picard tells his crew. The *Star Trek* bridge exemplifies the common movie trope of the control center, where a decisive commander with a smartly competent crew issues orders that instantaneously result in action at a distance. Found also in military recruitment ads, particularly for the US Air Force, this image captures the allure of both camaraderie and command. The crew contributes effectively and willingly to the shared mission; the wise and clever commander's power requires no coercion, which would break the moment's grace. In many such scenes, maps and glowing screens add visual mystery and drama, while the control center itself is often hidden from outsiders—a secret place known only to initiates.

Both autonomy and synchronization are illusions, of course, requiring drastic simplifications of reality. Autonomy suggests that we can shed the constraints of complex relationships, whether familial ties or electrical grids, without sacrificing their benefits. Synchronization omits the trials and rehearsal that real coordination requires. It hides conflict and disguises the compromises necessary to achieve apparent harmony. It assumes goals that are not only shared but worthy. (In some of the most famous movie command centers, notably the war room in *Dr. Strangelove* [1964], effortless synchronization turns ominous.) These graceful visions remain pleasurable because discordant elements can be concealed in space or time.

———

In an essay, the author Michael Chabon, whose work often explores themes of illusion, idealism, and escape, recounts a lesson one of his childhood religious-school teachers gave on the dangers of fantasy and escapism. The teacher told the class about a boy who, enthralled with Superman, had tied a red towel around his neck, leapt from the roof, and tumbled to his death. Moral: Don't succumb to glamour.

Or at least don't try to reify it. The lesson confused two different ways people use glamour: as an imaginative respite and as an inspiration for real-world action. The first is rarely dangerous and often life-affirming. Nobody dies from simply reading superhero comics or fashion magazines, however much their fantastic images may offend sober-minded pedagogues. Nor, surely, would Chabon's Jewish ethics teacher have condemned Anne Frank for brightening the walls of her Secret Annex with photos of movie stars and princesses rather than remaining realistically focused on her likely fate.[38] Escapism per se is no problem.

The costumes in studio-era films were often so tight that actresses like Jean Harlow, shown here with director George Cukor, could not sit down between takes but instead reclined on "leaning boards." *Photofest*

The dangers arise when glamour inspires real-world action. As an imaginative process, glamour provides inspiration and illumination, pleasure and escape. It can enhance self-knowledge and affirm self-worth. It focuses desire and suggests possibilities for fulfillment. But glamour can rightly be only a guide, not a destination. It leaves things out, and, in the real world, those things matter. The very grace that makes a glamorous image so compelling to the imagination makes the ideal impossible to reproduce in reality.

If you expect your vacation to be a series of perfectly composed still photos, with no baggage carousels or sandy bathing suits, you won't have a good time. If you demand "happily ever after," you won't be content with "for better or worse." If you don't want your clothes to wrinkle, you'll never

be able to sit down. Many of the costumes for studio-era Hollywood films were, in fact, so tight or heavy that the actresses who wore them could not sit down between takes but instead had to recline on "leaning boards."[39]

Translating glamour into real-world action requires editing back into one's projections the likely costs, distractions, and anomalies. Many an alluring architectural model or urban plan has turned dysfunctional when the real places were subjected to the stresses of wear and weather—or the actual, rather than imagined, behavior and preferences of their human occupants. Dramatic plazas become windswept no-man's-lands; floor-to-ceiling windows have to be covered for privacy; high-rise housing projects turn into crime-ridden fortresses; residence-only suburbs require constant trips by car. Similarly, new transportation projects often require heavy use to justify their construction costs, but they're sold to the public with graceful imagery representing the opposite assumption: that few people will crowd the highways, the trains, or the newly accessible skies. The trick is not to forswear glamour but to preserve the inspiration and insight it offers while remembering what might be left out.

The alternative is disillusionment, or worse. Without a backstage, the quest for grace threatens to turn tyrannical, subordinating the complexities and flux of life to a unitary and artificial ideal. In *The Second Sex*, Simone de Beauvoir decries the constraints imposed on fashionable women by the canons of mid-twentieth-century elegance. The transformation promised by the right dress, she argues, is dangerous. Its glamour undermines a woman's self-confidence by making her identity dependent on the vagaries of appearance and social recognition. A real woman is not a static icon, and a real gown is not the magical garment of fairy-tale dreams. Both inevitably suffer the indignities of dwelling in time and space, where true grace is ephemeral.

Accidents will happen; wine is spilled on her dress, a cigarette burns it; this marks the disappearance of the luxurious and festive creature who bore herself with smiling pride into the ballroom. . . . [I]t becomes all at once evident that her toilette was not a set piece like fireworks, a transient burst of splendour, intended for the lavish illumination of a moment. . . . Spots, tears, botched dressmaking, bad hair-dos are catastrophes still more serious than a burnt roast or a broken vase, for not only does the woman of fashion project herself into things, she has chosen to make herself a thing.[40]

More charitably, one might say that she has chosen to make herself a work of art; de Beauvoir's harsh judgment reveals the intellectual's contempt for sensory pleasures, at least those of the bourgeoisie. But she correctly highlights the cost and fragility of the illusion. The accident turns image into actuality. The real-world gown is not a costume designed for the "transient burst" of a photograph or a movie take, after which the star can return to her dressing room for repairs. Entropy has no place to hide.

What's true for individuals is even more true for societies. All utopias, whether hateful or benevolent, trade in glamour. As literature, they offer only a graceful setting—no narrative, no conflict, no depth of character, no change. They edit out the dynamism and complexity of social interactions to compose a static image of the ideal. As philosophical thought experiments, utopias can be illuminating. As political programs, they are at best impractical. At the extreme, they become deadly, as the quest for grace becomes a demand for purity, with no room for anything or anyone that might disrupt the guiding vision—whether religious dissenters or ethnic minorities, competitive markets or artistic innovation, scientific discoveries or contradictory ideologies. Perfect grace cannot tolerate the unpredictability and diversity of real human beings.

⁓

The flip side of glamour is horror. Glamorous archetypes like the vampire, the con man, the femme fatale, and the double agent remind us of how easy it is to succumb to manipulation and desire. The glamour-smitten Madame Bovary ruins her family financially and dies a ghastly death. In *Frankenstein,* Victor carries out his ill-fated experiments enraptured by a glamorous vision of scientific glory. He labors tirelessly, barely noticing the gory details of cadavers and mismatched body parts. When he succeeds, however, the glamour vanishes.

> I had worked hard for nearly two years, for the sole purpose of in-
> fusing life into an inanimate body. For this I had deprived myself
> of rest and health. I had desired it with an ardour that far exceeded
> moderation; but now that I had finished, the beauty of the dream
> vanished, and breathless horror and disgust filled my heart.[41]

Desire morphs into revulsion, as Frankenstein's beautiful illusion bursts
into a nightmarish new reality.

To destroy the glamour of someone or something, critics seek to reveal
the ugly secrets hidden offstage. Military action, they declare, is alluring
because we do not see the carnage, smoking because we do not see the
ruined lungs, a life of parties because we do not see the hangovers and
financial ruin. "Che was a murderer, and your T-shirt is not cool," declared a Facebook group aimed at the ubiquitous silhouettes of the Cuban
revolutionary.[42] In the early 1970s, the American Cancer Society created
a poster with the headline "Smoking Is Very Glamorous," below a closeup
of a worn, poor-looking woman with a bad haircut puffing a cigarette.[43] To
attack the fashionable glamour of fur, People for the Ethical Treatment of
Animals runs ads in which a beautiful singer holds up the flayed carcass of
a fox. "Here's the rest of your fur coat," they announce.

Most of the time, however, glamour conceals mundane imperfections, making its deflation a better subject for comedy than horror. In the
1970s, the comedian Gilda Radner spun one such (presumably fictional)
incongruity into a famous *Saturday Night Live* routine. Portraying the
self-absorbed motormouth Roseanne Roseannadanna, she launched into
a monologue about her evening at a glamorous restaurant, where she enjoyed watching celebrities with spaghetti sauce on their lips. On this visit,
she saw Princess Lee Radziwill, the sister of Jacqueline Kennedy Onassis,
coming out of the ladies' room.

> She was dressed up like a doll in this slinky basic black dress and
> she's got real skinny arms with expensive jewelry hangin' off of
> 'em. But then I noticed that Princess Lee had a little teeny-tiny
> piece of toilet paper stickin' to the bottom of one of her Gucci

shoes. She—listen to this—she was just walkin' around, up and down, with that little piece of toilet paper just trailin' behind her, wouldn't fall off! And the more she walked, the dirtier that toilet paper got. And things started stickin' to it. There was a fuzzball, a hair, gum, a bug. There was even some fettucini alfredo and a piece of Romaine lettuce! Well, let me tell you that I, Roseanne Roseannadanna, started to lose my appetite. And I yelled, "Hey! Princess Lee! Take that toilet paper off your shoe! What are you tryin' to do? Make me sick?"[44]

While other diners come to the celebrity-filled restaurant to feel part of an exclusive crowd, for Roseanne Roseannadanna the pleasure comes from peeking behind the curtain and puncturing celebrity glamour. The joke's toilet humor is particularly appropriate, because in real life the bathroom functions as a safe place offstage, where we conceal not only the ugliness of excrement but also the secrets of the toilette. It is "the powder room," where women go to maintain their elegant façades. The toilet paper is a reminder of entropy and so are all the things that stick to it, tainting Princess Lee's polished image. Like a momentarily clean restaurant floor, we are all subject to the accretions of time.

Our yearning to escape entropy explains why "timeless glamour" is almost as much a cliché as "effortless glamour." As an advertising slogan, the phrase may signify little more than "classic style," but it has far more resonance. Classic style offers merely a respite from transitory fashions. Timeless glamour promises something greater: escape from age and loss, decay and death, into the "artifice of eternity." This is the promise of the pristine white of Julius Shulman's walls and the eternally youthful contours of Greta Garbo's face. "Stars are ageless, aren't they?" says Norma Desmond (Gloria Swanson) at the climax of *Sunset Blvd*. The line, like the 1950 film, is an ironic deconstruction of Hollywood glamour. While autonomous and synchronous moments do exist benignly in real life, they are just that: moments, "transient bursts" made glamorous by concealing what comes before and after. Garbo disappeared from public view when she was only thirty-six, and Shulman's photos offer no hint of how drab concrete-block screens appear after a few decades. From Alexander the Great to JFK, the most glamorous figures are often those who die young.

Whether expressed as simplicity or harmony, autonomy or synchronization, grace lifts the glamorous object out of time, creating a perfect moment. Even as it stops time, however, glamour often invites the audience to project itself into the imagined past or future, exotic regions where the ideal has been safely and enticingly displaced. In the world of glamour, as in Einstein's universe, time is but another dimension, another site of escape and transformation, another hiding place for imperfections. It offers another means of giving objects the third element essential to glamour: the mystery and distance that invite desire.

The mysterious Greta Garbo maintained an eternally youthful image by disappearing from public view when she was only thirty-six. *Photofest*

Icon
WIRELESSNESS

In the middle half of the twentieth century, the designer Raymond Loewy stream-lined products ranging from locomotives to pencil sharpeners, wrapping the complex gears, pumps, and combustion of modern machinery in sleek shells that promised progress and forward movement. He crafted an equally glamor-ous image for himself and the profession he christened "industrial design."[1]

Loewy's image making is evident in this office mock-up, which was ex-hibited at the Museum of Modern Art in 1934. For the photo, the designer poses among his vehicle designs in a setting where the desks, chairs, and even the walls are curved, with black metal piping to create a sense of motion. This glamorized workspace includes no trash cans, and its two lamps operate without electrical cords or outlets. The office embodies streamlined autonomy.

For years, the museum's industrial design collection reflected the same fan-tasy. When Paola Antonelli arrived as design curator in 1994, she discovered

Industrial designer Raymond Loewy poses in a mock-up of his office, whose lamps apparently operate without electrical cords or outlets.

Library of Congress

that someone had systematically vandalized the collection's lamps and electrical appliances. Their cords had been cut off. Instead of a working artifact capable of lighting a room or whipping up a soufflé, every piece that used electricity had become an inert sculpture. These icons of modern design could no longer tap the electric power that had once defined modernity. Antonelli never found out who was responsible, but she can imagine the reasoning: "The cord is not pretty."[2]

Flip through a home-furnishings catalog or an interiors magazine, and you'll find the same selective vision. Where possible, stylists hide cords for a photo shoot, taping them behind sofas or under windowsills. Where that's not possible, Photoshop eliminates the evidence. "A lamp's power cable must no more break the line of a designer table than a finger should obscure the serif of a corporate font," says the Sydney-based photographer Robin Ford. "In the 'high church of style' cables are ritually cut and their very absence is a symbol of sanctification."[3]

Removing cords enhances a setting's glamour. As interiors stylist Adam Fortner notes, cords are unruly objects that tend to twist their own way, destroying a scene's carefully composed lines. "They're really random."[4] While we usually ignore them in real life, cords attract attention in a still photograph. To charm viewers into imagining how the room or the lamp might fulfill their lifestyle dreams, the cords must go. No one is supposed to notice their absence, however. Removing them represents darkroom grace, a tool of seduction but not a seductive end in itself.

In other cases, however, wirelessness is itself the object of desire. From the radio to the iPad, wireless devices have long been among the most glamorous of new technologies. They promise to cut the ties that bind us to our desks, our homes, our mundane existence. Wireless technology bestows on ordinary mortals the power to pluck from the atmosphere unheard voices and unseen images. It creates the illusion of proximity, immediacy, even intimacy. It transports us from our real surroundings and embodies escape.

"The first wireless product with glamour would have to be the pocket transistor radio," says David Hall, who runs Plan59, an online museum of mid-century advertising images.[5] In the 1960s, the tiny radios came to symbolize the footloose freedom of youth. The classic 1964 movie *The Endless Summer* follows two surfers traveling the world with their boards and, almost as prominently, their transistor radio.

Three decades later another glamorous image captured a similar dream: the laptop computer at the beach. A popular stock photo in the 1990s, it evoked an alluring mix of escapism and productivity. With the right technology, the image suggested, you could do your work and have your fun at the same time. As laptops became ubiquitous, experience largely destroyed the fantasy. People discovered that working at the beach is still working—and that laptops and cell phones only make escape more difficult. The stock photos still sell well, but now they're as likely to illustrate articles on how to avoid stress on vacation as to promote the dream of a mobile, entrepreneurial lifestyle.

Still, there is something truly liberating about the power to choose where to work, not to mention the ability to summon libraries of information, impeccable directions, or thousands of movies from the air. The dream of autonomy exerts a potent influence on the shape of new technologies, spurring demand for wireless networks and cloud computing. Apple can celebrate the iPad as "magical" in large part because the device can operate for such long periods without wires or visible connections.

But, alas, wirelessness still remains something of an illusion. "Magicians who use wires in their act don't let you see them, but that doesn't mean they aren't there," cautioned the technology columnist Chris Taylor after Apple introduced the iPad 2. "In this case, the wire is the same old white cable that you'll have to use to sync your iPad to your PC or Mac from Day One." It was, he said, a "clunky throwback" for "a device that's supposed to be about effortless connecting."[6] Wireless syncing has since done away with that cable, but electric current still requires connections, if only to recharge batteries. The wires have become less numerous, but they haven't entirely disappeared.

Icon
THE SUPERHERO

Up, up, and away! Superman's famous exclamation, first heard in a 1940s radio serial, captures the allure of superheroes in a single phrase. Who wouldn't be transported by the dream of flying above Metropolis, swinging through the canyons of New York, commanding the elements, or becoming invisible at will? Even the supposedly unenhanced Batman possesses agility and tools far beyond the reach of real-life billionaire geniuses.

Comic-book connoisseurs may thrill to complex plots and revisionist re-imaginings, but the enduring appeal of superheroes is broader and far more elemental. Not even the most glamorous golden age movie star embodies escape and transformation, grace and mystery as surely as these costumed characters, with their origin stories, uncanny abilities, secret identities, and distinctive disguises. Detached from any narrative, superheroes show up in places as diverse as children's birthday cakes and M•A•C cosmetic cases, drawing us

Photofest

into a world where the normal constraints of physics, biology, economics, law, and bureaucracy don't apply. "If you feel insecure, look at yourself in the mirror and through the reflection remember to be the Wonder Woman you can be," said the fashion designer Diane von Furstenberg, introducing a 2008 collection inspired by the Amazon princess.[1]

The classic superhero starts out ordinary and becomes extraordinary, or seems to be one thing but is really another. Clark Kent is really Superman, and Clark Kent is us—which, in a moment of imaginative transposition, allows us to be super as well. As if enacting the audience's own dreams, the nerdy, angst-ridden Peter Parker achieves his own ideal self when he becomes Spider-Man. The web-slinging hero, writes the psychologist Robert Biswas-Diener, is "the positive counterpart to all of Peter's failings: Spidey is strong and athletic, outgoing and witty, adventuresome and risk-taking. No wonder Parker wants to put his life on the line night after night."[2] Though Peter Parker's life is usually a mess, Spider-Man embodies grace. When most people see the superhero, they don't think about his alter ego's stressful personal life. They imagine the joy of swinging through the skyscrapers.

Photofest

It's a fantasy, of course, like all glamour. But it's particularly honest about the illusion. You might imagine that a spy's life resembles James Bond's or that the right pair of Christian Louboutin pumps will make you irresistibly sexy. But not even the most susceptible audience expects to develop superpowers. Though felt to be true, these illusions are always known to be false. That's part of their appeal.

"Like those superheroes who were able to move through walls or become invisible to their enemies, we appreciated the liberty that comics gave us: we were free to move in and out of what we could see was an illusion," writes the essayist Geoffrey O'Brien, recalling his childhood pleasures in the 1950s and '60s. "We could allow it to be as real as we wanted it to be; we could dissolve it at will."[3]

A common solvent is humor. Marvel is famous for

injecting knowing wisecracks into *Spider-Man* and *The Fantastic Four*, creating what O'Brien calls a "utopian parody" that preserves the earnest idealism of the original while laughing at its extremes.

> On the one hand, the Marvel heroes weren't kidding. (Reed Richards of the Fantastic Four: "I wonder if the world will ever know how close it came—to an almost incomprehensible fate.") On the other hand, they were always kidding. (The Thing, in response: "Don't worry! There'll always be some loudmouth like you around to spill the beans!")[4]

The comics historian Gerard Jones argues that this double vision goes all the way back to the original superhero. "The humor and excess of *Superman*," he writes, "made it possible to laugh along with the creators while still thrilling to the fantasy of power. . . . You could want the invulnerability and the power, but you had to laugh to keep people from knowing how badly you wanted it."[5]

This knowing humor is not the destructive ridicule of camp but an irony far more difficult to achieve and sustain. Like a Warhol portrait of Marilyn Monroe, it acknowledges the absurdity of the artifice without sacrificing its allure. It owns up to glamour without destroying it—preserving the pleasures of imagination by not demanding that dreams come perfectly true.

Andy Warhol's *Superman* (1981).

© Christie's Images/Corbis

FIVE

LEAVE SOMETHING TO THE IMAGINATION

The fastest way to look glamorous is to put on sunglasses. The right shades instantly associate even the most ordinary face with movie stars and jazz greats, ski resorts and beach vacations. *Vogue* editor in chief Anna Wintour wears sunglasses on the front row at fashion shows. Jay Z wears them on the front row at NBA games. Audrey Hepburn wore them playing Holly Golightly. Steve McQueen wore them pulling a heist in *The Thomas Crowne Affair* (1968). General Douglas MacArthur wore them wading ashore on his victorious return to the Philippines. Jacqueline Kennedy Onassis wore them everywhere. Sunglasses are the quintessential glamorous accessory.

The connection between sunglasses and glamour goes deeper than their association with iconic people and places. It's also aesthetic. Sunglasses enhance the wearer's appearance by implicitly enlarging the eyes and obscuring bloodshot irises or unsightly bags. They add grace. Most important, they create mystery—the third essential element of glamour. Someone wearing sunglasses is intriguing: "Who's behind those Foster Grants?"[1] While we may guess what the wearer is looking at, we cannot be certain. Sunglasses hide emotion. They create an impression of coolness and detachment. Someone wearing sunglasses is visible yet veiled.[2]

If the longing for escape and transformation is glamour's emotional core, and grace glamour's central illusion, then mystery is glamour's defining perceptual quality. "Everything at a distance turns into poetry: distant mountains, distant people, distant events," wrote Novalis, the eighteenth-century German Romantic poet and theorist.[3] Every object of glamour is in some way exotic to its audience—displaced in time, space, culture, or social milieu, inhabiting a different biological, physical, or economic reality. This distance allows the other to become an ideal extension of the self. Mystery encourages projection. It makes glamour work.

© Norman Parkinson Ltd./Courtesy of Norman Parkinson Archive

"The women had so much mystery," says the fashion designer Carolina Herrera, explaining why Alfred Hitchcock's heroines were paragons of glamour, "and they all looked so effortless."[4] When Ben Brantley, now the *New York Times* theater critic, saw Greta Garbo on the street in 1985, the aging star looked neither chic nor beautiful. Her face was without makeup, her expression clenched, her clothes nothing special. But, he recalls, "she was wearing six decades' worth of well-documented silence. And that made her the most glamorous creature I had ever set eyes on."[5] Rock stars were more glamorous, suggests the music critic Brian McCollum, when fans knew them only from liner notes and grainy photos. "Mystique is the lifeblood of key qualities such as glamour and cool," he writes, but "in today's buzzing Information Age, mystique—that intangible it—is getting harder to pull off."[6]

Silence, distance, mystery. By veiling reality and obscuring details, they permit the audience to mingle its desires with the visible characteristics of the glamorous person, place, or thing. The less we know of the person behind the persona, the more we can fill in the gaps with our own yearnings. "It may be the goddamnedest put-on of all time," said the director Billy Wilder, "yet Garbo is the quintessence of what a star should be. . . . She said and did nothing and let the world write her story."[7] On a more contemporary note, *British Vogue* comments that "by refusing to speak to the press even when assailed by controversy, Kate Moss has become a true icon—an image onto which we can project whatever meaning we desire."[8] The supermodel's image is everywhere, but she remains silent. "To be the one person who won't talk to anyone but then also be everywhere visually," says the fashion journalist Angela Buttolph, "is beyond genius."[9]

What's true of people is true also of settings: distance feeds glamour. It's easier to imagine an ideal life in a time or place you know only from selective images. California and Paris, "the Orient" and New York were most glamorous when they were still difficult to reach. They could live in the imagination. "I never went to Africa," admits Ralph Lauren. "But if I had, I might never have done the clothes that I did." His safari collections represented "a mysterious world that didn't exist anymore, or never existed, but inspired a mood about dressing and desire."[10] His imagined Africa was glamorous. The promotional photos that re-created it were staged in Hawaii.

In his 2011 film *Midnight in Paris*, Woody Allen plays with the idea that even the most glamorous of eras can look that way only to outsiders.

Glamour is neither opaque nor transparent. It is translucent, existing on the border between the obvious and the hidden. *Geoff Lung*

With a beautiful fiancée and a successful career as a Hollywood screen-writer, protagonist Gil Pender (Owen Wilson) has a life that itself would seem glamorous from afar. But his future wife shares none of his interests, and he feels like a hack. Wandering the streets of Paris one night, Gil is magically transported back to his ideal setting—the Paris of the 1920s. There, amid the full cast of modernist icons, he meets the lovely Adriana (Marion Cotillard). They fall in love. But Adriana perceives no glamour in the 1920s. She dreams instead of Paris in the 1890s, *la belle époque.* "I love it so much," she says. "Everything was so perfect." When she and Gil suddenly find themselves in that era, she decides to stay. But what about the twenties? "It's the present," pouts Adriana. "It's dull." Not to Gil, of course, who announces that he's from 2010 and declares the 1920s the golden age. "But *I'm* from the twenties," Adriana insists, "and I'm telling you the golden age was *la belle époque.*" The artists of *la belle époque,* meanwhile, dream of the Renaissance.

The moral of the story, in Allen's downbeat summary, is "It's always rotten to be where you are, and then when you get where you want to go, whether it's back in time or to a different country, then it's rotten too."[11] Familiarity breeds discontent. There's no glamour without mystery.

———

The mystery essential to glamour is not complete inscrutability. Glamorous sunglasses, after all, highlight as well as veil. They call attention to the face, most of which remains visible, and even the darkest lenses allow a hint of eye to show every now and then, when the light is just right. (Mirror shades, by contrast, are less glamorous than intimidating.) Glamour, as noted in chapter one, is neither opaque nor transparent. It is *translucent,* balancing attraction and denial. Glamour exists, as a French book describes the folding screen, "*à la frontière entre l'évident et le caché,*" on the border between the obvious and the hidden.[12] "You can create instant glamour with candlelight, which covers up anything," advises tastemaker Carolyne Roehm.[13] But the cover-up is not complete. Candlelight not only conceals but illuminates. It creates an enchanted circle, drawing guests closer. By highlighting some qualities and obscuring others, mystery creates a compellingly stylized version of reality that heightens grace and focuses desire. "The most essential thing about my style was working with shadows to design the face instead of flooding it with light," wrote the Hollywood photographer George Hurrell.[14] One way or another, all glamour follows the formula he laid out: "Bring out the best, conceal the worst, and leave something to the imagination."[15]

In constructing glamour, mystery is both a tool and an essential element. As a tool, mystery does two things: it provides imaginative space for the audience to project its own desires onto the glamorous object, and it enhances grace by obscuring preparation and flaws. As an essential element itself, it captures and holds the audience's attention. It fascinates and intrigues.

We can see mystery playing all these roles in one of the twentieth century's most glamorous figures: Jacqueline Kennedy Onassis. In her biography *Mrs. Kennedy*, Barbara Leaming portrays the first lady deliberately crafting her image, adjusting it for the audience and circumstances but always relying on concealment and distance to maintain an alluring façade:

Portrait of Carole Lombard by George Hurrell: "The most essential thing about my style was working with shadows to design the face instead of flooding it with light." *Courtesy of Pancho Barnes Trust Estate Archives, © Estate of George Hurrell*

> Like so much in her life, the aim of her signature style was concealment. A chemical straightener disguised the naturally kinky hair she hated. The teased bouffant masked a low hairline. Kid gloves covered large, strong, mannish hands. . . . The cut of her suit jacket artfully concealed the breadth of her shoulders, and her muscular back and arms. The skirt disguised hips she thought much too broad. The shoes were specially cut to make large feet look smaller and more feminine. Sunglasses hid brown eyes set so far apart that her optician had had to special-order a suitably wide bridge. Dark

lenses had the additional advantage of guarding emotions that since childhood she had taken tremendous pains to hide.[16]

The first lady's mystery hid her artfulness; the enchanted public saw only the results.

Though Jackie was famous for her sunglasses, in two of her most evocative portraits her face is masked in other ways: by a black mourning veil in one of the funeral photos immortalized by Andy Warhol and by her hair in Ron Galella's famous "Windblown Jackie."[17] Like Garbo, she also remained largely silent. The young Mrs. Kennedy gave a few campaign interviews and recorded her White House tour for CBS, but once her husband had been killed, her voice was almost never heard again in public.[18] "Silence fertilizes fantasy; had Jackie hosted a talk show, she would doubtless have lost cachet," writes Wayne Koestenbaum in his meditation on "icon Jackie," a glamorous dream figure only somewhat related to the real woman.[19] Like many glamorous figures, from Barack Obama and Kate Moss to James Bond and Mr. Spock, the public Jacqueline Kennedy Onassis was famously composed and self-contained.[20] Her poise and reserve protected her privacy but also made her a blank screen onto which the public could project its fantasies and desires.

This mysterious blankness recalls actress Hedy Lamarr's famous, possibly apocryphal, remark that "Any girl can be glamorous. All you have to do is stand still and look stupid."[21] In fact, the highly intelligent Lamarr had mastered a compelling form of mystery. She was, said Hurrell, "one of those actresses who can wear an absolutely blank expression and yet convey an attitude of complete intrigue."[22]

Intrigue. Hurrell's word choice is suggestive. Mystery makes its subject intriguing. Secrets engage our attention. Secret agent, secret admirer, secret society, secret rendezvous—all are redolent of glamour. "The commonest thing is delightful if one only hides it," Basil Hallward, Oscar Wilde's alter ego, advises Dorian Gray.[23] The allure of lingerie comes from such partial revelation. A woman's underwear, writes the fashion historian Valerie Steele, constitutes "a type of secret, sexual clothing," revealing more

Kate Moss: By staying silent yet visible, she becomes "an image onto which we can project whatever meaning we desire." *Photo by Martin Karius/Rex/Rex USA, courtesy of Everett Collection*

than street clothes while still concealing—and in some cases perfecting—the nude form. "A woman in a corset is a lie, a falsehood, a fiction, but for us this fiction is better than the reality," observed the nineteenth-century writer Eugène Campus.[24]

Whether a road stretching over the curve of the horizon or lace stretching across the curves of a woman, mystery invites the audience to linger and explore, to imagine crossing the frontier and discovering the hidden. "A stricter silhouette may cover more," says the fashion designer Peter Som, "but at the same time it makes you wonder what's underneath. It's a subversive kind of glamour."[25]

Partial revelation tantalizes and mesmerizes. It strengthens glamour's hold on the imagination. "It wasn't simply her veiled glance, her famous legs, that strange hint of a deeply knowing smile that fascinated," the biographer Donald Spoto writes of Marlene Dietrich. "She was *there*—on the local screen—but she was certainly never fully comprehensible. She was, quite literally, alluring: she captivated, enticed, drew us on."[26]

Marking Michael Jordan's fiftieth birthday, sports writer Phil Taylor makes a similar observation about the basketball star, whose public persona is simultaneously affable and reserved. Jordan's "refusal to lay himself open," he writes, has

helped him maintain a bit of mystery, and with it, a certain cachet. In a culture that cycles through celebrity athletes in a heartbeat—think Dennis Rodman and Terrell Owens—Jordan abides, still with a modicum of cool even as he pitches products as decidedly unhip as Hanes underwear. It's because even after all these years, we feel that we don't know everything about him, that we're not through with him yet. Some athletes chase our attention. Jordan lets us chase him.[27]

Intrigue is not as neutral a noun as *mystery*. It goes beyond the merely unknown or unfamiliar to suggest deliberation and complicity. Intrigue is mystery for a purpose. Hurrell's formulation suggests the active construction of glamour, with its intention to seduce or persuade. Take *Mad Men*'s iconic title card. It features a silhouette of protagonist Don Draper seen from behind, all grace and mystery with his arm casually draped over the back of a sofa and a cigarette dangling from his fingers. The silhouette is both glamorous and intriguing. As pure image, it suggests success and confidence: a figure worth emulating. As advertising for a television drama, however, it invites the audience to meet the man behind the mystery—to enjoy the illusion Don presents to the world while sharing his secrets. "It's the iconography of Movie Hero or Leading Man," says series creator Matthew Weiner, "but Don Draper is a disaster inside."[28]

—

Mystery plays a central role in distinguishing glamour from another alluring quality: charisma. Though writers sometimes use the words *glamorous* and *charismatic* interchangeably, these concepts are quite different. In its precise sense, charisma (originally a religious term) is a quality of leadership that inspires followers to join the charismatic leader in the disciplined pursuit of a greater cause. More colloquially, charisma is a kind of personal magnetism that inspires loyalty.

Charisma in either sense is a *personal* characteristic like intelligence. A place, an idea, even an object can be glamorous, but only a person can be charismatic. And while glamour depends on the audience's receptive imagination, even unsympathetic audiences can feel the power of charisma. (Charisma in someone hostile is quite frightening.)

GLAMOUR	CHARISMA
Cool	Warm
Distant	Personal
Admiration	Loyalty
Audience defines meaning	Charismatic person defines meaning
Desire	Commitment
Still photo	Live performance
Sales	Leadership
Good for campaigning	Good for governing

Most important, glamour requires mystery, allowing the audience to fill in the details with their own desires. Glamour doesn't persuade the audience to share a leader's vision. Instead, it inspires the audience to project their own longings onto the leader (or movie star, vacation resort, or new car). The meaning of glamour, in other words, lies entirely in the audience's mind, making glamour most effective at a distance. Charisma, by contrast, works through personal contact. A still image, the ideal medium for glamour, cannot capture charisma, which requires a live performance or, at the very least, a video recording. Charisma draws the audience to share the charismatic figure's own commitments, seeking that person's affection or approval. Charisma enhances leadership; glamour enhances sales.

This distinction explains a common political confusion. If you think of Barack Obama as a charismatic president, it is hard to explain why he has had so much trouble persuading the public that elected him to support his policies. But if you understand his appeal as glamour, in which the audience supplies the meaning, then it's not surprising that Obama means different things to different people and thus, especially in his first term, often had difficulty rallying his supporters in favor of a given course of action. Glamour is an asset in a campaign, but charisma is more useful once you're elected. A few particularly gifted leaders—Ronald Reagan, Nelson Mandela, and, outside of politics, Steve Jobs—have had both.

GLAMOUR	CHARISMA
Barack Obama	Bill Clinton
Che	Castro
Thomas Jefferson	Andrew Jackson
Jackie Kennedy	Eleanor Roosevelt
Michael Jordan	Earvin "Magic" Johnson
John Lennon	Janice Joplin
Leonardo	Raphael
Spock	Kirk
Tupac Shakur	Snoop Dogg
Joan of Arc dead	Joan of Arc alive
Early Princess Diana	Late Princess Diana

It's rare for a charismatic leader to be as self-contained as Reagan or Mandela, which is one reason glamour rarely accompanies charisma. But, for the right audience, distance can provide the requisite mystery. On a trip to London some years ago, I happened to catch a television special on the evangelist Billy Graham's landmark 1954 crusade there. Like most successful preachers, Graham possessed considerable charisma. But it had never occurred to me that he might be glamorous. In the Bible Belt where I grew up, Graham was simply too familiar. But here were British interview subjects talking about him as a tall, handsome representative of exotic American culture—not just a persuasive Christian evangelist but an evocative, mysterious, exciting contrast to the grayness of postwar "austerity Britain." A stranger from a distant land, Graham was, in midcentury London, not only charismatic but glamorous.

Death, the ultimate mystery, marks the sharpest distinction between glamour and charisma. Not only does glamour survive death, but death at a young age often amplifies glamour, preserving the grace of youth and the mystery of what might have been. Charisma, by contrast, perishes with its possessor. Charismatic figures are remembered only through accounts of their charms or the effects of their actions. As time passes, their personal magnetism becomes less and less understood, especially if there are no video recordings of them. Historians can tell us plenty about Jacksonian democracy's significance in American political history, but we can no longer fully comprehend why Andrew Jackson, the charismatic general and seventh president, was its representative.

After death, charisma is sometimes transmuted into glamour. The charismatic figure loses his or her individuality to the audience's mythmaking desires. Joan of Arc may be the preeminent example of this phenomenon. "Instead of a bold and charismatic leader, talented soldier, and quick-witted girl, she was recast symbolically as an agent of God, a simple peasant girl chosen to humble the great and powerful," writes the historian

Larissa Juliet Taylor in *The Virgin Warrior: The Life and Death of Joan of Arc*, which seeks to separate the woman from the myth. Over the centuries, Taylor notes, Joan "has become everything to everyone—a Catholic, a proto-Protestant, a right or left wing partisan, anti-Semitic, nationalist, anti-colonialist, and even the face on cheese, chocolates, baked beans, and cosmetics."[29] In the various retellings of her story, another historian suggests, Joan has become "akin to a beautiful work of art."[30]

By contrast, the evolution of Princess Diana suggests that, in life, glamour can sometimes be replaced by charisma—as the fairy-tale iconography of the youthful bride gave way to the personal magnetism of the flawed "people's princess," with her sometimes scandalous behavior. When Diana died, however, her image shifted again. Replacing the racy or unflattering photos that had only recently filled British tabloids were memorial books of officially sanctioned images in which Diana deployed her signature "Shy Di" pose, with its tilted head and upturned eyes. "She is codified in these publications as mother, princess, wife, humanitarian, beautiful, and never, ever 'inappropriate' or 'unfeminine,'" notes the art historian Jill R. Chancey. "It is only in death that her visual biography has begun to fit the fictional narrative of ideal womanhood."[31] Upon her death, Diana's charisma vanished. But with distance and discretion, the mystery and glamour returned.

—

Constructing glamour requires mystery, but not every situation permits simple concealment. There are, however, other options. Mystery comes in different forms, each of which withholds information in a different way. Consider the diverse aesthetic tropes associated with glamour. There is, first and most obviously, the mystery created by shadows, spiral staircases, silhouettes, smoke, sunsets, and streamlining: the mystery of *the veiled, the distant, and the unseen*. Call it the mystery of *shadow*. From shadow arises the glamour of hats and veils and folding fans; of skylines viewed from afar (especially at night); and of the many images of Paris in the rain, which turn the City of Light into a place of shadows and fog. "It is necessary to photograph certain subjects in the rain," Brassaï declared in *Paris de nuit*, "since it is the rain that makes them 'photogenic.'"[32]

Glamorous portraits often deploy shadow literally, as Hurrell did, or they create metaphorical shadow by directing the subject's gaze away from the audience or, just as effectively, right through the viewer to some distant focal point. The result, in either case, is a mysteriously self-contained contrast to the open, ingratiating smiles common both in snapshots and on the covers of American fashion magazines. Shadow also accounts for the enduring appeal of black-and-white photography as a medium for glamour. "I like the mystery," says the fashion photographer Patrick Demarchelier, explaining why he often works in black and white. "A nude in color looks cheap and vulgar. In black and white, there is a veil."[33]

What, then, are we to make of the headline in *The Wall Street Journal*'s magazine, promising "Instant Glamour" in the form of diamond hair clips? Or of *Lucky* magazine's feature on jewelry teased with the same cover line? Why does a *New York Times* report say an iridescent umbrella "adds instant glamour to gloom"? Glitter and flash seem the antithesis of mystery—as "cheap and vulgar" as a nude in color—and yet they're often equated with glamour.[34]

Glittering jewels and metallic fabrics are luxurious and eye-catching, of course; perhaps they're symbols of wealth and attention. Or maybe writers just love the alliteration of "glamour and glitz." As the iridescent umbrella hints, however, there is in fact a genuine aesthetic association—and a second kind of mystery—at work. Glitter, sparkle, and shine not only grab the eye. Like the shifting colors of iridescence, they also confuse it. We cannot quite focus on the light's source, and when we try to, it seems to move elsewhere. Like shadows, glittering objects distort perception. In great quantities, they overwhelm, dazzling the audience to produce spectacle. But in moderation, they fascinate, feeding glamour. They represent the mystery of *the chameleon, the paradoxical, and the ambiguous*: the mystery of *sparkle*.

Sparkle informs the allure of Shakespeare's Cleopatra, whose contradictory and changeable nature makes her endlessly fascinating to men:

> Age cannot wither her, nor custom stale
> Her infinite variety. Other women cloy
> The appetites they feed, but she makes hungry
> Where most she satisfies.[35]

The British artist Marc Quinn, who has created several sculptures of Kate Moss, describes the supermodel's mystery in similar terms. "Her image is elusive, and you can never fix it," he says. "Even if you make it in solid gold," which he has, "another image will appear. . . . It's a special quality, which means she continues to carry on and gets more and more mythical. It's the mystery of the Sphinx."[36]

Sparkle also explains the connection between glamour and androgynous style: Marlene Dietrich in a tuxedo, David Bowie as Ziggy Stardust, Helmut Newton's *Le Smoking* photos for Yves Saint Laurent. Like a mirror ball, androgynous style confuses, tantalizes, and intrigues. It makes us look again. Who is that really, and why is he/she dressed that way? Dietrich's tuxedo, suggests the biographer Donald Spoto, signified her "mysteriously unpredictable nature. . . . She defied categorization. Something essential about her was unknowable."[37]

Marlene Dietrich's masculine attire, suggests biographer Donald Spoto, signified her "mysteriously unpredictable nature." Like a mirror ball, androgynous style confuses, tantalizes, and intrigues.

Courtesy of Everett Collection

Describing her taste in interior design, Candace Bushnell, the author of *Sex and the City*, combines sparkle with a third form of mystery: "I love things that are old and glittery," she says, "that come with layers of glamour and past lives."[38] In this idea of layers, the past is not a discrete and stylized moment—"Paris in the 1920s"—but a mysterious, unpredictable process that leaves an accordingly rich residue. From layers emerge the sensory qualities of pearls and lacquerware; of great perfumes, whose scents reveal themselves over time; and of the beautifully irregular patterns of natural stone: marble, agate, lapis lazuli.

This form of mystery hides information not through concealment or confusion but through complexity and depth. We don't know what history or nature will produce; there are too many variables and too much detail to comprehend in a glance. Hence the mystery of rugged coastlines, verdigris patina, and twisting woodland paths. As a design element, such mystery appears in Alexander McQueen's 2009 Plato's Atlantis collection, with its phosphorescent sequins, opalescent beads, and jellyfish and reptile-skin prints. This is the mystery of *the layered, the fluid, and the fractal*: the mystery of *complexity*.

These three types of mystery—shadow, sparkle, and complexity—are not mutually exclusive. To the contrary, they're often complementary, both as styles and as metaphors. The touchstone glamour of art deco and of Hollywood's studio-era costume and set design combined the aesthetics of shadow and sparkle. Frank Gehry's signature buildings are simultaneously sparkling and complex. So is the sapphire-and-diamond Julia necklace Marc Newsom designed for Boucheron, based on fractal geometry. Animal prints mingle the distance (shadow) of exoticism with the complexity of biological patterns, which themselves create camouflage by emulating the play of light and shadow. In his famous meditation on traditional Japanese aesthetics, *In Praise of Shadows,* Jun'ichirō Tanizaki writes eloquently of the interplay of shadow and sparkle with the complex layers of lacquerware, reminding moderns that such works (like the gilded altar pieces of European churches) weren't meant to be experienced under electric lights:

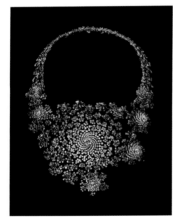

Based on fractal geometry, Marc Newsom's Julia necklace for Boucheron combines complexity and sparkle. © *Boucheron International*

Lacquerware decorated in gold is not something to be seen in a brilliant light, to be taken in at a single glance; it should be left in the dark, a part here and a part there picked up by a faint light. Its florid patterns recede into the darkness, conjuring in their stead an inexpressible aura of depth and mystery, of overtones but partly suggested. The sheen of the lacquer, set out in the night, reflects the wavering candlelight, announcing the drafts that find their way from time to time into the quiet room, luring one into a state of reverie.[39]

As stylistic elements, the forms of mystery are particularly intriguing together.

But shadow, sparkle, and complexity are more than literal aesthetic prescriptions; glamour is not, after all, a style. They are also metaphors that illuminate the different sources of mystery and, thus, the diverse strategies available for creating it. Understanding the varieties of mystery offers hints of how a person, a travel destination, or a brand might create and maintain translucence in what the writer David Brin has aptly dubbed "the transparent society."[40] How can mystery survive the overexposed age of high-definition reality TV?

Consider Paris, a place so enduringly glamorous that many English speakers assume, incorrectly, that the word *glamour* must come from the French. The city is known for the grace of its people and places, and the idea of Paris suggests many different forms of escape and transformation: to the bohemian life of the artist, the cosmopolitan sophistication of the diplomat, the chic polish of the *Parisienne*, or the café camaraderie of writers and intellectuals. But what makes Paris mysterious?

The city long relied on the allure of the unseen. It was the distant capital to the provinces, the foreign to those abroad. "Paris, more vague than the ocean, glimmered before Emma's eyes with a silvery glow," writes Gustave Flaubert of his provincial protagonist in *Madam Bovary*.[41] For centuries, Paris was the subject of song, story, and cinema (not to mention enticing product names) in large part because it could represent a dream city—and, thereby, a dream life—which the audience had never experienced. "How," muses the style historian Joan DeJean, "would the modern perfume industry have marketed its mythical scents without the mystique of Paris to back them up?"[42]

Reinfried Marass

Yet despite the relative ease of travel today, Paris has not lost its mystique. Emma Bovary (and *Sex and the City*'s disillusioned Carrie) notwithstanding, those who come to Paris often find the city more intriguing as they get to know it. What a guidebook calls the city's "enduring air of romance, mystery, and sophistication" arises not only from shadow but from complexity—the sense that there is always more to discover.[43] This mystery is symbolized by the tradition of the wandering *flâneur*, by the twisting streets of the Marais, and by the unknown treasures of the flea market, Les Puces. The search for antiques is like doing intelligence work, says a Paris antiquarian, noting that both endeavors involve "uncovering the hidden, discovering the disappeared, deciphering the secret."[44] Layers and complexity provide a mystery that remains intriguing even after repeated exposure.

So can the ambiguity, paradoxes, and changeability of sparkle. In an interview on the eve of the opening of *Elizabeth*, the 1998 movie that made her a star, Cate Blanchett acknowledged the realities of the transparent society. "You can go mad trying to control your image," she said. "In Elizabeth's day a painter would take a couple of months to paint your portrait. Now you can be photographed walking down the street in your pajamas and there's nothing you can do—you just have to grin and bear it."[45]

Yet Blanchett has managed to maintain her mystery. "She goes out of her way to give nothing away," notes the journalist Miranda Sawyer, profiling Blanchett for *Glamour UK*. "She's elusive and vague, which means women like her, but we're not sure why."[46] Compounding that elusiveness is her choice of roles. As an actress, Blanchett is a chameleon, playing characters who look and behave in radically different ways. We can't assume her roles say anything about who she really is. In person, the critic John Lahr writes, she is similarly ambiguous: "both candid and private, gregarious and solitary, self-doubting and daring, witty and melancholy." Her favorite word, he observes, is *fluidity*. Blanchett need not go mad controlling her image, because she has no single image to begin with. "Ambiguity is not absence," she says, discussing how to play a scene. "It's a wildly contradicting series of actions, emotions, and intentions."[47] By wedding sparkle to complexity, Blanchett not only gives her characters believable motivation and depth but preserves the mystery of her own secret self.

As an exceptionally versatile actress, Blanchett may be an extreme case. But like Paris, she illustrates a broader phenomenon. People who bemoan the death of mystery and, thus, of glamour are wrong. Mystery may be difficult to sustain through concealment alone, but even in our "buzzing Information Age" much public disclosure is still a matter of choice. (You don't have to leave the house in your pajamas.) Most important, blending shadow with sparkle or complexity can preserve mystery in ways that make the glamorous even more intriguing.

For the audience, maintaining the balance between the obvious and the hidden requires restraint—a willingness to let the unknown remain so and not to turn on the electric lights, look behind the curtain, and reveal the secrets. "After a time," counseled Mr. Spock, "you may find that having is not so pleasing a thing, after all, as wanting. It is not logical, but it is often true."[48] Glamour can be a powerful spur to both action and inquiry but, in the process, information and experience often destroy glamour's essential mystery, dispelling the illusion that was once so inspiring. You may find, like Simon Doonan, that the Beautiful People are boring.

One reason that still images are so effective at creating glamour is that they can fix the mysterious moment for all time, refusing access to any further information. Consider what may be the most glamorous of the many female nudes in Western art: Diego Velázquez's *Rokeby Venus*. The beautiful young woman reclines on her right side, holding up her head to look in a mirror held by Cupid. We see her blurred reflection in the glass, while, as in a rearview mirror, she gazes at the onlooker. This is not Venus surprised at her toilette by an intruder or voyeur. She isn't doing her hair or applying her makeup, nor, as in some other paintings, is she asleep. She is calm, composed, graceful, and, for all her bare skin, mysterious. Working in the seventeenth century, Velázquez may not have known the concept of glamour, but he knew how to produce the effect.

Unlike the reclining nudes produced by the painter's contemporaries in Venice, observes the art historian Andreas Prater, this figure "is not stretched out passively before us, but supports her head in an almost up-

Diego Velázquez's *Rokeby Venus*: Perhaps the most glamorous female nude in Western art, it suggests and preserves the moment before intimacy replaces idealization. *Fine Art Images/ Superstock/Everett Collection*

right position that is a continuation of the rising curve of her back" and the artist "places the focal point much lower, so that we do not look down on the scene, but stand directly before it.[49] Psychologically, the eye-level view invites projection and perhaps identification. The art critic Edward Snow argues that even for male viewers, "The long lines, the bounded musculature, the sensual contact of flesh and fabric: all appeal less to visual delectation than to those gender-indifferent kinesthetic instincts that cause bodies to identify with other bodies, and to imagine what they feel."[50]

Whether the painting engenders identification or merely projection, Velázquez's nude is clearly not just beauty on display, something easily known and possessed. This is another person, an independent consciousness, and therefore intriguing—all the more so since we cannot really see the face that might provide hints of her attitude toward her audience, or of her inner life. The mirror at once discloses and obscures. It provides only a secondary, tantalizingly indistinct image that invites further looking.

That invitation is particularly appropriate since, unlike most of the period's nudes, the woman Velázquez represents as Venus is neither a goddess nor a prostitute but a bride, as indicated by the pink ribbons symbolizing "the fetters of love representing the bond of marriage."[51] The painting was most likely a wedding gift, to be displayed in the private, marital bedroom of Don Gaspar de Haro y Guzmán and his young bride, Doña Maria Antonia de la Cerda, who was described at the time as "the most beautiful woman in the world." Though not intended for public display, the painting would therefore have anticipated a female as well as male audience—the bride along with the groom.

The image thus suggests and preserves the moment before daily intimacy replaces idealization.[52] Glamour is both the painting's effect and, in this way, its subject: here is what it is like to admire and be admired, to desire and be desired—and to imagine and be imagined, but not to know or truly be known.

Glamour provides a lucid glimpse of desire fulfilled. It captures moments, not stories. It seems timeless.

To identify the common characteristics shared by all types of glamour, the preceding chapters have deliberately taken examples from different times, places, and circumstances. But glamour, like any product of human culture, exists in history. Its elements remain constant, but its forms and meanings evolve. Like art, literature, or fashion, glamour develops over time. Old objects yield to new ones, and audiences change.

Now that we understand what glamour is and how it works, we can tell its story. In the following chapters, we'll explore critical episodes in its history and discover ways in which glamour itself shaped history.

Icon
THE WINDOW

In the opening sequence of *Breakfast at Tiffany's* (1961), Holly Golightly (Audrey Hepburn), wearing a black evening dress with an elaborate pearl necklace, gets out of a cab on a deserted, early-morning Fifth Avenue and walks slowly toward Tiffany's. Pulling a pastry and cup of coffee out of a paper bag, Holly drinks and munches as she gazes at windows filled with jewels and chandeliers.

Audrey Hepburn in *Breakfast at Tiffany's* (1961): The image of the window balances disclosure and denial. *Courtesy of Everett Collection*

Although she looks like an elegant lady, her longing suggests she does not shop at Tiffany's. Her jewels are paste, her finery an illusion. Her appearance is a glamorous façade, and the store's windows represent not the life she actually lives but the one she yearns for.

Windows are common in the iconography of glamour, because a window, despite its transparency, creates mystery. It may let in light and air, sounds and sights, but it also sets boundaries, balancing disclosure and denial.

From medieval romances to the 1989 movie *Say Anything*, young men have serenaded their lady loves through open windows. The woman is accessible yet hidden within. If the serenade succeeds, she will appear at the window—visible, yet still elevated and enclosed. The window serves as a symbol of tantalizing desire, an object so close and yet so far. Later in *Breakfast at Tiffany's*, the movie reverses the classic serenade scene, as Holly sits on her window by the fire escape singing "Moon River" while her love interest Paul (George Peppard) looks down from his window above.

Glamorous window views are not voyeuristic; the viewer is not furtive. Window shopping is a public activity, and the serenading lover hopes his lady will look back and respond. The mystery surrounds not the observer but the observed. By simultaneously withholding and revealing information, a window makes the scene on the other side intriguing.

Voyeurism is invasive and revelatory; the voyeur wants to see as much as possible. Glamour, by contrast, needs room for imaginative projection. To preserve the illusion, the audience must keep its distance. "I look out at dozens of neighbors who live in apartment buildings, town houses, and even an artist's atelier, but I cannot see them with the naked eye," John Berendt, the author of *Midnight in the Garden of Good and Evil*, writes of his New York apartment. "I am content to leave to my imagination exactly who they are and what they do. Peering at them up close through a telescope would not only breach an unwritten code of urban ethics, it would probably reveal their lives to be far less glamorous than I like to think they are."[1] The allure of a cityscape at night lies in the alternative lives suggested, but not revealed, by all those glittering windows.

By limiting the view, a window frame creates mystery and intrigue. Its limits are especially suggestive when the frame itself is an image: a frame within a frame. The effect is heightened further when the window appears in the middle view, where in real life the audience might draw closer, change the angle, or pick up the forbidden telescope. In a picture, the view is fixed. Only the imagination can fill in what lies beyond the frame.

Lillian Bassman, "More Fashion Mileage per Dress." New York, 1956.
© *Lillian Bassman*

Many window images are doubly glamorous. Like Holly Golightly or the condo dwellers in chapter one, the picture's subject experiences the glamour of looking through a window and the picture, in turn, arouses glamour in the audience. When the subject is right up against the window, the view beyond is often blurred, adding mystery and allowing the audience to fill in their own desires. We glimpse only hints of Tiffany's chandeliers and jewels. The glamour of Lillian Bassman's 1956 photograph "More Fashion Mileage per Dress" comes from the feeling of anticipation we share with the stylish woman as she rises from her bus seat to look out at the excitement of the city—however we might imagine it. All we actually see are blurry reflections in the glass.

Whether a barely glimpsed apartment or a department store vignette, the other side of a window represents a different life. The Romantic writers and artists of the nineteenth century depicted the view from the inside out, contrasting contemplative domesticity with nature, adventure, and action, the cozy with the expansive. "The window is like a threshold and at the same time a barrier," writes the art critic Lorenz Eitner. "Through it, nature, the world, the active life beckon, but the artist remains imprisoned, not unpleasantly, in domestic snugness. The window image illustrates perfectly the themes of frustrated longing, of lust for travel or escape which run through romantic literature."[2]

In the iconography of glamour, windows serve more varied purposes, because glamour encompasses a wider range of desires—and definitions of escape—than does Romantic poetry. Commuting home one evening, Shohei Sugiyama (Kôji Yakusho), the unhappy accountant in *Shall We Dansu?* (1996), looks through the window of his train and sees a beautiful young ballroom dance instructor gazing wistfully from the window of her studio. Repeated over several nights, this double window view sets in motion the movie's plot, in which Mr. Sugiyama finds in dance a more joyful existence. He escapes not from his setting, his family, or his occupation, but from the confines of social convention and daily routine.

Or take the image at the beginning of this chapter: Julius Shulman's famous 1960 photograph of Pierre Koenig's Case Study House No. 22, a building that seems to be all window. This twilight portrait of two young women conversing in a living room thrusting out toward a lighted city grid is intensely glamorous. But the ideal it evokes is modern, urban (or suburban) domesticity—the antithesis of Romantic longings. The women ignore the view.

The genius of Shulman's composition is to include both the domestic scene and the city sprawling below: both idealized, both remote. The photograph makes us yearn to claim not only the home but also the city, the perfect combination of tranquility and excitement. Architecture critic Paul Goldberger aptly describes the photograph as "one of those singular images that sums up an entire city at a moment in time."[3] It is Los Angeles as it longed to be, and as we wish it were.

Icon
SHANGHAI

For twentieth-century Westerners, the glamour of Shanghai was personified by Marlene Dietrich and Anna May Wong in *Shanghai Express* (1932). The two beautiful courtesans, with their feathers, veils, furs, silk, and jewels, represented the forbidden pleasures of a distant land, a place exotic yet, thanks to its colonial concessions, not entirely foreign. Shanghai's glamour, audiences understood, disguised a city of heartbreak and vice—all the innuendos contained in Dietrich's famous line, "It took more than one man to change my name to Shanghai Lily." Yet the dark side only added to the allure.

The very word *Shanghai* was enticing. It promised "mystic ecstasies," as the background copy whispered in an ad for Lenthéric's "Shanghai" perfume. *The Lady from Shanghai*, the 1948 Orson Welles film starring Rita Hayworth, went through two other working titles before settling on that alluring, and largely irrelevant, final choice.[1] Like a femme fatale, Shanghai was dangerous, mysterious, and irresistible.

The city held a different sort of glamour for Chinese: the promise of a better life. They came to escape famine and civil war and, like the immigrants who squeezed into the tenements of New York, to claim their portion of a widely shared dream. "Shanghai is a golden city, a city beyond the imagination,"

Two versions of Shanghai's pre–World War II glamour: for Chinese, a modern Shanghai woman, and for Westerners, Anna May Wong's courtesan in *Shanghai Express* (1932).

Courtesy of Everett Collection; Advertising Archive/Courtesy of Everett Collection

says a farmer in a 1935 short story by the Shanghainese author Mu Shiying.[2] The popular cartoonist Feng Zikai captured the promise in a 1932 drawing that shows a peasant father and son looking across fields toward a distant train. "Heading for Shanghai," reads the caption. The pair seem to wish they were, too.

For Chinese as well as Westerners, Shanghai represented an intriguing zone between the familiar and the foreign. A Francophile Chinese intellectual could walk the streets of the French Concession and imagine himself in Paris.[3] Yet the city was overwhelmingly Chinese.

Most of all, in a land of Confucian tradition and peasant agriculture Shanghai was modern: a commercial city of trade and industry, with electricity and skyscrapers, movie palaces and department stores. "Nothing enthralled the Shanghainese more than modernity," writes the cultural historian Lynn Pan, whose family fled the city in 1955. "While the rest of the nation was still sunk in rusticity, here were young girls clacking about on Italian heels, photographic studios, department stores, special offers and seasonal sales."[4] A poster from the 1930s shows a modern Shanghainese woman, her bobbed hair in fashionable marcel waves, wearing a form-fitting *qipao* and Western shoes. Through the window behind her, we behold an electrified city of bright office buildings and neon-lit towers. The caption declares Shanghai "a prosperous city that never sleeps." The subtext, notes an art curator, is "Come to Shanghai to find a modern woman!"[5]

The *qipao* embodied Shanghai's glamour, balancing the familiar and the new. Streamlined with Western-style darts, it was nonetheless unmistakably Chinese—a sleek Shanghainese reworking of the loose and cumbersome Manchu robe. And it struck a balance of mystery and disclosure. With its side slits and close fit, a *qipao* provided suggestive hints of the wearer's body, even as it covered her from neck to toe. Unlike a Western outfit, its allure didn't come from showing skin.

After the Communists took power, Shanghai acquired a new sort of mystery. It became a legend, a lost civilization. Many of its people went into exile, taking with them an evocative idea of Shanghai. "All Chinese Asian cities were modeled on Shanghai in some way," says the writer Tina Kanagaratnam, a Shanghai resident born in Singapore. "So Shanghai has this allure, this glam-

David Bulow

our."[6] In every city of the Chinese diaspora, she notes, you'll find a Shanghai Hair Salon, its name asserting a claim to stylishness.

Now the city is back. "By far it's the most glamorous city in China," says the Shanghai restaurateur Michelle Garnaut, who opened the Glamour Bar in 1999.[7] Back then hers was the only hot spot on the legendary Bund, whose historic buildings once housed foreign banks, clubs, and trading companies. The Bund now bustles with sightseers. "Glamour Reborn on the Bund," declares the home page for Shanghai's Peninsula hotel.[8]

But contemporary Shanghai's glamour does not really lie in its art deco past. From the windows of the Peninsula or the roof deck of the Glamour Bar, guests look across the Huangpu River to the towers of the city's Pudong district, all built in the past two decades. Bright with lights against the evening sky, Pudong's skyline is modernity reincarnated. "Built to be impressive, not enjoyable," with vast, impersonal plazas and wide boulevards unpassable by pedestrians, writes architecture critic Daniel Brook, "Pudong is meant to be viewed from across the river on the Bund—and in photos or films shot from the Bund—rather than from its own streets; for Pudong is less a city than an ad for a city."[9] It is the image that now signifies Shanghai in sports car ads and fashion shoots: a "futuristic" backdrop symbolizing the glamour of a resurgent China, at home and abroad.[10]

III.

THE EVOLUTION OF GLAMOUR

FROM A MUSE OF FIRE TO THE GLEAM OF A THOUSAND LIGHTS

In *The Princess Bride*, William Goldman's affectionate send-up of the fairy-tale adventure genre, the narrator establishes the story's mythic setting with a series of parenthetical asides. The tale, he says, takes place "before Europe" but "after Paris," "just after America but long after fortunes," and "after taste" but "before glamour." The asides, Goldman tells us in his own fictional persona, drove the book's copy editor crazy. "How can it be before Europe but after Paris?" she demanded. "And how is it possible this happens before glamour when glamour is an ancient concept? See 'glamer' in the Oxford English Dictionary."[1]

This elaborate joke points to a real issue. The old magical term notwithstanding, glamour as a concept with a distinctive word to describe it is far from ancient. As we saw in chapter one, *glamour* in its modern usage dates only to the nineteenth century. The more interesting and difficult question is whether glamour is an ancient *phenomenon*, regardless of whether that phenomenon might have been recognized or named.

Now that we've established what glamour is and how it works, where should we begin the history of glamour?

Here, as *The Princess Bride* suggests, glamour does resemble Europe, a land mass that existed before it was a cultural concept with defined borders and a specific title. Glamour is not like the stirrup, the telescope, the lightbulb, or the microprocessor. It was not invented but evolved along with human minds and human culture. Once its usefulness was discovered, however, glamour, like an agricultural plant, was tended and strengthened through deliberate action. That's why so many people assume glamour must have originated with Hollywood producers, New York ad men, or Parisian courtesans; although these figures did not invent glamour, they did effectively cultivate it.

Like a plant, glamour flourishes more in some environments than in others, and it also requires certain preconditions to survive. These preconditions not only explain why glamour seems to be, in the historian Stephen Gundle's words, "a quintessentially modern phenomenon" but also suggest where and in what forms glamour might have arisen in premodern cultures.[2]

In his 2008 book *Glamour: A History*, Gundle rightly distinguishes glamour from the luxurious trappings of aristocratic courts. "Although monarchs, courts, and aristocrats offered examples of luxurious living and high style," he writes, "it was the fabrication of these by the emergent men and women of the bourgeois era, by the new rich and commercial establishments and the world of entertainment that was glamorous. . . . Glamour contained the promise of a mobile and commercial society that anyone could be transformed into a better, more attractive, and wealthier version of themselves."[3] Gundle's formulation is a more generous and insightful version of John Berger's pronouncement, cited in chapter two, that "glamour cannot exist without personal social envy being a common and widespread emotion."[4] Both associate glamour with upward social mobility, calling to mind the visions that entranced Joan Crawford as Marian in *Possessed* or the "poor man's son" imagined by Adam Smith.

But Gundle's phrase "anyone could be transformed" hints at a precondition not found exclusively in modern, commercial societies. Glamour, as we saw in chapters two and three, offers a lucid glimpse of desire fulfilled.

Its promise of escape and transformation lets us project ourselves into a setting or identity in which we feel our unarticulated longings realized. It thereby persuades us (or at least lets us entertain the belief) that our desires are achievable and that we are not stuck with the life we have. The first precondition for glamour, then, is *the willingness to acknowledge discontent with one's current situation along with the ability to imagine a different, better self in different, better circumstances.* Glamour is incompatible with fatalism; they repel each other. For glamour to work, the audience must be able to envision their lives transformed. The imagined transformation may be improbable (and, of course, glamour hides the difficulties). It may even be fantastic and thus literally impossible. But it cannot be inconceivable. The surrounding culture must therefore offer some avenue, however far-fetched, through which such transformation becomes imaginable.

By opening up opportunities for economic advancement and offering goods and services that beautify, educate, and otherwise promote self-improvement, modern, commercial societies provide many such avenues. To these promises of transformation, such trends as urbanization, rapid transportation, colonial expansion (for the colonizers), and mass immigration add the prospect of escape—a new life in a new location. Modern commercial societies thus afford abundant material for constructing and experiencing glamour. In this way, glamour does seem quintessentially modern.

But while premodern societies provided fewer opportunities for escape and transformation, and therefore fewer sources of glamour, fewer does not mean none. Nor for glamour to exist must it appeal to every segment of society. Even in a relatively static society, there may be groups or individuals who long for different circumstances and are susceptible to images representing escape and transformation. Without records of such audiences' reactions, however, we can only infer the existence of the allure from the popularity of such pictorial or verbal images. Consider the handsome young samurai evoked in a song popular in mid-seventeenth-century Japan:

On a spring day, through gossamer and dandelion fuzz
Who is breaking off the willow branch?
It's the young lord on white horseback.

The song paints a glamorous picture of the young lord. Hearing it, one might imagine himself cutting a similarly dashing figure, and, although samurai status was hereditary, white horses, the era's chicest mode of transportation, were available for rent.[5]

Or take the romances so popular in medieval France. In a world where marriages were contracted for economic or political advantage, the idea of romantic love itself could be glamorous. Less obviously, the medievalist Sarah-Grace Heller argues, the romances offered a second appeal to male audiences: they allowed young men of talent and ambition but no inheritance to imagine acquiring the arms and clothing needed to become knights. In one such tale, *Amadas et Ydoine*, written around the turn of the thirteenth century, the duke of Burgundy knights not only the hero but a hundred other young men, furnishing them all with new equipment. "The narrative," Heller writes, "offers the fantasy of a place to get new clothing and arms, essentials for earning a fortune, and thereby the means to obtain further new arms and clothing. This dream was a typical one in romances of the period."[6]

In other tales, the economic transformation comes through love, with varying degrees of fantasy involved. In the late twelfth-century story *Lanval*, "wealthy and generous supernatural women fall in love with the impoverished heroes, take them as lovers, and provide them with funds," while in *Jehan et Blonde*, from the thirteenth century, Blonde's inheritance gives Jehan the money he needs. "While still a fantasy economic scheme," comments Heller, "marrying an heiress is a much more practical strategy than attracting a wealthy fairy."[7]

Whatever their details, Heller argues that these scenes of sudden abundance enabled young men to imagine having the chance to "outfit themselves according to their tastes and their social ambitions," and thus led to the eventual development of a consumer-driven fashion system. "Desire for change," she writes, "must be present to cause the actual marketplace to evolve."[8] Heller's argument about medieval romances thus recalls Sally Alexander's, cited in chapter three, about the role that the films and advertisements of the 1930s played in enabling working-class British housewives to imagine an end to drudgery. The romances focused the audience's discontent and provided a vision of a better life.

Those popular medieval stories not only illustrate how the first precondition for glamour might be satisfied in a premodern culture but also suggest a second prerequisite. If glamour emerges, like humor, through the interaction between object and audience, that object must come from somewhere. Glamour is the product of communication. It requires, therefore, *the creation and transmission of images that invite projection.* These images may be evocative word pictures or visual art, theatrical performances or live glimpses of people, places, or artifacts. But, whatever the medium, the audience must be able to see themselves in the picture somehow—to identify with the glamorous person, imagine themselves in the glamorous setting, feel transformed by the glamorous artifact, identify with the glamorous concept. Not just any image, however beautiful or sublime, will do.

Here, again, we see why glamour seems like a modern phenomenon, since mass media carry a profusion of images, including ones consciously designed to elicit longing in order to sell commercial goods. And just as modernity opens up more opportunities to change one's status, it also offers more role models through whose popular images one may imagine a different life. Charles Dana Gibson succinctly captured this sort of glamour at work in a 1903 illustration titled *The Seed of Ambition.* In Gibson's

THE SEED OF AMBITION.

drawing, a young shopgirl or servant is on her way to deliver a large package when a theatrical poster catches her eye. She gazes longingly at the leading lady decked out in eighteenth-century finery. Whether lured by the fame or the costume, the girl seems destined for the stage.

Yet we need not wait for modern, commercial society to find imagery created to evoke projection and yearning. What travel brochure or perfume ad could ever equal the promise of "a land flowing with milk and honey"? Or consider the famous Saint Crispin's Day speech from Shakespeare's *Henry V*, in which the king rallies his outnumbered troops before the Battle of Agincourt. With a beginning that invites each man to assume he'll be one who "outlives this day, and comes safe home," the speech skims over present difficulties to paint an evocative picture of future fellowship and hearty celebration.

> He that shall live this day, and see old age,
> Will yearly on the vigil feast his neighbours,
> And say "To-morrow is Saint Crispian:"
> Then will he strip his sleeve and show his scars.
> And say "These wounds I had on Crispin's day."
> Old men forget: yet all shall be forgot,
> But he'll remember with advantages
> What feats he did that day: then shall our names,
> Familiar in his mouth as household words,
> Harry the king, Bedford and Exeter,
> Warwick and Talbot, Salisbury and Gloucester,
> Be in their flowing cups freshly remember'd.
> This story shall the good man teach his son;
> And Crispin Crispian shall ne'er go by,
> From this day to the ending of the world,
> But we in it shall be remember'd;
> We few, we happy few, we band of brothers;
> For he to-day that sheds his blood with me
> Shall be my brother.[9]

Instead of focusing on the suffering they're about to face, the men project themselves years ahead, to the happy time when they will be old and honored, with even the meanest of their number elevated to gentry status as the king's brothers-in-arms. With this vivid picture of their glorious future, the king moves the troops to conquer their fears and follow him to victory.

A much quieter invitation to projection hangs in the Florentine abbey called La Badia. Painted around 1485 by Filippino Lippi, *The Vision of Saint Bernard* portrays a scene from the life of Bernard of Clairvaux, a twelfth-century Cistercian monk and theologian who was known for his devotion to the Virgin Mary. According to legend, once when Bernard was too feeble from ill health to continue his work, the Virgin appeared to him, giving him comfort and courage. In Filippino's rendition, Bernard looks up from the homily he is composing on the Annunciation to see the loving face of Mary, as she extends her hand toward him. "Mary comes to him just as Gabriel came to her, to announce salvation," notes the art historian and Catholic priest Timothy Verdon. The painting's composition draws the viewer into the intimate space in which this moment of grace occurs. Writes Verdon,

> This entire episode is isolated in the foreground of the picture: the other monks, beyond the rock formation, do not see Mary but only a light in the sky. We by contrast—like Saint Bernard himself—see first hand the help Mary gives the saints: Filippino in fact concentrates our attention on the large figures in the foreground, enclosing the event in the tightly packed "psychological space" that extends from the viewer to the wall of rock.[10]

That privileged space includes Mary, her accompanying angels, Bernard, the painting's patron Piero di Francesco del Pugliese (shown in prayer in the right-hand corner), and, by implication, us. Unlike many religious paintings of the period, Filippino's work is not a scene designed strictly for adoration and devotion, like Mary on her throne or Jesus on the cross, but one that deliberately encourages projection. Like Piero, we are not only witnesses to the miracle but, as witnesses, invited to partake in the experience. The audience shares with Bernard this special confirmation of faith, just as King Henry shares with his men the honors of victory. Although its subject matter is far from the luxury and fame so often associated with modern glamour, to the monks for whom the painting was originally created, this vision of the religious life rewarded could not have been more alluring. What we find glamorous does, after all, depend on what we desire.

Despite their obvious differences, Henry's speech portraying the honors of the active life and Filippino's rendering of the consolations of contemplation share certain important qualities. Both transport the audience out of present realities and into an ideal and distant state. Both focus on the moment of reward, not the hardships along the way. Both exemplify a rhetoric of seductive, aspirational imagery. And both suggest modes of transformation that are open, at least in theory, to broad audiences—the brave or the pious—whatever their birth.

It is this quality of tacit egalitarianism that makes glamour seem so modern to many analysts, since rigid political and social hierarchies hinder projection. Yet through the centuries before the emergence of modern social mobility, there did exist avenues of aspiration where identifying with the great was not only permissible but in some cases encouraged: religious devotion, masculine martial prowess, and seductive feminine beauty. All three furnished imagery, ideas, and exemplary lives capable of sparking glamour.

Religion may seem a questionable source of glamour, yet escape and transformation, grace, and mystery all have religious resonance, and eschatology is the most common form of displaced meaning. Religions also depend on persuasion to sustain the faithful and win new converts, making the nonverbal rhetoric of glamour as useful to religious institutions as it is to commercial or patriotic enterprises. Particularly in situations where one's status in this world is unlikely to change, the love of God and hope of a glorious afterlife offer imaginative refuge. The religious life also provides models who inspire emulation and longing. If the mysteries of cloistered contemplation could be glamorous to Mary Gordon in the 1950s, they likely held similar allure in eras with fewer competing alternatives.

Then there is the enduring, and problematic, glamour of martyrdom, a state more pleasurably contemplated than experienced. In the glamorous version, the martyr's faith never wavers and is thereby demonstrated to be true. Death comes gracefully, with dignity, resolve, and, at least in the artistic portrayals, calm beauty. (Think of all those paintings of Saint Sebastian.) Above all, martyrdom makes the individual believer significant. "The early church," notes the contemporary Anglican theologian Andrew Shanks, "used its martyr stories, as a source of glamour, for recruiting purposes."[11]

One need not actually die to enjoy the glamour of martyrdom. It is an imaginative experience, one that survives to this day. While the phrase "glamour of martyrdom" now usually applies to Palestinian and jihadi suicide bombers, who are more soldiers than religious exemplars, the more traditional, less martial concept still inspires longing among some contemporary Christians. Interviewed at a 2007 gathering sponsored by the evangelical group Voice of the Martyrs, a fifteen-year-old aspiring missionary named Mercy Grace was asked what she thought of dying for her faith. She grinned and replied, "It would be neat!" Even her amended response, "It would be a privilege," suggests that in some parts of twenty-first-century America, the glamour of martyrdom endures.[12]

⎯

For all the power of religious glamour, the warrior and the beauty are the incarnations in which we find the most likely sources of premodern glamour, and the most ancient. They are central to Homer's *Iliad*, the oldest work of Western literature. We will never know when the first shoots of glamour appeared, but we can answer the question raised at the opening of this chapter. Glamour was indeed an ancient phenomenon. It goes back to Achilles and, in a more ambiguous way, to Helen.

Statue of Achilles at the Achilleion Palace in Corfu, Greece: Achilles is the first Western figure we can plausibly describe as glamorous to someone in particular. *Photo by Elizabeth Ellis as Flickr user izzie_whizzie under Creative Commons Attribution-NoDerivs 2.0 generic license*

Achilles is the greatest and most heralded of the Homeric Greek warriors, "the paragon of male courage" to the ancient Greeks and for many centuries that followed.[13] For the lyric poet Pindar, writing in the fifth century BC, he represents the aristocratic ideal, "the splendor running in the blood."[14] The son of a goddess, Achilles is strong and swift, tall and handsome, a singer and healer, and, above all, unmatched in battle—the "best of the Achaeans." He is also the youngest. He comes to Troy knowing he will die there, choosing immortality in song and story rather than a long and quiet life at home. Without Achilles, his allies face defeat; with him comes the promise of victory. He is the indispensable man.

But Achilles is more than an exemplary hero. He is the first Western figure we can plausibly describe as glamorous to someone in particular. Four centuries after Homer, nine after the Trojan War, he inspired Alexander III of Macedon, later dubbed by the Romans "the Great."[15] From childhood on, Alexander imagined himself as Achilles, copied the legendary warrior, and sought to surpass him. Alexander's boyhood tutor Lysimachus of Acarnania even nicknamed him Achilles. During his campaigns, the adult Alexander slept with a copy of *The Iliad* under his pillow; when he seized a jeweled casket from Darius of Persia, he chose Homer's book as the most fitting treasure to store in it. On reaching Asia, the young conqueror paid homage at Achilles' tomb in Troy, where he expressed his longing to have, like Achilles, "in life, a faithful friend, and in death, a great herald of his fame." Alexander cast his own friend Hephaestion in the role of Achilles' friend Patroclus and, when Hephaestion died, reportedly cut his hair over the corpse in emulation of Achilles mourning Patroclus. His Roman biographer Arrian found the story credible, "considering his envy of Achilles, with whom he had had a rivalry (*philotimia*) from boyhood."[16]

Achilles may have lived in a fatalistic universe, but Alexander did not. His biographers attribute to him a driving *pothos*, or yearning, "to do something new and extraordinary," something inspired by but beyond the achievements of his ancient hero.[17] "Alexander spent his life, short as it was, trying to surpass Achilles, a task in which inevitably he failed, as every warrior must," writes the defense intellectual Christopher Coker. "Our fictional heroes are beyond reach because they are archetypes, not

Alexander the Great's look of *pothos*, or yearning, became a visual representation of the visionary leader that persists to this day. *AISA/Everett Collection*

flawed human beings. But at least Alexander died in the knowledge that after Achilles he would be considered supremely worthy of emulation."[18] Like Achilles, Alexander himself became an icon of martial glamour.

Unlike modern readers, however, Alexander did not doubt that the "fictional" Achilles had really lived—any more than Julius Caesar doubted the existence of Alexander or Naomi Wolf doubts the reality of Angelina Jolie. Rather, like any good student of Aristotle, he understood that Homer's fiction lay in idealizing his hero. The poet, as Aristotle wrote, had created a "likeness which is true to life and yet more beautiful," downplaying Achilles' flaws and highlighting his virtues so as to "preserve the type and yet ennoble it."[19] Time and art obscured the details and defects of the real warrior, leaving ample room for the ambitious Alexander to project his own yearnings onto the glamorous figure of Achilles.

If Achilles was, at least for Alexander, an object of glamour, Helen is something more complicated and intriguing. Although *The Iliad*'s Helen is the most famous, the classical texts offer many versions of the world's most beautiful woman, with others suggested by the archeological evidence and still more added down through the ages. Helen is a figure of mystery, "an icon of beauty who flees from view."[20] People have imagined her many different ways. Among her various guises, writes the scholar Robert Emmet Meagher, "Helen is goddess, queen, trickster, witch, seeress, scapegoat, prize, curse, devoted wife, whore, weaver of tapestries and of fates, phantom, seductress, victim, the promise of bliss, and the assurance of doom."[21] Radiant and golden-haired, Helen shimmers when she walks, and her identity metaphorically sparkles as well—now one thing, now another. She is ambiguous, fascinating those who contemplate her.

The one consistent fact about Helen is that she is overwhelmingly beautiful, "the face that launched a thousand ships." Watching her move along the battlements of Troy, the city elders murmur:

> Ah, no wonder the men of Troy and Argives under arms have suffered years of agony all for her, for such a woman.
> Beauty, terrible beauty! A deathless goddess—so she strikes our eyes![22]

Helen's beauty is both a treasure men fight to possess and a spell that warps men's minds. It is disarmingly, frighteningly powerful. The longing she stirs can override virtue, honor, and reason.

To some, Helen is the ultimate glamorous woman, the figure you long to be or be with. Christopher Marlowe in *Dr. Faustus* portrays her as a supernatural version of the femme fatale. But in the ancient world, Helen's beauty was more than dangerous. It was godlike and awe-inspiring—more sublime than glamorous. "If we understand the Spartan Queen the way the ancients did," writes the historian Bettany Hughes, "her beauty cannot simply be viewed, it is coercive; she forces men and women alike into a state of longing, she forces them to act. Those who look at her cannot walk away unscathed. She catalyses desire. She is an *eidolon* that burns with projected emotion."[23] In this reading, Helen is less a person than a phenomenon.

Player's Cigarettes

Helen of Troy

An *eidolon* is an image, a phantom, an illusion—the deceptive product of the sort of magic the Scots once called *glamour*. In one version of her story, the real Helen never goes to Troy. She is whisked by the gods to safety in Egypt, while the Trojans and Achaeans battle over a mere eidolon sent to satisfy Aphrodite's promise to give Paris the world's most beautiful woman. Plato, in *The Republic*, uses the eidolon Helen as a metaphor for illusory pleasures.[24] Euripides, who judges Helen harshly in his Trojan tragedies, turns the eidolon story to comedy in *Helen*, creating an adventure with a happy ending. One reading of that play, however, makes it bitterly consistent with the poet's darker works. "Instead of rebuking men for creating endless misery in their quest for unworthy ends (Helen the slut)," writes the critic Jack Lindsay, "he tells them that their wars and greeds have a mere illusion or mirage as their goal."[25]

An image that burns with projected emotion, whose identity is both idealized and elusive, which engenders longing, hides difficulties, and moves audiences to sometimes-foolish action—in Helen we see the first shoots of glamour as not just a phenomenon but a concept. Helen is a beautiful illusion: glamour personified. "Helen was put on earth to catalise desire," writes Hughes.

> And for three millenia she has been hated for it: because in entertaining desire, we recognise our needs and our disappointments. . . . Here is a narrative not just of beauty, sex and death, but of eternal longing, a story born out of the first civilisation on the Greek mainland. Civilisation is restless, greedy—it always wants more, what it does not have. Longing propels us into uncharted territories, we go willingly and yet come to resent the journeys we have embarked on.[26]

Seen this way, Helen's tale becomes a lesson in the power and consequences of glamour.

In the conflicting interpretations of Helen we find the ambivalence that inevitably accompanies glamour and its objects. She is false or unworthy, and look at all the tragedy she causes. Yet the pleasure of seeing her cancels out the pain. She also represents love and beauty, which are genuine values. Sappho, writing in the seventh century BC, cites Helen to demonstrate that the most beautiful thing on earth is whatever one loves.[27] Three centuries later, the rhetorician Isocrates praises her beauty for its intrinsic worth—"the most august, most precious, and most divine of all things"—and her cause for uniting the Greeks: "It is owing to her that we are not the slaves of the barbarians."[28]

Above all, Helen inspires heroic deeds and enduring art. Distraught at Patroclus' death, Achilles rails that he is "in a distant land, fighting Trojans, and all for that blood-chilling horror, Helen!"[29] Yet we know Achilles has not come to Troy out of any deep concern for Helen or her wronged husband, Menelaus. The queen's abduction and her husband's offended honor merely provide the occasion that allows Achilles to achieve glory. Without Helen's "terrible beauty," there would be no songs of heroes ringing down the ages, no one remembering the names of the dead.[30] *The Iliad* is full of such names, from those who appear only as they die to others "familiar in our mouths as household words," a phrase used in explaining the spelling choices in the translation by Robert Fagles.[31] The Shakespearean echo is deliberate.

"Zeus planted a killing doom within us both," Helen laments to Hector, "so even for generations still unborn we will live in song."[32] Marlowe was onto something when he had Faustus beg Helen to "make me immortal with a kiss." What Helen offers is not just the pleasure of sex but the promise of immortality—glamour worth dying for.

Love and war, death and immortality. This is high-stakes glamour. The transformations proffered are the most transcendent, the illusions the most dangerous. Critics from Euripides to the present have decried martial glamour as a meretricious inducement to needless slaughter. Other voices, equally ancient and modern, have condemned beauty as a prison for women and a snare for men. How we feel about these forms of glamour ultimately depends not on their truth or falsity but on our attitudes toward the actions they inspire. We are still talking about Helen and Achilles more than three thousand years after the fall of Troy. The glory was real, but was it worth the cost?

———

From antiquity, then, we can find enough scattered written and pictorial evidence to infer the existence of glamour and occasionally its deliberate construction, particularly to inspire military action. It's incorrect to declare glamour uniquely modern. Yet that notion isn't altogether misguided. Until relatively recently, glamour did not appear to be a widespread or common phenomenon.

Then something happened. We see it in Edo (now Tokyo) in the late seventeenth century, in London and Paris in the eighteenth, and in New York and Chicago in the nineteenth. In these vast commercial cities, each with more than a half million residents, glamour underwent a phase change. What had been once a rare or occasional experience became all but unavoidable. Instead of a handful of manifestations, glamour took on many forms, embodying a diversity of desires in a wide array of objects. As novel types of glamour emerged, they created an environment hospitable to still more incarnations. Glamour became so common that it soon furnished the subject for literary works, social criticism, and moral anxiety. And, of course, it eventually got a name.

Even as the commercial metropolis amplified and diversified glamour, it also softened it. No longer did escape and transformation demand the commitment of body or soul. They could seemingly be bought for the price of a ribbon, an embroidered garment, a Persian carpet, a railway ticket. The city abounded with sights to invite projection and spark desire, not only in would-be saints or heroes but in ordinary people seeking mundane forms of fulfillment. "Today a low song of longing had been set singing in her heart by the finery, the merriment, the beauty she had seen," writes Theodore Dreiser in *Sister Carrie*, his 1900 novel of urban glamour and its disappointments. Through the plate-glass windows of office buildings, in the display cases of department stores, amid the broad lawns of grand houses, Carrie glimpses intriguing hints of a better, more joyful existence: "She imagined that across these richly carved entrance ways, where the globed and crystalled lamps shone upon paneled doors set with stained and designed panes of glass, was neither care nor unsatisfied desire. She was perfectly certain that here was happiness. If she could but stroll up yon

Henri Gervex's *Une soirée au Pré-Catelan*, painted in 1909, depicts a number of celebrities of the day, including the courtesan Liane de Pougy, in the center window with the large black hat. © *Musée Carnavalet/Roger-Viollet/The Image Works*

broad walk, cross that rich entrance way . . . how quickly would sadness flee; how, in an instant, would the heartache end."[33]

In the great commercial city, glamour expanded beyond the subjects of epic poetry, history paintings, and theatrical tragedy—grand and fraught with moral significance—to the more intimate seductions of lyrics and novels, portraits and domestic scenes, comedy and melodrama. The pursuit of happiness largely superseded the pursuit of immortality. Here emerged the culture that fostered what Colin Campbell calls "modern, self-illusory hedonism." Contemplating the future enjoyment of goods and experiences became one of the "pleasures of the imagination," a characteristic eighteenth-century expression. This new urban glamour was more banal than its predecessors, but also more benign. It could therefore appeal to a vastly larger audience.

Among the objects of glamour was the city itself, as seen or imagined from afar. Considered at a distance, the great metropolis shimmered in the imagination like the Emerald City rising before Dorothy and her companions—the representation of all that was marvelous, mysterious, and missing from the audience's life. "The gleam of a thousand lights is often as effective as the persuasive light in a wooing and fascinating eye," writes Dreiser.[34] Out in the provinces, Emma Bovary buys a map of Paris and traces her fingers down its boulevards, closing her eyes to "see in the darkness the gas jets flitting in the wind and the steps of carriages lowered noisily in front of the theatre-entrances."[35] For those discontented with the familiar life of town or countryside, the city was a place of dreams, including the tantalizing promise of like-minded fellowship and a true home. As a young man in provincial Montpellier in the late nineteenth century, Paul Valéry, the future poet and author, thanked a friend for his letters from the capital: "You cannot imagine what a few pages . . . from Paris mean, from Paris, which is alive and intelligent."[36] Arriving from Edinburgh in 1762, the young James Boswell looked down upon London from the top of Highgate Hill. "My soul," he recalled in his journal, "bounded forth to a certain prospect of happy futurity."[37] The city was the geographical embodiment of escape and transformation.

Its allure from afar fed the city's growth, which in turn supported the new sources and types of glamour found within its bounds. These forms of glamour arose from the great metropolis's two defining and mutually reinforcing characteristics: its large population and its consumer culture. The city was not only mysterious at a distance; it was too big to be fully known even by its inhabitants. By virtue of its size alone, it offered a diverse sample of humanity. The metropolis was, in Boswell's words, "a place where men and manners may be seen to the greatest advantage"—a place to see and be seen, with every person a potential object of glamour.[38] In the juxtapositions of everyday experience, city dwellers glimpsed more alternative lives than did their country cousins. As one of Boswell's less enthusiastic contemporaries complained, in bustling London people from all "departments of life are jumbled together—the hod-carrier, the low mechanic, the tapster, the publican, the shop-keeper, the pettifogger, the citizen, the courtier, *all tread upon the kibes of one another*."[39]

At the same time, money dissolved some of the status barriers that had formerly limited the aspirations of the lowborn and thus the scope of glamour. Even in rigidly hierarchical Edo, samurai and merchants mingled in the Yoshiwara pleasure quarter, where money rather than class differentiated customers. The actors and courtesans of the demimonde, officially below even merchants in the social hierarchy, set the styles for the rest of society—just as in nineteenth-century Paris.[40] "With money," the literary scholar Howard Hibbett writes of Edo, "a fishmonger's son could be a social lion. Careers of beauty were never more accessible. An obscure shop or tea-house might blossom into splendid profit; whereupon its owner would 'train an epicure's palate, renew his wardrobe, and yearn for the exquisite in all things.'"[41] However different the institutional details, much the same could be said of London, Paris, New York, or Chicago.

Urban mixing was never complete, however. Rather, lives and classes hovered at a suggestive distance. Translucence, in other words, replaced the old opacity—and the old transparency. In the great city, you could be lost in the crowd, seen without being known. After a visit to the country, Joseph Addison, the eighteenth-century essayist, returned to London eager to "get into the crowd again as fast as I can, in order to be alone. I can there raise what speculations I please upon others, without being observed myself."[42]

Although some found such anonymity disorienting or demoralizing, for others it represented liberation. Metropolitan life offered a chance at re-invention, not to mention pleasures forbidden at home, giving substance to the image of transformation and escape. Writing from nineteenth-century Paris, two young women from provincial Limoges described the city as "an emancipation, a dream. . . . What charmed them specially was 'that no one spied upon anyone.'"[43] Young men loved Paris, Ralph Waldo Emerson observed, "because of the perfect freedom—freedom from observation as well as interference—in which each one walks."[44] Boswell, too, relished the city's privacy and freedom. "The satisfaction of pursuing whatever plan is most agreeable, without being known or looked at, is very great," he wrote.[45] It wasn't really true, of course, that residents were never spied on, observed, or looked at, as Addison's desire to "raise what speculations I please upon others" demonstrates. Rather, such scrutiny came mostly from strangers and so was usually of little consequence. Mystery and distance, essential to generating glamour, arose naturally from the city's sheer size.

From the enticing lovelies of poster art to shop windows bright against the night, the commercial metropolis forged the vernacular of glamour. Glamour in turn shaped the city. Despite vastly different cultural and political arrangements, certain commonalities emerged. Consider the theater, one of the defining institutions of urban life. Boswell, later famous for his biography of Samuel Johnson, regularly attended plays and argued their merits; he had affairs with actresses; he circulated among playwrights and actors. By the end of *Sister Carrie*, the protagonist enjoys a comfortable living as an actress, a career unimaginable in her small hometown. In cities as different as London and Edo, theater enthusiasts purchased popular prints of their favorite actors and read books about performers' real or imagined lives. Stage productions seem as intrinsic to urban life as crowded streets.

The crowds allowed theaters to flourish. In the age before film, only a geographically concentrated population could furnish the consistently large audiences needed to sustain frequent performances by multiple professional companies. As cities grew, audiences swelled to astounding num-

A London theater at the turn of the nineteenth century: The theater established a way of looking that primed city dwellers for other forms of glamour. *Mary Evans Picture Library/Everett Collection*

bers. "In the 1880s and 1890s," writes the historian Eugen Weber, "half a million Parisians went to the theater once a week, more than twice as many once a month. 'The population of Paris,' a journalist observed, 'lives in the theater, for the theater, by the theater.'"[46]

Along with a lively social space, the theater provided an imaginative respite from the constraints of everyday life. "Players made the stage seductive: their glamour and beauty, the virtuosity of their performances, their private lives, at once the focus of polite society and yet disreputably on its margins, all made the theatre a place of exciting dreams, fantasies and illusions," the historian John Brewer writes of eighteenth-century London. "Actors enjoyed the privilege of behaving on stage in ways which thrilled the audience with their impropriety."[47] In Edo, kabuki heroes embodied a different sort of escape, fulfilling the public's longing for what the Japanese scholar Nishiyama Matsunosuke calls "power to the weak." Like today's superheroes or action stars, kabuki "street knights" (*kyōkaku*) captivated audiences with their manly postures and effortless swordsmanship as they righted the wrongs of the oppressed. These characters displayed not only remarkable grace—made all the more impressive by their hugely oversized weapons—but also an unfailing sense of justice rarely found in their real-world counterparts.[48] Featuring "dreams of bravado, a show of forbidden ostentation, and not a few satirical comments," the kabuki theater, Howard Hibbett observes, represented "an escape from life and a criticism of it."[49]

Beyond the particulars of setting or plot, the theater established a way of looking—a habit of projection and model of spectatorship—that informed how city dwellers experienced daily life and primed them for other forms of glamour. In the commercial metropolis, every urbanite was both an audience and a performer for passersby, and every street a stage. "In Paris," wrote a nineteenth-century observer, "everyone is posing, everyone tarts themselves up, everyone has the *air* of being an artist, a porter, an actor, a cobbler, a soldier, a bad lot, or extremely proper."[50] Around 1900 the London couturier Lucile (Lady Duff-Gordon) applied the psychology of theatergoing to sell her fashion line. To great acclaim, she produced the first fashion show featuring a promenade of live models, then called mannequins. "All women make pictures for themselves," she explained in her memoirs,

> they go to the theater and see themselves as the heroine of the play . . . it is themselves they are watching really, and when the lights are lowered to a rosy glow, and soft music is played and the mannequins parade, there is not a woman in the audience, though she may be fat and middle-aged, who is not seeing herself looking as those slim, beautiful girls look in the clothes they are offering her. And that is the inevitable prelude to buying the clothes.

By transforming pretty working-class girls into polished, graceful goddesses with countless rich suitors, Lucile wound up selling more than her dresses. When word got out that she was hiring a second contingent of models, more than two hundred young women applied.[51] To market one vehicle of transformation, her designs, she had created another: the modeling profession.

The great nineteenth-century department stores also turned shopping into theater, mingling glamour and spectacle as they seduced shoppers

with image-laden publicity and colorful displays of
abundant merchandise. "Dazzling and sensuous, the
Bon Marché became a permanent fair, an institution,
a fantasy world, a spectacle of extraordinary propor-
tions, so that going to the store became an event and an
adventure," writes Michael B. Miller, a historian of the
pioneering Parisian store.[52] Unlike traditional shops,
department stores invited even the casual browser to
fondle and caress the goods, knowing that such contact
would kindle longing, projection, and, with some regu-
larity, the impulse to buy. In *The Ladies' Paradise*, his
novel set in a store modeled on the Bon Marché, Émile
Zola depicts the financially pressed Madame de Boves
"having all sorts of laces handed down, simply for the
pleasure of seeing and handling them. . . . [H]er fingers
trembling with desire, her face gradually warming with
a sensual joy" as she dives her fingers into the mounting

pile. Her "furious, irresistible passion for dress" eventually gets the better of
her, and she is caught shoplifting.[53] To guard against such sticky-fingered
customers, stores installed glass cases, making their merchandise still tantalizingly visible. "Any clerk can sell the customer the goods she came in
and asks for," opined a trade magazine, "but it takes a 'Silent Salesman'
All-Glass Show-Case to sell goods that the customer never knew she
wanted until she saw them displayed."[54]

Such seductive and novel pleasures excited warnings that their pur-
veyors were up to no good. "These are not merchants that you are visiting,"
a French association of small shopkeepers cautioned consumers in 1888.
"You are visiting artists, *fantaisistes*, idealists, psychologists, the inventors
of tricks, the disciples of Dr. Charcot, the emulators of Robert Houdin."[55]
Unlike the old shops, which might deceive customers with shoddy goods
or sharp dealing, the great department stores trafficked in more subtle
illusions. Their merchandising sold dreams of an ideal life—of comfort,
stability, leisure, sociability, luxury, and beauty. A contemporary historian
scoffs at the deception. "When a shopgirl buys a silk dress to fulfill a per-

sonal fantasy," writes Rosalind H. Williams, "she steps out onto the street and discovers that thousands of other women have had the same dream and bought the same type of dress. For all of them the illusion of wealth is shattered."[56] But the glamour was not so easily spoiled. Consumers seemed to enjoy the illusions, which transported them from the everyday and, however false in their details, honored the truth of customers' desires. The rustling skirts of a silk dress, even a common one, could make a young working woman feel like a lady—and shopgirls, of all people, were surely aware of what other women were wearing. To the disgust of critics, customers rewarded the *fantaisistes* with patronage and cultural influence.

Not all new forms of glamour were so deliberately constructed, however. Some arose spontaneously. In the crowded city, an ordinary stroll offered a series of evocative scenes and characters, and certain locales became known as promenades. Walking down Broadway with a friend, Dreiser's Carrie finds "herself stared at and ogled. Men in flawless top-coats, high hats, and silver-headed walking sticks elbowed near and looked too often into conscious eyes. Ladies rustled by in dresses of stiff cloth, shedding affected smiles and perfume. . . . With a start she awoke to find that she was in fashion's crowd, on parade in a show place—and such a show place!" Later, recalling the experience, she is overcome with yearning:

> Oh, these women who had passed her by, hundreds and hundreds strong, who were they? Whence came the rich, elegant dresses, the astonishingly colored buttons, the knick-knacks of silver and gold? Where were these lovely creatures housed? . . . Oh, the mansions, the lights, the perfume, the loaded boudoirs and tables! New York must be filled with such bowers, or the beautiful, insolent, supercilious creatures could not be. Some hothouses held them. It ached her to know that she was not one of them.[57]

Knowing nothing of the strangers' lives, Carrie fills the gaps with her own desires.

By multiplying the sources and types of glamour, the city also inevitably increased the chances of disillusionment, even horror. Carrie achieves everything she dreams, only to find that neither wealth nor acclaim brings happiness. Boswell contracted gonorrhea. In nineteenth-century Paris a third of the babies were born out of wedlock, and many were abandoned.[58] Bourgeois gentlemen went bankrupt lavishing gifts on Parisian courtesans. Department-store bounty tempted respectable women into kleptomania, a term coined specifically to apply to this new kind of theft.[59] And while the courtesan's wealth, beauty, and apparent independence made her glamorous in some eyes, her cultural prominence suggested the ever-present risk of a fall into less genteel forms of prostitution. The view from afar obscured the presence of crime, disease, dissipation, and financial ruin.

Mystery and desire, anonymity and yearning, could prove a particularly dangerous combination. The con artist is an urban character. So is the serial killer. In *The Devil in the White City* (2003), his nonfiction narrative of Chicago in the early 1890s, Erik Larson portrays a man who was both. Using aliases and phony corporate identities, Henry Holmes cheated creditors and suppliers, building impressive homes and businesses that made him appear a respectable and desirable figure. He then hired, seduced, and killed a series of young women (and a few other victims), offering anyone who inquired a plausible story for each person's disappearance. People were, after all, constantly coming and going in the great metropolis. "Holmes adored Chicago," Larson writes, "adored in particular how the smoke and din could envelop a woman and leave no hint that she ever had existed, save perhaps a blade-thin track of perfume amid the stench of dung, anthracite, and putrefaction."[60]

Few city dwellers wound up murdered, of course. The more common dangers presented by the ubiquitous glamour of the great metropolis were psychological, not physical. For sensitive and yearning souls like Dreiser's Carrie (or Helga Crane in Nella Larsen's *Quicksand*, discussed in chapter three), glamour focused a vague and permanent dissatisfaction on particular objects, suggesting that attaining them would bring happiness. Nothing, however, could resolve the fundamental discontent of such a restless temperament. Glamour thus proved disappointing, even when it spurred ambition and achievement.

In others, the desire was more specific: to be loved or recognized or socially superior. Here, the city offered greater possibilities of satisfaction—the prospect of finding like-minded companionship or a romantic soul mate really does improve as the population grows—but, again depending on temperament, urban life could also exacerbate feelings of envy and failure. The streets were full of sights reminding the city dweller of the material goods, social prominence, sexual allure, professional accomplishment, or countless other desirable states he or she did not possess. Constant exposure to out-of-reach luxuries, Dreiser writes in *Sister Carrie* "to the untried mind is like opium to the untried body. A craving is set up which, if gratified, shall eternally result in dreams and death."[61] A 1910 *Atlantic Monthly* column titled "The Immorality of Shop-Windows" denounced stores on Fifth Avenue for displaying luxurious furnishings, artworks, jewels, and clothing where any passerby could see and long for them.

> Somebody has the price, for the shops are ever open, the allurement of their windows never less. But not you, who gaze hungry-eyed at these beautiful objects, and then go to a Sixth Avenue department store and wonder if you can afford that Persian rug made in Harlem, marked down from $50 to $48.87. . . . Envy gnaws at your heart. And yet you had supposed that yours was a comfortable income.[62]

This atmosphere produced two common responses, illustrated by the different ways in which two minor figures in *The Ladies' Paradise* react to the great department store. First, there is Madame Guibal, who "walked about the shop for hours without ever buying anything, happy and satisfied to simply feast her eyes." She derives enjoyment from the store's sensory and escapist pleasures, without needing to possess its wares. By contrast, Madame de Boves, whom we previously met fondling the lace and shoplifting, responds with envy and resentment. "Short of money, always tortured by some immoderate wish," she "nourished a feeling of rancor against the goods she could not carry away."[63]

In one of his journal entries, Boswell drew the same contrast between envy and enjoyment. He recounted a dinner conversation with fellow

Scottish emigrés in which they had debated whether a young Scotsman with only a modest fortune would be better off in London or Edinburgh. Boswell's friend Lady Betty, whose family was only modestly endowed, argued that Edinburgh would be preferable, because the sight of so many wealthy Londoners and particularly so many splendidly outfitted coaches would be depressing to a man who couldn't afford such luxuries himself. The longing unleashed by these sights would be unendurable. "Lady Betty," replied Boswell, mocking her envy with a glamour-deflating literalism, "you want to have the solid equipages themselves, to embrace and carry in your arms the thick tarry wheels."

In contrast to his friend's narrow materialism, Boswell went on to declare that for "a person of imagination and feeling," the sights of London provided "lively enjoyment," regardless of whether one could actually own the city's luxuries.[64] A grandly outfitted coach, like an exotic sports car today, might spark envy in some onlookers, but it could also be appreciated aesthetically as rolling sculpture, or provide a moment of transitory glamour—the pleasures of picturing what it would be like to inhabit the vehicle, and the life it represented, without an urgent or lingering craving to do so.

Glamour not only focuses longings. It reveals character. As the commercial metropolis grew, its plentiful glamour did more than inspire envy and frustration. It opened space for positive aspiration, and it rewarded those who could savor its pleasures without being tortured by the gap between reality and dream. Over time, glamour's very abundance also inoculated its audience against some of its immediate effects. As people grew up in a glamour-saturated culture, "untried minds" became rarer. Experience made the audience wise to the most obvious illusions. But glamour, too, evolved. Its forms became increasingly sophisticated, its audience greater, its objects more numerous and grand. Early in the twentieth century, glamour entered its golden age.

Icon
THE HORSEMAN

Centuries before the airplane or the automobile, the aviator or the race-car driver, another masculine icon represented power, control, grace, mystery, and escape: the horseman. "Out of a thousand centuries they drew the ancient admiration of the footman for the horseman," John Steinbeck writes in *The Red Pony*, as the boy Jody shows off his new colt. "They knew instinctively that a man on a horse is spiritually as well as physically bigger than a man on foot."[1] He is certainly more glamorous.

From the knight to the cowboy, the samurai to the jockey, versions of the horseman gallop across the history of glamour, channeling different longings for different audiences. Some represent wealth and status—the glamour of the "horsey set." Others exemplify chivalric nobility and courage. Some bring justice, some defy authority, and some do both. All are masters of their swift, sure steeds.

Photofest

Whatever other yearnings he represents, the glamorous horseman always embodies grace, as both an element and object of glamour. In the fifteenth-century *Book of the Courtier*, Baldassare Castiglione praises the accomplished rider as an exemplar of *sprezzatura*, the graceful nonchalance that makes difficult tasks appear effortless. The ideal horseman, he writes, "appears to give no thought to the matter and sits on his horse as free and easy as if he were on foot."[2] Horse and rider seem to act as one. The training that permits such perfect harmony is, of course, hidden.

The horseman is also a man of mystery. Traveling faster on land than anyone else in the preindustrial world, he could appear seemingly from nowhere and disappear just as swiftly: a rescuer to some, a threat to others. "A stranger comes to town" is the classic setup for a movie western. Alfred Noyes's 1906 poem "The Highwayman" places the horseman in an equally mysterious landscape, amplifying his glamour:

The wind was a torrent of darkness among the gusty trees,
The moon was a ghostly galleon tossed upon cloudy seas,

The road was a ribbon of moonlight over the purple moor,
And the highwayman came riding—
    Riding—riding—
The highwayman came riding, up to the old inn-door.[3]

In his glamorous literary and theatrical incarnations, the highwayman—a sometimes murderous criminal in real life—has an air of danger, a bad boy's allure. Playing on one legendary highwayman's appeal, a 1934 poster promoting the London & North Eastern Railway's service to York contains no sign of a train. It portrays instead the black-clad highwayman Dick Turpin galloping to York on his horse, Black Bess.

In modern parlance, "the man on horseback" signifies a populist hero who promises to rescue the nation by becoming dictator, tapping the public's desire to effortlessly achieve order and justice—a dangerously seductive idea. The 1930s westerns that made John Wayne a star offered audiences a similar fantasy of escape from the conflicts of Depression-era political and economic life. The movies' plots, argue Wayne biographers Randy Roberts and James S.

DICK TURPIN'S RIDE

TO YORK
TRAVEL BY TRAIN
FULL INFORMATION FROM L·N·E·R OFFICES & AGENCIES

Playing on his legendary appeal, a 1934 poster promoting railway service portrayed the black-clad highwayman Dick Turpin galloping to York on his horse, Black Bess. © *NRM/ Pictorial Collection/SSPL/The Image Works*

Olson, "suggested that the source of the country's problem was bad people, particularly bad businessmen. . . . All that was needed was a man on a white horse to ride into town and restore the community's natural balance."[4]

Other versions of the glamorous horseman focus a yearning for freedom. In the nineteenth century, English audiences collected pictures of fox hunters bounding over country hedges, allowing their horses to freely extend their heads and necks in contrast to European riding styles. To the traditionalist residents of country homes, these exhilarating images represented both English political liberties and escape from an otherwise dull rural winter.[5]

A wilder icon of freedom came out of the American West: the cowboy, a self-sufficient man amid the vast and lawless expanses of the frontier. Real cowboys might have been a hardworking, hard-drinking, sexually promiscuous, poorly dressed, and illiterate lot, but their glamorous counterparts were paragons of competence, independence, good looks, and manly virtues. Writing of Zane Grey's pulp westerns in 1939, the critic Burton Rascoe observed that the novels "brought about the vicarious wish-fulfillment of millions of sedentary workers in the office warrens of cities and industrial towns—of imprisoned men to whom a new Zane Grey novel was a splendid escape into a wild, free dreamland of limitless horizons . . . where man may breathe in freedom."[6]

Equestrian circus acts brought an alluring glimpse of a bigger world to sleepy rural towns, and parents feared that the "glamour of the circus" would seduce their children. *Library of Congress*

In the unknown West, readers or moviegoers might imagine a life unfettered by the regimentation of work or the demands of family life. "Very seldom was the hero of a B western laden with the responsibilities that beset the ordinary man," writes the cowboy-film historian Buck Rainey. "He seldom, if ever, was married, seldom presented as a widower with children, and almost never had a mother or father or maiden aunt to look after."[7] The audience might have no serious desire to abandon their loved ones for the wide-open spaces. But, like movie fantasies of a kept woman's luxuries and leisure, the glamorous portrayal of the unencumbered cowboy—who never missed a shot, dirtied his clothes, or, no matter what wild stunts he did, lost his hat—provided an enjoyable moment of escape.[8]

iStockphoto

For unadulterated glamour, however, nothing beat the equestrian circus performers who brought excitement to sleepy rural towns in the nineteenth and early twentieth centuries, giving residents a brief and alluring glimpse of a bigger world. Parenting manuals and children's literature sought to dispel the "glamour of the circus," lest innocent minds succumb.[9] In *Boy Life on the Prairie*, his 1899 account of growing up in the two decades following the Civil War, Hamlin Garland describes the potent allure that circus horsemen held for farm boys:

> Forth from the mystic gateway came the knights and their ladies, riding two and two on splendid horses, and the boys thrilled with the joy of it. . . . Oh, to be one of those fine and splendid riders, with no more corn to plough, or hay to rake, or corn to husk. To go forth into the great, mysterious world, in the company of those grand men and lovely women; to be always admired by thousands, to bow and graciously return thanks, to wear a star upon his breast, to be able to live under the shining canvas in the sound of music.[10]

No wonder parents feared their children would run away to join the circus.

Icon
THE GIBSON GIRL

Charles Dana Gibson maintained that he never intended to create an ideal or archetype. "I was trying to realize on paper the real American young woman — pretty, well-gowned, high-bred, distinctive," he declared in 1908.[1] Although she was just one of the many figures who peopled the artist's gently satirical and sweetly romantic illustrations of life among the American gentry, the Gibson Girl quickly became the figure young women longed to be and young men to be with. In the 1890s, "she looks like a Gibson Girl" was the highest of compliments. As popular as the movie stars of a later era, her image was ubiquitous, appearing not only in magazines and books but on pillowcases, dinner plates, and souvenir spoons.[2]

Tall and slim, with a long neck, tiny waist, and thick, abundant hair, the Gibson Girl had a preternatural grace most easily achieved in pen and ink. The illustrator, observed a *New York Times* writer in 1934, "drew the girl of

Author's collection

the period as his own young eyes saw her—that is to say, as she was, but clothed with a glamour that made her stiff shirt-waist and pompadour crow's nest topped by a hard straw hat, accessories of grace—circumstances of beauty and not of burlesque."[3]

Popular with both men and women, the Gibson Girl balanced the turn-of-the-century aspiration for modernity with a reassuringly traditional feminine charm. In an 1898 profile, a female journalist applauded the artist for abandoning the "doll-like inanely pretty faces" of Victorian illustrations for a more vigorous and intellectual model. "His girls look as if they would have opinions of their own and would act with discrimination in the affairs of life," wrote Sara Crowquill. "They are tall and graceful and although not in the least like fashion plates, their clothes are becoming and fit perfectly."[4]

The Gibson Girl rode bicycles and drove cars, played golf and tennis, swam in the ocean and hiked in the mountains. She was flirtatious yet haughty, capable of unwavering devotion and heartbreaking scorn. Suitors followed her wherever she went, and she was not above using her charms to entice them into manual labor or an advantageous marriage. "As you look on a Gibson

Author's collection

girl," declared an 1896 article, "you feel that she has a mind or a heart, that she thinks and feels; that she is an influence for good or for evil—but always a factor that has to be reckoned with."[5] In her most appealing incarnations, she found true love. In one illustration she and her beau sit on a fence embracing, oblivious to the pouring rain, while in another they kiss on the beach as the rising tide drenches them.

Not everyone approved. Imagining an encounter between the icons of two different eras, a 1901 *Atlantic Monthly* story drew invidious comparisons between the Gibson Girl, with her "mannish" clothes and direct ways, and the refined and delicate Steel-Engraving Lady of Victorian illustrations. "When a man approaches," the Gibson Girl told her shocked counterpart, "we do not tremble and droop our eyelids, or gaze adoringly while he lays down the law. We meet him on a ground of perfect fellowship, and converse freely on every topic." The Gibson Girl's aspirations to "be up and doing" and pursuing a "distinct vocation" led the Steel-Engraving Lady to wonder why a woman's home was not sufficient occupation. "Hail the new woman—behold she comes apace," the story concluded. "WOMAN, ONCE MAN'S SUPERIOR, NOW HIS EQUAL!"[6] Reviewing the piece in the *New York Times*, a writer deemed the Gibson Girl a passing fad and declared the Steel-Engraving Lady "the enduring type" of "the feminine woman, faithful to Puritan ideals."[7]

Nowadays, by contrast, critics tend to emphasize the uncomfortable corset implied by the Gibson Girl's S-shaped curves or the ethnic exclusion suggested by her pale skin, delicate features, thick silky hair, and extreme height. They complain that the popular icon was not a political or sexual radical.[8] Less anachronistically, the feminist historian Lois Banner observes that the Gibson Girl represented "a fantasy figure in whom the problem[s] of poverty, immigration, and labor strife were denied and through whom people could identify with a world of glamour."[9]

The fantasy expressed a widespread and powerful yearning for a new model of womanhood. "Importantly," the illustrator's sister observed decades later, "she carved a new kind of femininity suggestive of emancipation."[10] The Gibson Girl, wrote Charlotte Perkins Gilman in her 1898 feminist classic *Women and Economics*, was a "noble type," a popular heroine who was replacing the "false sentimentality, the false delicacy, the false modesty, the utter falseness of elaborate compliment and servile gallantry" of Victorian romances. For all her artificial grace, Gilman argued, the Gibson Girl represented a refreshing new frankness. Inspired by her example, she suggested, "women are growing honester, braver, stronger, more healthful and skillful and able and free, more human in all ways."[11] A pioneer of modern glamour, the Gibson Girl gave women a way to see themselves as both desirable and independent, active and adored.

Author's collection

Courtesy of Jeffrey Wendt

SEVEN

THE WORLD OF TOMORROW

When people think of glamour as "modern," the rise of bourgeois culture isn't usually what they have in mind. They don't imagine ladies in bustles examining Bon Marché lace selections or the Gibson Girl playing golf in a corseted shirtwaist. They picture movies, skyscrapers, red lipstick, ocean liners, airplanes, and shiny evening gowns: Machine Age modernity and old Hollywood glamour. They envision the 1930s. "The most timeless, most modern decade," the fashion designer Norma Kamali called it in the introduction to her fall 2012 collection.[1] Had she added "the most glamorous," few looking at her embellished necklines would have disagreed.

Kamali took her inspiration from the late thirties, specifically citing 1939 for its classic movies and visionary World's Fair. She didn't mention that 1939 was also the tenth year of the seemingly endless Great Depression and the year Hitler invaded Poland. An era of economic hardship, political extremism, and looming world war isn't an obvious place to look for glamour.

Yet no one can doubt the association. The 1930s largely created "glamour" as we think of it today. The movies introduced the styles and imagery that became its visual shorthand: the high-contrast surfaces and streamlined forms of American art deco, the satin gowns and dramatically lit portraits of screen goddesses, the distant shots of the New York skyline, the sleek nightclubs and penthouse apartments, the languorous cigarette smoke. Thanks to imaginative re-creations by writers exiled from Manhattan to Hollywood, in the thirties New York gradually displaced Paris as the touchstone of glamorous urbanity.[2]

Nor, for all their power, were the movies the era's only new sources or objects of glamour. The 1933 and 1939 World's Fairs captured the public's imagination with alluring visions of a "Century of Progress" and "The World of Tomorrow." *Mademoiselle* featured the first beauty makeover, and other magazines followed.[3] Julius Shulman began his photographic transfigurations of modern architecture. Sunglasses became popular accessories.[4] Comic book artists and writers created the first superheroes. *Buck Rogers* aired on the radio. *Fortune* published photographs and illustrations that turned factories and their products into glamorously abstracted still lifes. The Golden Gate Bridge opened. So did Frank Lloyd Wright's Falling Water. Industrial designers wrapped electrical appliances in streamlined shells, giving radios and vacuum cleaners a seductive aura of effortlessness and speed. "Streamlined styling romanticised technology," writes the architecture and design historian Michael Johnson. "It helped to make it glamorous."[5]

Although the thirties marked its zenith, this profusion of modern glamour began in the 1920s and stretched into the Second World War.[6] The period amplified and diversified the forms that had developed in the commercial city while giving rise to new ones. New themes emerged, tapping new longings and addressing the old ones in new ways. Understanding why this particular period generated such a memorable outpouring of glamour tells us something about the conditions that produce glamour and the purposes glamour can serve.

The common explanation for the prevalence of glamour in the 1930s is escapism. Times were bad, and people wanted to take their minds off their problems. Clothing design and apparel advertising, notes the fashion curator Dennita Sewell, tended to refer either to the past, with historicist styles, or to ideals of the future. The message, she observes, was "Anywhere but here."[7] Many movies were frothy fantasies, as were many Broadway shows. In both types of theater, writes the cultural historian Morris Dickstein, "much of the Depression audience chose to entertain itself with a memory of the 1920s, a carefree fantasy of 'easy living' that was already a dream *in* the 1920s."[8]

As this statement suggests, however, the profusion of glamour predates the Depression. The prosperous twenties also dreamed glamorous dreams, suggesting that the glamour of the thirties is better seen as the evolution of an existing trend rather than primarily a reaction to hard times. Nor can "escapism" by itself account for why the 1930s, of all the terrible periods in human history, were particularly marked by glamour. Bad times do not necessarily produce escapism. To take a minor counterexample, in response to the 1971 recession, apparel retailers slashed their advertising in *Vogue* and *Harper's Bazaar*, leading to the ouster of the legendary *Vogue* editor Diana Vreeland in favor of a more "realistic" approach to fashion, using "natural" models in "typical" environments.[9] In that case, tough economic times produced an anti-escapist shift toward literalism and practicality.

Most important, the "Depression escapism" explanation ignores the nature of glamour. All glamour is escapist, but not all escapism is glamour. The escape that glamour offers is of a particular type. Glamour is a way of "seeing what is not there," not simply forgetting what *is* there. Although glamour does provide immediate pleasure, it doesn't numb or distract desire. To the contrary, it intensifies longings by giving them an object. Glamour thus implies and fosters hope, from individual aspiration to collective utopian dreams. It requires not only discontent with one's current situation but also the ability to imagine a different, better self in different, better circumstances. The prevalence of glamour suggests not despair but ambition and rising, if temporarily suspended, expectations.

Responding to a sociologist's inquiry, a twenty-two-year-old British clerk illustrated the way Depression-era glamour operated on its audience's imagination. Surveyed in 1945, the young woman explained how movies like *Hi, Gaucho* (1935) and *The Mark of Zorro* (1940) had stoked her yearning to travel and inspired her to study Spanish. Her friends warned her, she said, that movies "have made me discontented with my monotonous suburban life, and have led to periods of unhappiness and depression. But I am glad. For they have given me ambition, ideals, something to work hard for, something to set my head above the boredom of routine."[10] Glamour provides an escape from the "boredom of routine," not from stabs of disappointment or desire. It makes restless imaginations more restless still.

———

So if the Depression alone doesn't explain why we remember the thirties as the golden age of glamour, what does? Why not, say, *la belle époque*, with its department stores, theaters, bejeweled courtesans, and bohemian cafés?

One important difference was the size of the audience. After World War I, glamour became a truly mass phenomenon, no longer limited by geography. Although cities continued to grow, a person no longer had to move to the metropolis to be constantly exposed to glamour. Mass media substituted for dense populations, bringing to small towns sights formerly reserved for the big city.

Some of those sights came in the mail, or to the local newsstand. Large-circulation magazines had been around since the late nineteenth century, when better paper, high-speed printing, and favorable postage rates allowed publishers to slash prices. (Once the press was running, an additional copy cost very little.) Turn-of-the-century magazines had spread glamorous imagery such as Charles Dana Gibson's idealized young women. But the real explosion of magazine glamour came in the 1920s, with the growth of consumer products—automobiles and appliances, cosmetics and packaged goods—and the advertising that promoted them.[11] Some of the ads themselves deployed glamorous images; think of the princess endorsements of Pond's cold cream and Lux laundry soap mentioned in chapter two, or the countless car ads promising speed, power, freedom, and the good life. Most important, consumer-product advertising supported new magazines whose editorial contents featured glamorous ideas and images, from travel stories and fashion spreads to beauty advice and, of course, photos of movie stars.[12] In the 1930s, the daughter of a London stevedore recalls in a recent oral history, "magazines opened up a whole new world."[13] The ads, articles, short stories, illustrations, and photos all combined to reinforce the promise of escape and transformation.

The movies were even more influential. In the new age of mechanical reproduction, audiences in great cities and small towns alike could share the same theatrical experience, at prices almost anyone could afford. Like consumer magazines, the movies spread the old forms of glamour more widely. Three decades after Lucile hired models to display her London fashions to a social elite, moviegoers could watch Joan Crawford parade in not one but three fashion shows, including a lingerie collection, in *Our Blushing Brides* (1930), one of the many movies with such scenes.[14] Within the film, the audiences were rich New Yorkers with accents and surnames suggesting old money, but out there in the cinema seats, viewers spanned

Joan Crawford and Clark Gable in *Possessed* (1931): "My life belongs to me."

Photofest

geography, ethnicity, and social class. "Paris fashion shows had once been accessible only to the chosen few," remarked moviemaker Cecil B. DeMille's brother William. "C. B. revealed them to the whole country, the costumes his heroines wore being copied by hordes of women and girls throughout the land, especially by those whose contacts with centers of fashion were limited or nonexistent."[15] Like magazines, motion pictures created a common culture of glamour, in which people far removed from each other could feel the same aspirations embodied in the same imagery.

That culture crossed national boundaries. Shanghai-made movies featured the same shiny surfaces, geometric patterns, and art deco streamlining used to signify wealth and modernity in Hollywood productions. "In a scene from one of [actress] Ruan Lingyu's films, *Good-bye, Shanghai*," notes Lynn Pan, the Shanghai cultural historian, "the style is emphasized by a framed poster of an ocean liner with the sharply raked prow, seen from below and disproportionately large, that is still familiar to us from the travel graphics of the Deco era, a time when speed and transportation were exalted." Affluent Chinese families filled their homes with white-painted "Shanghai Deco" furniture that mimicked movie style.[16]

Despite competition from such local productions, Hollywood movies dominated the world's cinemas, enchanting audiences with their glamorous visions of love and success.[17] In 1934, in the small town of Los Toldos, Argentina, fifteen-year-old Eva Duarte was utterly captivated by Norma Shearer's performance as Lady Mary Rexford in *Riptide*. She "found in the beautifully gowned star her ideal of elegance," writes the Hollywood historian Howard Gutner. "She packed up her belongings and went to try her luck in Buenos Aires, and by the time she met General Juan Perón she had seen Norma Shearer in *Marie Antoinette* [1938] six times."[18] Peronism might be a homegrown political movement, but its glamorous symbol—the poor girl turned fashionable lady—was a Hollywood creation.

Opened in 1930, the Pantages Theatre in Hollywood was one of the movie palaces with luxurious interiors that offered excitement and escape even before the film began.

J. Christopher Launi Photography

The future Evita responded to the movies' glamorous images in much the same way that Theodore Dreiser's Carrie reacted to the elegantly dressed women on Broadway: "It ached her to know that she was not one of them." But watching a movie was not the same as walking a crowded city street or viewing a play. The relationship between the audience and the actors was both more intimate and more distanced. The new medium not only reached a mass audience; it affected them in a new and powerful way.

Unlike strangers on the street or the characters of a play, the people in a movie were not really there. Yet they seemed intimately near—because they were huge. With their emphasis on the closeup, Hollywood films enhanced and intensified identification, while the immersive quality of movies encouraged projection. "We look *into* the screen, *through* the images displayed upon it, and *at* whatever those images represent," observes the philosopher Colin McGinn.[19] The same can be said of reading a novel, but unlike the mental pictures conjured by literature, movie images were the same for everyone, and photography made them seem all the more real.

As a medium for glamour, motion pictures did have one problem, however. They moved. One scene led to the next, pulling the viewer along without time to linger over evocative moments. Their plots also required conflicts, tensions, complications, and revelations that could destroy the characters' mystery or mar their grace. And every movie eventually left town, disappearing into the studio's vaults.

The pervasive glamour of the movies, then, derived less from the films themselves than from a combination of memory and photography, which heightened both mystery and grace. The most resonant scenes stayed in the audience's imagination, freezing moments to serve the viewers' own longings rather than the movie's plot. Decades later when British women recalled the movies of their youth, writes the film scholar Jackie Stacey, their memories were often snapshots of "'pure image': be it Bette Davis's flashing and rebellious eyes, Doris Day's fun outfits or Rita Hayworth's flowing hair."[20] Audiences who saw Fritz Lang's *Metropolis* (1926), notes the science-fiction author Gregory Benford, took home not the director's dystopian vision of oppressed workers slaving below ground but "images of the sparkling towers; the light, airy suspension bridges; and the swarms of strange vehicles in the sky. They wanted that, and forgot about the basements."[21]

Adding to individual memories, promotional photos turned ephemeral scenes into permanent stills. We remember many of the most famous movie scenes—the robot in *Metropolis*, Rick and Ilsa's farewell in *Casablanca*, Gilda smoking in her strapless gown, Holly Golightly with her cigarette holder and jewels, Marilyn Monroe holding down her billowing white skirt—not from seeing them flashing by on the screen but from their repetition as printed photographs.[22] Such images lift scenes out of the narrative flow, intensifying their grace and, with it, their glamour. These iconic shots were particularly significant before television, when movies vanished from public view once their theatrical runs were complete. Like wedding portraits or vacation postcards, the photos preserved transient experiences, distilling them into ideal moments.

Even more important were the stars' studio portraits, which were published in magazines and sent out in response to fan mail. Movie characters might come and go, but the stars endured, transformed in their portraits into timeless objects of contemplation and projection. While a movie might reveal a character's inner life, a portrait offered only hints (and sometimes false ones) of the star's true self. It was these portraits, more than what appeared on screen, that defined Old Hollywood glamour. "The movie itself was only a passing story," writes the Hollywood historian Tom Zimmerman, "while the great studio portraits were romanticized ideals caught frozen in time: lasting objects of perfection to hold in your hands."[23]

———

We remember this period as glamour's golden age, then, because it expanded the audience for glamour, established a common international culture of glamour, and intensified the identification between audiences and glamorous icons. But there is more to it than that. Interwar glamour was culturally consequential, for reasons Norma Kamali hinted at when she paradoxically called the late thirties both "timeless" and "modern."

The two terms ought to be contradictory. The word *modern* means "of the present," as opposed to the past. Something "modern" belongs to *now* and not to *then*. Yet when Kamali described the thirties as both "timeless" and "modern," her audience knew exactly what she meant. More than seventy years have passed, she noted, but "Cary Grant and Carole Lombard . . . would still be considered fashion style powerhouses. Their wardrobes could walk any red carpet today." A designer in 1939 could never have said such a thing about the 1860s or even the 1910s. Grant's and Lombard's clothes still look modern, in the sense of current, because they were modern in another sense.

In the early twentieth century, the word *modern* ceased to be only a neutral synonym for *current* or *contemporary* and took on a second, more resonant meaning. For good or ill, these were, as the 1936 Charlie Chaplin movie title put it, *Modern Times*. The word was everywhere. "Modern Electric Cookery frees the modern mother," declared a typical advertising headline from 1929.[24] The world seemed full of new possibilities, tantalizingly near but as yet only partially perceived. The confluence of developments in science, technology, economic organization, and social mores promised a new kind of life—a *modern* life—but what exactly that meant wasn't clear. Artists and intellectuals elaborated and debated their own theories about what modernity implied. But most people got their concept of the modern not from rationalist arguments or purist manifestos but from experience and association—and from glamour.

Think about how glamour works. Like humor, it emerges from the interaction between an object and an audience, which may be a single person. (Recall Yiyun Li's candy wrapper from chapter one.) Glamour begins in the individual mind, and it may conceivably go no further.[25] But glamour persists, spreads, and flourishes in social groups, which reinforce the sensation and encourage the repetition of glamorous tropes, strengthening their meaning. Members of these groups share similar longings and resonate to the same objects embodying them. The most memorable forms of glamour are those that affect the largest groups and become part of the general cultural background: the glamour experienced and recognized by just about everyone.

In the golden age, those universally recognized forms of glamour shared common versions of escape and transformation. One way or another, they allowed audiences to project themselves into an alluring vision of modern life, giving lucid imaginative form to the possibilities shimmering just out of reach, whether in time, space, or social milieu. Rather than offering a blueprint or manifesto, they embodied overlapping themes: streamlined forms, independent women, easy transportation, labor-saving machines, technology, efficiency, excitement, freedom. These themes created a sort of collage or pointillist

portrait. Just as a composite "dream city" arose from films set in New York, so a glamorous idea of "modernity," and its companion and alter ego "the future," emerged from the striking artifacts and imagery that gave common themes believability and coherence.[26]

One reason we remember the period's glamour so vividly, then, is that it proved socially significant. Glamour became more than just a tool for selling consumer goods or a form of escapist entertainment. It became a way of exploring—individually and collectively, consciously and unconsciously—what it meant to be modern. That exploration was not systematic, and it was not always consistent. It was often simply a form of play. But over time it produced a recognizable culture whose traces still inform contemporary life, and whose stylistic representations we still call "glamorous."

As portrayed in movies, fiction, journalism, and graphic art—and embodied in the design of all sorts of new artifacts—modernity seemed to promise a future that was freer, more convenient, more youthful, more efficient, more healthful, more scientific, and more fun than the past. What the cultural historian Lynn Pan writes about Shanghai in the 1930s could be said, with only minor revisions, about many other places at the time:

> What was smart and what was in vogue were inextricably intertwined with what was modern—or *modeng*, as the Chinese called it. *Modeng*, a word quickly absorbed into the Chinese lexicon, was much bandied about in the interwar period, popularly understood in the sense which *Modern Cinema* gives it when, in an issue published in 1933, the magazine breaks it down to ballroom dancing, brilliantined hair, crimson lipstick, multi-coloured nail polish, automobile, Western-style villa, Western food, handbag, high heels, falling in love, feeling depressed and so on. But these are all signs of an inauthentic modernity, the magazine writer goes on to say, authentic modernity being defined by a strong, supple and healthy physique, and an interest in knowledge of science, particularly social science.[27]

In its glamorous version, "modern" was not just a desirable attribute (a "modern" stove) to serve other ends (easier cooking). Like wealth, beauty, or respect, modernity seemed to be an end in itself. People wanted to be modern, whatever that meant.

"*Poudre de Début* is truly a *modern* powder for modern times," proclaimed an American cosmetics ad that ran in 1929.[28] Framing text in which the word *modern* appeared six times were stylized illustrations portraying the many incarnations of the glamorous modern woman: in an evening dress with a deep plunging back; in a cloche hat and short, leg-revealing skirt; sunning herself in a bathing suit; tossing a beach ball with bare arms and legs; wearing an aviator's helmet and goggles; and, prominently placed above the product logo on the bottom right, at the steering wheel of a car. The ideal modern woman was beautiful, of course, but she was also slim, fit, active, public, leisured, capable, independent, and not afraid to tastefully show some skin. It was all very appealing.

Unlike a modern stove, Poudre de Début offered no significant technological advance. Science wasn't what made it modern. Culture was. The face powder claimed to be modern by association with the glamorous lifestyle of the modern woman. Whether represented by Poudre de Début's leisured debutantes or the shopgirls and stenographers making mascara and colored nail polish fashionable, the modern woman embodied the alluring promise of a new era: she took charge of her own destiny.[29] Modernity was itself an object of desire. It meant agency, efficiency, novelty, and stimulation, with technology and science in service of those ends.

"You don't own me," Joan Crawford's Marian tells her hometown boyfriend in *Possessed*, when he grabs her arm and tells her she's not going anywhere. "Nobody does. My life belongs to me!"

"And you'll make a fine mess of it," he warns.

"It'll still belong to me."

Few moviegoers would have abandoned marriage and children for Marian's unencumbered but insecure and disreputable life as a kept woman. But they enjoyed the escapist fantasies of fancy apartments, beautiful clothes, lavish entertainment, and freedom from family responsibilities—and they embraced the idea of a woman making her own way.

The "fast-talking dames" of comedies in the thirties and forties advanced a similarly independent image. They "paved a way for a new class or sort of woman who finally would answer to no one but herself," writes the literary scholar Maria DiBattista. Their grace shone in their mastery of language—"the pleasure of saying the thing you mean to say the moment you mean to say it"—which signified a more general competence. Capable and cynical, these characters were usually out for money and security. But, as DiBattista notes, "they lived in a comic universe" that delivered love as well.[30] Here we begin to see why Carole Lombard's dresses still look "modern" to us (although many of today's fashions would look strange to her). Like her characters, she lived a modern life, and she dressed accordingly.

To be modern meant to adopt attitudes, activities, habits, and goods that replaced the encrustations of tradition with less-encumbered forms—an idea of modernity embodied not only in the much-debated figure of the modern woman but in the clean lines and polished surfaces of modern, and "modernistic," design.[31] "Travel the Modern Way" suggested a 1937 ad for the Lincoln-Zephyr, posing the streamlined car next to an ocean liner.[32] Such smooth, tear-dropped shapes were more than functional problem solving, more than marketing gimmicks. They were symbolic. "Streamlining has captured the American imagination to mean modern, efficient, well-organized, sweet[,] clean and beautiful," Egmont Arens, an industrial designer who promoted "streamlining for recovery," excitedly telegrammed President Roosevelt in 1934. "You would love it."[33] While streamlined pencil sharpeners, science-fiction pulp illustrations, Joan Crawford characters, and art deco dressing tables might not measure up to intellectual ideals of the modern, they made modernity seductive.

Rayon spools captured by Margaret Bourke-White, whose photographs made the products and processes of industry appear sensuously glamorous. *Getty Images/Margaret Bourke-White*

The New York journalist Joan Kron recalls sitting on the floor with her brother as a child in the 1930s, cutting out pictures of ever-more-streamlined cars from the newspaper. "I was fascinated with car design, these modern cars," she says. "Industrial design was very much on our minds. It wasn't just to look at. It was bringing us the future." A new, streamlined radio meant new forms of entertainment; a new car provided a way to go to the seashore; a "cute refrigerator with round edges" replaced the "klutzy" icebox. "These things were glamorous," she says, "not just because of the way they looked but because of what they brought to us. They brought us a better, more interesting life."[34] Not just easier but *more interesting*. The word the Lincoln-Zephyr ad used was *stimulating*. The glamour of modernity countered the "boredom of routine."

If modernity meant agency, efficiency, novelty, and stimulation, then transportation vehicles, with their promise of mobility, were its ideal representatives. Like the streamlined forms of industrial design and the speed lines of graphic art, the trains, planes, cars, ocean liners, and dirigibles that figured so prominently in the glamour of the period pulled the audience effortlessly forward— toward the future. "Speed is the cry of our era," wrote the industrial designer Norman Bel Geddes in 1932.[35] They represented a hope, a promise, even an expectation that this mysterious destination would be something wonder-

J. Christopher Launi Photography

ful. "All I wanted to do," says Kron, recalling her childhood, "was go into the World of Tomorrow." She's talking about the Futurama exhibit at the 1939 World's Fair. But she's also expressing a more general sentiment. In those days, *the future* and *tomorrow*, like *modern*, resonated with glamour.

Among the most glamorous modern images created in the 1930s are Margaret Bourke-White's industrial photographs for *Fortune* and *Life*. Through repetition and abstraction, the photographer turned dynamos and dams, plow blades and whirling spools of rayon into alluringly sensuous patterns. "When Margaret focused on the boring, forbidding instruments of technology," writes her biographer Vicki Goldberg, "they suddenly became accessible, beautiful, and unexpectedly glamorous." Or, as her *Fortune* colleague Dwight Macdonald sneered, "She made even machines look sexy."[36]

Bourke-White crafted her own image as carefully as her photographs, adding to the era's archetypes of the modern woman. She shot the swaying tower of the Chrysler Building from a beam eight hundred feet in the air and had her picture taken on a gargoyle. "This Daring Camera Girl Scales Skyscrapers for Art," declared a magazine headline in 1930.[37] The streamlined design of the studio she opened in the Chrysler Building, writes Goldberg, "announced that Margaret Bourke-White was poised on the edge of tomorrow."[38]

The photographer exulted in her own independence—one reason she loved heights was that "nobody can reach me to give me orders"—but the industrial images that made her famous left little room for the individual. Her stark geometries treated people as little more than props. When Bourke-White visited the Soviet Union in 1930, she approvingly observed that the government there believed that "it is for the artist to stir the imagination of the people with the grandeur of the industrial program."[39] She applied the same attitude to US industry. "Ore boats, bridges, cranes, engines—all are giant creatures with steel hearts," Bourke-White told an American interviewer. "They all have an unconscious beauty that is dynamic, because they are designed for a purpose. There is nothing wasted, nothing superficial. The realization of this idea will grow. It reflects the modern spirit of the world."[40]

Although enchanting to Bourke-White, that spirit frightened many others, as the popularity of Chaplin's black comedy *Modern Times* demonstrates. Labor-saving devices looked alluring to the exhausted housewife, but to her wage-earning husband "labor-saving" often sounded like a prescription for unemployment. Nearly a quarter of unemployed Americans receiving government relief in 1939 believed they'd lost their jobs to automation.[41] "Do you know the guy said that machinery is going to take the place of every profession?" says Jean Harlow's character in *Dinner at Eight* (1933), describing the book she's reading to look intellectual. A 1931 article in *Modern Mechanix* asked, "Is Man Doomed by the Machine Age?"[42]

Modernity threatened to make human muscle power redundant. It's not surprising, then, that themes of strength, efficacy, and physical prowess are prominent in the era's male-oriented glamour. Think of sports stars and

Above his crude bed, a
Depression-era migrant
worker has pasted photos
of new cars, offering a
glamorous respite after a
hard day's work.

*Farm Security Administration/Office
of War Information Collection, Library
of Congress, photographer Arthur
Rothstein*

aviators, gangster films and superhero comics. The awkward Clark Kent
was a milquetoast with a modern job as a newspaperman. His alter ego,
a hero to adults as well as children, was a man of steel able to lift a car or
stop a train with a single hand. In a 1941 animated short, Superman even
vanquished a squadron of robot thieves.[43] The desire to be strong is eternal,
but the Machine Age had also made it timely.

Here we see another reason for the vehicles so central to the era's
glamour. Automobiles in particular represented a modernity that ran
contrary to the regimentation of the factory and, indeed, to the imposed
schedules of the train—a modernity that promised the individual power
over time and space, and control over his own personal machine. Especially to men, cars embodied the modern promise of agency. "We will decide ourselves whether we drive fast or slow, where we stop, where we want
to pass through without delay," wrote a visionary German auto enthusiast
in 1903.[44]

Automobiles often turned up in the lyrics of blues songs as emblems
of sex appeal and sexual prowess. "Who's that coming, hey, with his motor
so strong?" sang Blind Lemon Jefferson in "D. B. Blues" (1928), whose lyr-

ics featured four different automobile makes, including the Dodge Brothers of the title. Cleo Wilson's 1929 song "I've Got a Ford Movement in My Hips" was more suggestive: "A Ford is a car everybody wants to ride. Jump in, you will see."[45] The car proved that machines could be sexy, and that modernity could bring the individual power.

A poignant 1938 image by the New Deal photographer Arthur Rothstein captures automotive glamour at work. On the unpainted wall adjoining a rough bed where migrant farm workers sleep, someone has pasted pictures of luxurious modern cars meticulously cut out of the newspaper. The bed is empty, but we can imagine the car lover lying there after a hard day in the fields, projecting himself into the pictures and dreaming of escape and transformation. The grilles of large vehicles point outward and, at the top of the display, a line of smaller cars in profile drives up the wall toward the ceiling, the edge of the photograph, and, the sense of motion implies, a better future.

Panel, Radio Broadcasting, from the Westinghouse Pavilion, "A Century of Progress" exposition, Chicago, IL, 1933. *The Wolfsonian–Florida International University, Miami Beach, Florida, The Mitchell Wolfson, Jr. Collection. XX1989.190a-c. Photo: Bruce White*

For many people in the twenties, thirties, and forties, the modern *was* the future. This was a period in which zippers and refrigerators were still novelties, and "radioman" was a glamorous, high-tech profession.[46] That a new technology or a new way of life existed somewhere didn't mean any given person had experienced it. A European aristocrat visiting New York in 1933 was dazzled by the electric eye that effortlessly opened doors. "I would like to see it adopted everywhere," Princess Bibesco wrote of the new technology, foreseeing its potential effects on traditional signs of deference: "If this fairylike invention spreads over the earth, it will abolish the chief gesture of English courtesy: 'I will open the door for you.'"[47] For New Yorkers, the electric eye was the present. Elsewhere, it was the future.

In the late 1930s, a series of picture cards inserted in packages of cigarettes honored "This Age of Power and Wonder." Some cards portrayed current marvels, including deep-sea diving suits, cinematic special effects, and the Thunderbolt car in which the Englishman George Eyston had set a land speed record. Others forecast the future, showing television studios, rooftop landing pads, and radiation treatments for cancer—as well as less prophetic designs for fruit orchards in the Arctic, a giant tower to light London, and invisibility rays. The mixture of current and futuristic images captured the way the two ideas intermingled. The present not only anticipated the future. It also seemed to *be* the future.[48]

The future had arrived but, as the novelist William Gibson famously said in the 1990s, it wasn't evenly distributed. A British woman interviewed by the film scholar Annette Kuhn about her memories of cinema-going in the 1930s recalls the futuristic visions presented in American films: "The women were always dressed in furs and fancy hats and lived in lovely homes and got *refrigerators*! I mean we hadn't

Author's collection

FIXTURE placement, as well as color and beautiful fixture design, heighten the charm of the modern bathroom. In this skylighted Crane room is illustrated how effective an unusual grouping can be. Between windows, whose panes are covered with decorated paper or printed fabric of a Japanese design, the mirror is set. Above it, false panes give the effect of one large window. Beneath is the center of interest, the *Elegia* lavatory, its exquisite form accented by its out-of-the-ordinary background. The *Elegia* is Lucerne blue twice-fired vitreous china; the bath the *Corwith*, either solid porcelain or enameled, in Lucerne blue. . . . Crane Co. is headquarters for *Bathrooms for Out-of-the-Ordinary Homes*. Write for the book of this title. And consult your architect and plumbing contractor about Crane quality and economy.

CRANE

FIXTURES, VALVES, FITTINGS, AND PIPING, FOR DOMESTIC AND INDUSTRIAL USE

got a refrigerator! . . . When we went to the cinema and [saw] people switching lights on and opening fridges and hoovering, it was a different world. I think it made us all a bit more ambitious."[49]

This unevenness produced an interesting dynamic between glamour and the future. By the 1930s, a century of experience had changed the way people thought about luxuries. Unlike diamond bracelets and silver tea services, new inventions tended to come down in price over time, making much of the lifestyle of the contemporary rich imaginable as the future of the middle and working class. By portraying the glamorous lives of the wealthy, then, the movies suggested marvelous things to come. The world of Fred Astaire and Joan Crawford was as futuristic as the adventures of Buster Crabbe, who played Buck Rogers and Flash Gordon—and equally stylized.

Take bathrooms. In 1940, just more than half of US homes had private baths and private flush toilets.[50] Movie characters, however, routinely inhabited bathrooms with huge, spa-style tubs. In *The Women* (1939), Crawford's gold-digger character even has a separate phone line installed next to the enormous tub where she takes bubble baths. "If the modern American bathroom is a clean and comfortable part of the modern American home, my pictures may have had something to do with that wholesome development," said Cecil B. DeMille, recalling the "dark, cramped" and cockroach-infested bathroom of his childhood. "When I had the opportunity to show on the screen that this room could be bright and clean and comfortable, I took it."[51] Although movie-size bathtubs didn't catch on until the spa fashion of the 1990s, Americans inspired by the movies did adopt tile, chrome, and "the tactile luxury of great fuzzy towels and rugs," write the Hollywood historians Richard Griffith and Arthur Mayer. By the end of the twenties, they note, "plumbing corporations which had never dared mention their wares in public were taking full-page advertisements to display bathrooms frankly modeled on the DeMille splendors."[52]

There was also the easy air travel suggested by the title of the first Fred Astaire–Ginger Rogers movie, *Flying Down to Rio* (1933). Movie characters seemed to go to faraway places with no more thought than a New Yorker might hail a cab. In *Top Hat* (1935), Fred's dance-star character Jerry pursues Ginger's lovely Dale by persuading his wealthy producer to charter an airplane for a weekend jaunt from London to Italy; he prom-ises they'll be back in time for Monday's show. Even without the dancing, it's quite a glamorous setup: gentlemen in tuxedos hiring an airplane on a whim. But the flight's glamour doesn't stop with easy money. Although the dialogue says the journey will take seven hours, the movie portrays it in barely more than a minute—without significant noise or turbulence. The trip appears effortless. "I came down on the fastest plane I could get," Jerry tells Dale. In the future, modernity promised to collapse the gap between destination and desire.

———

Competing with the composite and variable modern future that emerged spontaneously, like the dream city, from multiple images and aspirations was a different glamorous idea: planning. "A perfectly ordered mechanical civilization" could replace unpredictable, stressful, and seemingly haphaz-ard developments with something more harmonious and efficient.[53] Here was a future with a blueprint. Social and economic planning promised to control the turbulence that made modernity so unnerving—and to do so in a way that was as scientific as factory automation.

"One thing we are confident we know about this world we hope to build," wrote the industrial designer Walter Dorwin Teague, "and that is that it will be free from the confusions, wastes, and frustrations that we can see all around us today. . . . It will have the perfect integration of parts we see today in some of our products that machine production makes pos-sible."[54] Planning offered, wrote the British socialists Sidney and Beatrice Webb, "the only alternative to the anarchy of individual profit-seeking," with "its devastating alternation of booms and slumps."[55] Centralized coordination would eliminate wasteful competition and duplication. It would instantiate Bourke-White's "modern spirit of the world," allowing "nothing wasted, nothing superficial."

The glamorous ideal of planning did not imply a specific plan. It took many forms, permitting wide variations in political ideology and national culture. It could be democratic or fascist, socialist or corporatist, commu-nist or technocratic. Teague believed in merchandising beautiful products, while the Webbs treated such commercial, nonfunctional considerations as largely irrational. Hitler wrapped even his highway planning in German nationalism; new roads would honor the German landscape, "meld the German people into unity," and "put an end to the last remnants of particularistic thinking."[56] Soviet planning, by contrast, claimed an internationalist view. Americans, such as Teague, particularly liked metaphors from design and engineering. US planning advocates were drawn, the historian John M. Jordan argues, to the promise of "kinetic change made stable."[57] In a turbulent period, stability was an alluring idea.

The same mass media that made it easier to promote cosmetics, cars, and the life they represented also enabled political entrepreneurs to sell their ideas of planning. The golden age of glamour was a golden age of political propaganda, some of which employed glamour. The covers of *Gioventù fascista*, the official Fascist youth magazine, used stylized images of speeding vehicles to portray the party as "a progressive, dynamic force leading Italy into the future."[58] Soviet graphic artists developed photomontage techniques that, the designer and critic Steven Heller writes, "wedded truth to fantasy to convey a utopian idea."[59] A 1932 issue of *USSR in Construction*, a magazine sent to readers abroad, celebrates Stalin's electrification program with dramatic layouts juxtaposing photos of Soviet leaders, machinery, workers, and power lines. In one spread, a smiling Stalin, his face partially in shadow, is flanked by a nighttime photo of a brightly lit plant with search lights that point toward a third

A 1930 ad for Brunswick Radio's new Futura model captured the era's glamorous view of planning and control.

Author's collection

photo of an anonymous hand throwing a power switch. These designs create a sense of excitement, purpose, and accomplishment, while leaving enough mystery to disguise any inefficiency, costs, or hardship. They glamorize Soviet planning.

But no political campaign promoted the glamour of planning more effectively than the 1939 New York World's Fair, which blended political propaganda with commercial promotion. The social critic Lewis Mumford, who shaped the fair's theme, described its goal as telling "the story of this planned environment, this planned industry, this planned civilization."[60] At the fair's central exhibit, the Democracity housed in the signature Perisphere, visitors looked down on a model of the "perfectly integrated garden city of tomorrow." Carefully planned and built from scratch, Democracity encompassed a high-rise hub and seventy surrounding towns linked by highways and greenbelts. Democracity, the fair's design board chairman Robert Kohn declared, was "not a vague dream of a life that might be lived in the far future." It could happen immediately "if we willed it so," he said. "The great, crushing, all absorbing city of today . . . would no longer be a planless jumble of slum and chimney, built only for gain, but an effective instrument for human activities, to be used for the building of a better world of tomorrow."[61]

Along with this seductive model of a green and pleasant urban order, the fair included many corporate attractions, from Westinghouse demonstrating an automatic dishwasher to AT&T offering free long-distance calls—and, of course, the famous General Motors Futurama, which beat out Democracity as the fair's most popular attraction. Latter-day critics condemn the fair for allowing commercialism to taint its technocratic vision. The fair, its president Grover Whalen had written, would allow the visitor to "gain a vision of what he might attain for himself and his community by intelligent, cooperative planning toward the better life of the future." But, notes the cultural historian Jeffrey L. Meikle, the fair had also promised business exhibitors "'an opportunity to construct their *own* World of Tomorrow.' . . . In other words, the fair would embody 'the specifications' for a consumer society planned not cooperatively by its citizens but by producers and distributors who hoped to promote sales of individual products to individual citizens."[62] In short, argues the art historian Helen A. Harrison, the fair undercut its original purpose. "Conceived as a demonstration of the triumph of enlightened social, economic, and technological engineering," she writes, "it was in actuality a monument to merchandising."[63]

In fact, the fair's merchandising sold both political planning and commercial products—and packaged both in glamour. It encouraged visitors to project themselves into a future not only of abundant goods and impressive technology but of effortless harmony and order. The fair did not acknowledge any contradiction between individual choices in the marketplace and "cooperative" political planning. In its glamorous depictions of the future, all groups worked together in harmony, and individual and collective plans exactly coincided. By editing out conflicts, the fair heightened the allure of both its commercial exhibits and the politically directed future. It sold a world where everyone wanted the same thing, a world without trade-offs or losers.

Who could fail to want the World of Tomorrow, especially as presented in the Futurama Norman Bel Geddes created for GM? The designer used his considerable theatrical talent to draw visitors into an alluring version of 1960. Seated in special "sound chairs," fairgoers flew over a meticulously realized American landscape, with lighting adjusting to signify the passage of time. Looking through "airplane windows," they saw mountains and valleys; industrial parks, electric dams, and hydroponic farms; skyscrapers, stores, and houses; airports, railroads, and "ten thousand moving cars on the superhighways of tomorrow."[64] The young protagonist of E. L. Doctorow's semiautobiographical novel *World's Fair* (1985) describes the experience:

> No matter what I had heard about the Futurama, nothing compared with seeing it for myself: all the small moving parts, all the lights and shadows, the animation, as if I were looking at the largest most complicated toy ever made! In fact this is what I realized and that no one had mentioned to me. It was a toy that any child in the world would want to own. You could play with it forever. The little cars made me think of my toy cars when I was small. . . . The buildings were models, it was a model world. It was filled with appropriate music, and an announcer was describing all these wonderful things as they went by, these raindrop cars, these air-conditioned cities.[65]

The Futurama was enticing because visitors never considered what it might feel like to be someone else's toy. With its god's-eye perspective, the exhibit also gave visitors the illusion of experiencing the future without actually negotiating its quotidian details. The exhibit was exciting, so by implication the life it represented would be, too.

Sponsored by General Motors, the Futurama sold cars and the super-highways to carry them. But it didn't recreate the feeling of driving a car, even a fast one. Instead, it made visitors feel like they were flying. Since passenger air travel was still rare, that feeling itself felt futuristic. The Futurama anticipated a future of suburbs and interstate freeways that looked a lot like the real 1960. When we got that future, however, we didn't celebrate the highways. We called it the Jet Age.

In a 1956 issue dedicated to the "Air Age," *Life* magazine profiled a Pan American crew traveling on a "13,000-mile, seven-day flight" from New York through Paris, Rome, Beirut, Tehran, and back. The feature gave readers a behind-the-scenes look at airplane operations, complete with spilled trays in the tiny galley. But the main emphasis, captured in four pages of photos, was how the crew spent their time off: kayaking in the Mediterranean, buying Damascus brocades in a Beirut shop, visiting a modernist painter's gallery in Paris, dining near the Eiffel Tower. The copilot visited Left Bank jazz clubs, and the stewardesses went shopping for perfume. To the *Life* reader, it was all exciting and exotic—right down to the Paris hotel's six-foot-long bathtub, a favorite of the copilot, who said he "never saw a tub like this back in West Virginia."[66]

F. C. Gundlach, "Summer in Furs," Deborah Dixon for SWA Beirut/Lebanon 1963

Here was a new take on the old glamour of aviation, offering not a dream of individual heroism or a general notion of escape but an image of travel as stimulating and fun. When the *Life* article ran, a mere eight percent of Americans had ever taken an airplane flight, and international travel was similarly rare.[67] Aside from wartime postings, few people had ever left the country, let alone the western hemisphere. In the United States of the fifties and sixties, the word *international* possessed a glamour almost as intense as the word *modern*, making the ocean-hopping life of the Pan Am crew deeply alluring. For Americans in particular, what came to be called the Jet Age represented a new version of escape and transformation, one that addressed several widespread longings.

In the prosperous postwar period, Americans enjoyed a rising standard of living, embodied in suburban houses, push-button kitchen gadgets, and chrome-bedecked cars. Although extreme poverty lingered in some places, most people were no longer yearning for escape from hardship. More likely, the escape they wanted was from boredom, regimentation, and routine—an escape symbolized by international travel. If you flew, especially internationally, you were someone special. If not a hero like James Bond, you were at least a person of leisure: an international playboy, a college student traveling standby, a tennis player on the international circuit, a carefree adventurer with time to see the world. On the last page of its Pan Am feature, *Life* highlighted the contrast between the globe-trotting crew's adventures and mundane American life, showing the pilot returning home to his wife and daughters in a New York suburb. On the days off between flights, he said, "Sometimes I just stand in the yard watching the briefcase brigade go by."[68]

Having achieved a smoother passage through life, many Americans yearned for a more exciting one. The man or woman in a Pan Am uniform embodied that longing. So did other icons of Jet Age glamour. Take the

era's distinctive automobile designs. In the mid-fifties, American car makers abandoned streamlined styles in favor of the aviation-inspired "forward look," with its wrap-around windshields and winglike tail fins. The cars' shapes, their advertising, their names (the Pontiac Strato Star, the Oldsmobile Rocket), and their features ("flightomatic" transmission, "Jetway hydra-matic") all suggested high-tech aviation. Hood ornaments took on the shapes of jets. "Millions of Americans now drove with model planes in their peripheral vision," observes Grant McCracken, the cultural anthropologist. "These peripheral planes made a plane of the car and a pilot of the driver." Detroit's products, he writes, "impressed as cars. They wowed as planes."[69]

Then there were James Bond and his many imitators.[70] With their daring and mystery, spies and secret agents had long been glamorous fictional figures, but the popular culture of the early sixties produced a new version of the character. He was aptly dubbed "the international man of mystery" by the Austin Powers parodies of the 1990s. This spy was not a wartime hero but a jet-setting operative whose adventures transported the audience to exotic locales, exclusive venues, and the arms of beautiful women. Bond was the prototype, but television shows like *I Spy* (which premiered in 1965), *Mission Impossible* (1966), and *The Saint* (a British series that debuted in 1962 and began airing in the United States in 1967) picked up the theme.[71] The Jet Age secret agent was charming, omnicompetent, and exceedingly well traveled. No place was truly foreign to him, yet he was always having new experiences. He made the international intriguing.

Even as one sort of Jet Age glamour was informing spy movies, another was providing a respite from the high-stakes conflicts of the Cold War. This was the innocent internationalism reflected to this day in the opening ceremonies of the Olympics and the Miss Universe pageant, with their colorful costumes and shared aspirations, superficial exoticism and essential sameness. The same Jet Age optimism was depicted in *The Endless Summer* (1966), a documentary in which two young surfers fly around the world in search of the perfect wave. From Africa to Australia, everywhere they find friendly people who love the beach as much as they do. In the world of *The Endless Summer,* nobody worries about nuclear war.

The glamorous version of the *international* was peaceful and friendly, reflecting the sunny faith of Disney's "It's a Small World" and *Star Trek.* There were no differences that wouldn't disappear once you got to know people—yet it was all much more interesting than ordinary life. The essayist Sandra Tsing Loh captures the culture I remember from my own childhood:

> As a kid in the sixties, I remember drinking up everything international: Expo 67! UNICEF! The five intertwining rings of the Olympics! International . . . House of Pancakes! "Come in!" international people always seemed to be saying. "We don't care where the hell you're from. Have some flapjacks!"[72]

The popularly priced pancake house, founded in 1958, may seem the antithesis of glamour, but in 1960s middle America the chance to eat crêpes or blintzes, or even to order good old American pecan pancakes from a menu featuring such exotic fare, offered a bridge to a glamorous ideal. Unlike a Chinese or Italian restaurant, the International House of Pancakes featured representatives of many different cultures in the same place. Its menu "looked like the UN," a period phrase that suggested an intriguing mix of costumes and skin colors: *Star Trek* without the alien makeup. The glamour depended on that harmonious juxtaposition. A 1966 ad inviting tourists to visit UN headquarters shows a young American boy looking sideways at a Japanese attaché wearing a kimono and the Mali ambassador in a kufi and grand boubou, as they talk to the US ambassador. "A trip to United Nations Headquarters can be educational and inspirational," it declares. "What's more, it's fun."[73]

In 1957, the United Nations made an appropriately glamorous backdrop for a fashion shoot. *Mary Evans Picture Library/National Magazine Company/Everett Collection*

From Pan Am pilots and mass-market crêpes to the UN building and such popular foreign films as *La Dolce Vita* (1960), the representatives of Jet Age glamour made Americans feel cosmopolitan and worldly—none more so than the chic, French-speaking Jacqueline Kennedy. A friend advised the first lady on hosting small dinner parties at the White House: "Have pretty women, attractive men, guests who are *en passant*, the flavor of another language. This is the jet age, so have something new and changing."[74] The dinner parties' international flavor not only offered pleasure to the guests; it also provided a glamorously sophisticated ideal for the nation, one that Americans were, in that moment, surprisingly eager to embrace.

In 1962 Jackie took her children on vacation to Ravello on Italy's Amalfi Coast. They stayed in a nine-hundred-year-old palace rented by her sister, Princess Lee Radziwill. A year later, after the Kennedys' third child died shortly after birth, Jackie recuperated from the trauma with a Mediterranean cruise on Aristotle Onassis's yacht, again arranged by her sister. Franklin Roosevelt Jr., a family friend then serving as undersecretary of commerce, was dragooned into coming along as a sort of chaperone. After a while, he said later, "We began to look like a boat full of jet-setters, and President Kennedy didn't want that image."[75] They looked like jet-setters because that's what they were.

The president's concern was understandable. Since the Jacksonian era in the 1820s, American voters have been instinctive populists, wary of politicians who suggest social elitism or conspicuous consumption. They prefer the candidate born in a log cabin to the scion of a great family. But Jackie's jet-setting image doesn't seem to have been a political negative.[76] Something was different about the Kennedy moment. A young campaign organizer saw it back before the president's election, when he accompanied Jackie during the hotly contested Democratic primary in West Virginia. Charles Peters had been worried that she was "far too glitzy" for West Virginia voters but discovered he had seriously misjudged:

> There was no question that instead of identifying with the woman who was like them—Muriel Humphrey—they identified with the Princess. You could just tell they wanted Jackie. They had a wondrous look in their eyes when they saw her. After the dowdiness of Eleanor Roosevelt, Bess Truman and Mamie Eisenhower, they were looking for an aristocratic image. And the Kennedys did a superlative job of merchandising that image.[77]

At no other moment in American history has the public been so willing not merely to vote for but *to identify with* a political family representing a privileged, cosmopolitan elite. Although the 1960 election was closely divided, Jackie was always popular. In a June 1961 survey, Gallup asked, "What are your impressions of Mrs. Jacqueline Kennedy?" Sixty-six percent of respondents said "favorable," compared to only twelve percent "unfavorable." That same year she ranked second, after Eleanor Roosevelt, on Gallup's survey of the American public's most-admired women; after Roosevelt's death in 1962, she topped the list every year until 1968, when she fell to seventh after marrying Onassis.[78]

Once you've watched enough movies from the 1930s—and most of the voting public in 1960 would have been moviegoers in that decade—the appeal of the jet-setting, couture-wearing Jackie Kennedy becomes clearer. She was living the glamorous life depicted in those old films, the life the ladies of West Virginia had dreamed of and identified with when they were young. Movie glamour had been an illusion they knew to be false but one they had, in those moments of cinematic magic, felt to be true; Jackie similarly inspired not envy, resentment, or insecurity but identification and longing. She was the pink negligee against Muriel Humphrey's or Pat Nixon's blue gingham dress: impractical and a tad foreign, but the embodiment of desire. She represented something beyond ordinary life.[79] In the early years of the Jet Age, her international aura seemed somehow appropriate.

Familiarity eventually destroyed Jet Age glamour. "When the jet age was new and exciting, flying was a glamorous and sexy endeavor," the Virgin Atlantic website declared in 2006, pledging "to bring this glamour back."[80] It's a perennial promise in the contemporary airline industry, usually offered along with an announcement of new in-flight luxuries or styl-

Plan59.com

ish new crew uniforms. But however nice the amenities or attractive the uniforms, the old glamour never returns, because Jet Age glamour wasn't about the actual experience of flying. It was about the *idea* of air travel and the ideals and identity it represented.

Jet Age glamour expressed the longing to experience a world of variety and excitement, a fast-moving, dynamic, and diverse alternative to the familiar and routine. We now inhabit the real version of that world, a world glamour advertised and helped bring about. We can never bring the old illusion back. We can only invent new ones, reflecting new circumstances, new possibilities, new desires, and new versions of yearnings that never go away.

Icon
THE SUNTAN

When the young Archie Leach reinvented himself as Cary Grant, he sought to become what a biographer describes as "the epitome of masculine glamour." Toward that end, he copied the fine tailoring he'd seen on Douglas Fairbanks. He also adopted the older star's deep bronze suntan.[1]

In the West throughout most of the twentieth century, glamorous people had suntans. Golden skin marked Hollywood stars and international jet-setters, the bohemian writers of the 1920s and the flower children of the 1960s. The Beautiful People had suntans. So did John F. Kennedy and James Bond.

The conventional story is that once upon a time, most people worked outdoors and only the wealthy could maintain complexions unmarked by the sun. So light skin was prestigious. Then factories and offices replaced agriculture, making wan faces a sign of labor. The idle rich could escape to sun themselves year-round. Tans became markers of wealth and leisure.

This story isn't wrong, but neither is it complete. (The oft-told tale that Coco Chanel was the first to popularize the tan is, however, a myth.[2]) The glamour of

THE SUN BATHERS

what a 1929 *Vogue* article precisely termed a "cultivated coat of tan" evoked more than the longing for wealth and leisure.[3] It connected twentieth-century audiences to a new ideal of permissive sensuality—an ease with the body and with nature.

"Fashion's habit of following the sun has made the pink-and-white complexion as absurd as bathing stockings," declared a 1929 ad promoting a line of silks in "sunburn colors."[4] Like bonnets and parasols, bathing stockings were the cumbersome paraphernalia of a now-ridiculous modesty.

Bronzed skin, by contrast, recalled the exotic simplicity of distant lands. The 1929 *Vogue* report extolled the chicness of "a slim young person at Antibes, brown as an Indian, bare-legged, bare-armed, barebacked, in an evening frock of water-blue crêpe satin with slippers in the same blue hue, with not a jewel about her."[5] Against the fussy, showy lace and jewelry of the immediate past, all that brown bareness felt both excitingly primitive and sleekly modern. It seemed to do away with unnecessary artifice, promising a return to a more natural state.

"There is a nice Jean Jacques Rousseau spirit to this that is good for your general attitude toward life," declared a 1935 *Harper's Bazaar* article recommending a regimen of nude sunbathing. For those not up on pop versions of political philosophy, the accompanying Martin Munkacsi photo of a nude young woman running away from the viewer offered a visual translation.[6] The new sun worship promised to return us to a joyful state of innocence, effortlessly overthrowing the strictures of civilization.

The rage for suntans marked what the literary critic John Weightman, writing in 1970, called the twentieth century's "solar revolution," characterized by the "almost universal belief that sunshine is good for one, and is, in fact, an elixir of youth." Suntans, he argued, expressed new attitudes toward nature and the body. Some avid sunbathers were "would-be noble savages" seeking transcendence and morality in nature, while others were "pantheistic immoralists" pursuing self-realization and the pleasures of the moment.[7]

Whatever the dream, the tans themselves were in fact neither effortless nor natural. Glamorous images of bronzed sunbathers, often shot from the back to preserve modesty and enhance projection, disguised the truth that systematically baking in the sun is frequently boring, uncomfortable, and unattractive. A cultivated coat of tan requires patient, sweaty discipline.

By Weightman's day, suntans had long ago lost most of their association with wealth and leisure. Any suburban housewife could get one in her backyard. Only winter tans suggested privilege. But even a summertime bronze could still shine with rebellious sex appeal.

If Tarzan embodied Rousseau's moralistic ideal of the noble savage, Weightman argued, Brigitte Bardot, sunbathing nude as Juliette in . . . *And God Created Woman* (*Et Dieu . . . créa la femme,* 1956) represented "the new ideal of the amoral savage."[8] To midcentury audiences, particularly in America, Juliette's disregard for social conventions and emotional consequences was as foreign and intriguing as an undiscovered South Sea island.

Amid the polished ladies of the fifties, the bare-skinned, barefoot Bardot was a harbinger of a new glamorous icon: the uninhibited "natural" *jeune fille,* who lives for the pleasures of the moment.[9] Her teenage rebelliousness represented a feminine, French version of the bad-boy glamour of Elvis Presley, Marlon Brando, or James Dean, and her all-over suntan was central to her appeal. "It announced that she controlled her own body, and wasn't confined by the social norms of past eras," writes the biological anthropologist Nina G. Jablonski. "At the time, people who protested [suntanning] were not considered prudent, just prudes, and in the 1960s that was as good as being dead."[10]

Nowadays, neither uninhibited sexuality nor suntanned skin is especially glamorous. Both are too common and their complications too familiar. Having lost their mystery, they've become the stuff of life, not of dreams. Cultivated tans are just a style, and a somewhat down-market one at that. Sometime after the disco era of the late seventies, when bronzed Beautiful People in slinky outfits still exuded sexual license, a suntan ceased to represent anything more extraordinary than darkened skin.

Icon

THE STRIDING WOMAN

In 1973 Revlon introduced Charlie, a "lifestyle fragrance" aimed at young, liberated women buying perfume for daily pleasure, rather than for dressing up or attracting men. It was an instant hit. With first-year sales of $10 million, Charlie's introduction proved the most lucrative in fragrance history. Within three years it was the world's best-selling fragrance—the first American perfume to achieve that status.[1]

The most striking thing about Charlie wasn't its smell but its advertising. Instead of the usual evening gowns, starlit nights, or exotic locales, Charlie ads featured the blond model Shelley Hack striding along in a pantsuit, with no man in sight.[2] The "Charlie Girl" represented a new version of glamour: youthful, energetic, and supremely confident. The androgynously named Charlie

was "breeziness incarnate," writes *New York Times* style reporter Susan Joy.[3] Women didn't know where she was going, what she did for a living, or whether she had a boyfriend, but they knew they wanted to be like her.

"Charlie held the hopes and aspirations for a generation of women who thought they were headed for board rooms by day, and nightclubs by evening," recalls *Wall Street Journal* style reporter Christina Binkley.[4] The campaign, write the marketing historians Deirdre Bird, Helen Caldwell, and Mark DeFanti, "helped to popularize the image of the independent woman. . . . The advertising image of a young, liberated woman striding confidently across the page appealed to women of the 1970s."[5]

It had also once appealed to their grandmothers.

The striding woman first appeared as the embodiment of modernity and liberation in the 1920s.[6] Editorial fashion spreads at the time still featured static poses, confining long strides to candid photos of doughty, unglamorous social-ites at the beach, racetrack, or country house. But as early as 1920 advertisers began using illustrations of lean-limbed women taking extra-long steps. As the decade progressed, the images became more common.

"This is a portrait of a modern," declared a 1928 ad for Shaggy-Tex coats featuring a stylized woman striding with her Russian wolfhound, a classic art deco motif.[7] A 1929 ad for Duro Gloss coats depicted a cloche-hatted woman with a briefcase walking briskly toward the viewer. "Along the Boulevards they come," read the copy, "these smart young moderns."[8]

CANDEE
GUMMI *und* SCHNEE-SCHUHE

By the midthirties, editorial features had caught up. "Long Strides across Paris," read the headline of a 1935 *Harper's Bazaar* spread on the Paris collections. Photographer Jean Moral, who would make striding women a leitmotif for decades, captured models joyfully traversing the city in steps that were sometimes so long they strained midcalf skirts.[9] Like the Charlie Girl, these women were graceful, energetic, and independent, headed to some unknown but no doubt wonderful destination.

Marveling at the real women he encountered on a 1937 trip to New York, the illustrator Vertes captured the spirit: "They stride like giantesses, looking only forward. They walk alone, perfectly at ease, feeling no need for the company of dog or man."[10] A 1938 *Collier's* cover portrayed the quintessential American tourist as a young woman with a camera bag slung over her shoulder, taking a huge stride as she gazed at her guidebook.[11]

A decade later, these dynamic young women had largely vanished.

Glamorous models rarely strode, except in photos taken by throwbacks like Moral.[12] They sat. They leaned. They stretched out their lovely arms or brought their gloved hands to their mouths. Occasionally they danced. But, above all, they *posed*. The woman of fashion "has chosen to make herself a thing," Simone de Beauvoir charged in *The Second Sex*, published in 1949.[13] These were models for an audience yearning to be admired and doted upon.

But there was more to the story than the postwar return to domesticity and stereotypical gender roles. Women also weren't striding because they were sitting in, leaning against, entering, or exiting shiny new cars. In the United States at least, "going places" meant driving. Walking, however purposeful, had lost its allure.

Then came the youthquake of the early sixties. The miniskirt freed women's legs, but it didn't restore the striding woman's iconic status. Youth, legs, and liberation might be in, but so was sitting on the floor—whether you were a mod girl showing off your tights or Audrey Hepburn wearing a Givenchy evening dress of embroidered pink chiffon.[14] The studied informality emphasized the shift away from postwar decorum, but the models were as static as their forerunners in boning and gloves. When they got up and moved, they posed with their legs bent in unnatural but geometrically interesting positions. These were still lifes, objects in space, representing modern art, not modern life.

Even photographer Richard Avedon, now remembered for photos like "Homage to Munkacsi," his 1957 shot of the model Carmen leaping off a Paris curb, umbrella in hand, confined himself mostly to stilted, studio poses. When he photographed four representatives of "The This-Moment Woman" for the March 1964 issue of *Harper's Bazaar*, their legs were mostly cropped out, their hands stayed near their bodies, and their eyes focused on the camera. They didn't move. (Models China Machado and Suzy Parker also sat on the floor.)

Two things brought back the striding woman. The obvious one—the one that produced the Charlie ads—was the resurgence of feminism and the trousers that were its material representation. By 1969, retailers and clothing brands (including Anne Klein and

Diana Vreeland, soon to make her mark as a columnist and later as fashion editor of *Harper's Bazaar*, strides down a New York sidewalk in a 1936 photo by Martin Munkacsi for the magazine.

© Estate of Martin Munkacsi, Courtesy of Howard Greenberg Gallery, New York

Levi's jeans) were featuring striding women in their ads, and editorial spreads began to let their models off the floor. Within a few years, striding women were again everywhere. Charlie was part of a much larger trend.

The earlier, less obvious cause was the June 1963 death of Martin Munkacsi, the first fashion photographer to take outdoor action pictures. In the 1930s, Munkacsi's models strode along Wall Street, ran on the beach, and jumped puddles in the rain. "Never pose your subjects," he said in 1935. "Let them move about naturally."[15] His work was everything the images dominating the postwar period were not.

When he died, *Harper's Bazaar's* young art directors got out old volumes to see what the fuss was about. "His women, laughing out of their pages, dazzled the drawing boards," wrote Avedon in a remembrance published in June 1964. Seven of the nine accompanying Munkacsi photos, including the opening shot of a barefoot model at the beach, depicted striding women. Avedon's essay was a tribute to the power of their glamour.

When he was eleven years old, Avedon recounted, he had clipped a small gallery of Munkacsi photos out of his family's magazines, pasting them above his bed in a windowless corner of the small apartment. The images lifted the boy out of his depressed surroundings into a life of freedom and joy. "The longings of my almost adolescence were focused on them," he wrote. "Photographs of falcons, camels, and women . . . *his women,* striding parallel to the sea, unconcerned with his camera, freed by his dreams of them, leaping straight kneed across my bed." Those graceful, confident, joyful women represented the world as it ought to be. "The art of Munkacsi lay in what he wanted life to be," Avedon wrote, "and he wanted it to be splendid."[16]

For all her embodiment of feminist ambition, the striding woman held a more universal allure. Munkacsi's death reconnected Avedon with the glamorous images of his childhood and he, in turn, offered up a similar vision to a new generation. Two issues later, and for month after month thereafter, Avedon sent his once-static models striding across the page.[17]

EIGHT

THE USES OF ENCHANTMENT

Many of the styles and settings that spelled "glamour" in the twentieth century persist in the twenty-first, with their original meanings enriched by layers of historical associations. The fashion designer Michael Kors updates jet-set glamour with ads and collections evoking film sets and red carpets, safaris, yachts, and private planes. Chanel No. 5 shows actress Audrey Tautou encountering a mysterious stranger on the Orient Express. Dior's J'adore perfume digitally casts Grace Kelly, Marlene Dietrich, and Marilyn Monroe in a backstage fashion-show scene with contemporary actress Charlize Theron. A 2011 video rebranding British Airways evokes aviator glamour in a poetic celebration of the airline's heritage, from biplanes to the Concorde to the present.[1] And, of course, every awards show sparks talk of red-carpet looks exemplifying "old Hollywood glamour."

The phrase suggests that glamour is a specific style: draping and sparkle, with red lipstick and neatly waved hair. But, as we've seen, glamour is not a style. It is an endlessly generative mixture of imagination and communication. New forms displace the old or simply join them, reflecting new circumstances and new longings. Scarlett Johansson poses in a ball gown for Moet & Chandon champagne and takes down bad guys as a cat-suited action heroine in Marvel superhero movies. The first role is centuries old; the second, which in English-language media traces back to the *Avengers* TV show of the early 1960s, became a staple of female glamour only in the late 1990s.[2]

The action heroine's power and daring channel ambitions—and an idea of sexiness—that are hard to imagine in a prefeminist era. She is independent and supremely capable, not a woman who needs or wants protecting. She exhibits *sprezzatura* and self-command. With an assist from weapons and martial-arts training, and occasionally supernatural powers, she physically enacts a glamorous equality. (In *Mr. and Mrs. Smith*, the 2005 movie featuring Brad Pitt and Angelina Jolie as married assassins assigned to kill each other, the protagonists are so equally matched they prove indestructible, allowing love to triumph in the end.) The action heroine doesn't inspire her male admirers to want to shelter or indulge her; they instead long to join her, to be her partner or teammate, to have her back and impress her with their own heroics. At the same time, her sleekness and grace (and those of her masculine counterparts) contrast with the actual bodies of an increasingly obese and sedentary population. She is what her audience is not but, at least for the moment, yearns to be.

Sunglasses, airplane, and striding woman: Many of the styles and settings that spelled "glamour" in the twentieth century persist in the twenty-first. Walter Chin/Trunk Archive

When we understand its nature, we can detect new forms of glamour even amid old iconography. In the video for her 2007 song "Glamorous," Fergie drinks champagne in a gold lamé dress; disembarks from a private jet in a coat with a fur collar; and stars in a 1930s-style gangster film (titled *Glamorous*) while wearing diamonds and a white evening gown.[3] She recalls her youthful dreams of "the days when I'd rock on MTV," a glamorous vision of stardom that has now come true.

It's a wistful memory. Even as the video surrounds her with signs of wealth and fame, the song deglamorizes her pop-star life. Hectored by "people in my ear" as she sits alone in her plane, Fergie slams her cell phone across the cabin, knocking her champagne glass off the table. "It's been a long road and the industry is cold," she sings. The video then pivots to a less traditional sort of glamour, answering a different yearning. We see in a flashback a loving father, his face largely in shadow, advising his ballerina-clad daughter about the hardships of becoming a star. We never learn exactly what he says, only that he was present, supportive, and wise. "My daddy told me so," Fergie sings, as the song ends. "He let his daughter know." Lucky daughter, to have such a father. The longing for family, and particularly for fathers, is not something twentieth-century glamour often addressed.[4] Yet the image of father and daughter is the climax of "Glamorous." Her father's love enables the star to soar.

What people find glamorous suggests something about who they are and what they find absent in their lives. In the movies of the thirties, divorce was exotic and glamorous. Marriage was for most people a lifetime commitment, and at times a loveless prison, so "taking the train to Reno,"

the place for easy divorces, offered an escapist fantasy. In 1934 Ginger Rogers played the title character in the Astaire-Rogers movie *The Gay Divorcée* (which would, of course, mean something entirely different today). Like wearing evening gowns and making cocktails in silver shakers, getting divorced was one of the distinctive habits of the fictional rich. Now divorces are commonplace, a quarter of American children live in single-mother households, and fatherly advice is glamorous.[5]

Although many longings are eternal, others arise from specific cultural contexts. In some cases, the underlying desires have changed so much that some contemporary constructions of glamour would be incomprehensible to earlier audiences. Consider a 2011 ad: A beautiful woman sits barefoot on a weathered wooden boat among the lily pads and grasses of a swampy tropical lake. Her lightweight trousers are rolled up just below the knee, and her perfectly imperfect hair blows slightly in the breeze. She appears to be alone, lost in thought, a picture of contented solitude. Next to her, its straps over one shoulder, is a large tote bag whose earthy browns harmonize with the boat—all her needs, it seems, reduced to a modest single satchel.

We are back to the tranquility of Toni Frissell's 1947 portrait of the girl in tennis clothes, but with a radically different setting—not a pristine resort, but an overgrown swamp. It's hard to imagine mid-twentieth-century audiences finding this image glamorous. For all her beauty, the woman is too drably dressed, as if for gardening or housework, and the setting is too primitive and remote. It recalls the hardships and grime of *The African Queen* (1951) or of World War II's Pacific theater. The photo would make people think of discomfort and disease. They would see the elemental, not the glamorous.

Yet for today's wealthy Western audiences this image of Angelina Jolie in Cambodia, captured for Louis Vuitton by Annie Leibovitz, represents a new kind of glamour, one just as stylized as the old. Against the yearning for speed, it presents an image of perfect stillness; against the frenzy of conspicuous consumption, it posits graceful simplicity; against urban excitement, it offers a verdant landscape; against instant communication, it promises splendid isolation. This is glamour for an audience whose material yearnings have long since been satisfied, an audience that can imagine that escape from modernity would be enjoyable. Here we find no mosquitoes, mud, or dengue fever, only tranquility, self-sufficiency, and abundant nature. It is a vision that inspires yoga routines and organic menus, vacation plans and environmental policy. "A single journey can change the course of a life," reads the caption. The image and the slogan suggest transformation through escape—a richer, more meaningful life made possible by shedding the complexity and demands of contemporary civilization. The bag is merely a useful accessory to the experience. And though the slogan refers to a journey, the picture is all quiet destination.

Like other forms of glamour, the ad is evocative make-believe. It shows none of the hardships and limitations of rural poverty and conceals the technologies, conveniences, and wealth that make Jolie's globe-trotting life possible. It even hides a basic truth about contemporary journeys: The affluent foreigners who trek to swamps in Cambodia don't generally bring Louis Vuitton. They buy specialized adventure-travel clothing with quick-dry fabrics engineered to protect them from insects and sun, and they carry backpacks made of high-tech materials like ballistic nylon. High-end leather goods are for a different audience—one that dreams of the peaceful, "authentic" life but rarely tries to live it.[6] Louis Vuitton's Cambodia is, like Ralph Lauren's Africa, a mysterious world that inspires a mood.

When we understand how glamour works, we can see how objects that would seem improbable to one audience can become glamorous to another. Consider the glamour that vintage fashion holds for many younger enthusiasts. Solanah Cornell, a popular vintage blogger with a particular love of styles from the 1940s, recalls how she once overheard an elderly woman walking behind her on the street comment to her companion, "Oh poor thing, she has to wear

For young vintage enthusiasts like blogger Solanah Cornell, decades-old garments are glamorous in part because they embody an ideal of thrift and self-reliance. *Lara Blair Images*

her grandma's hand-me-downs."[7] Women who lived through World War II yearned for fashionable new clothes and an escape from the constraints of shortages and rationing. For them newness meant quality and progress. An old dress was the antithesis of glamour.

For young enthusiasts like Cornell, by contrast, decades-old garments are glamorous in part because they embody an ideal of thrift and self-reliance. "I really love the make-do and mend and DIY aspect of the war era, as it's something I can be creative with," Cornell says. She describes wearing vintage clothes as "a rebellion against the negative aspects of modern society," including "the lack of care and pride people place in their clothing and style, bad manners, poor eating habits, and value of quantity over quality."[8]

For this audience, material abundance isn't as appealing as it seemed in the 1940s. It feels sloppy, superficial, and, in its own way, insistent and constraining. The glamour of "vintage" thus offers an escape similar to the one promised in the Louis Vuitton ad: simplicity, harmony, and meaning. Wearing clothing from decades past is less about nostalgia—vintage lovers are quick to point out the faults in the past, particularly in the treatment of women, and many style themselves as environmentalists concerned about social justice—than it is a way of reaching for the ideal.[9] Cornell explicitly ties vintage to escapism, noting that "many vintage enthusiasts are very involved in various forms of fantasy, fiction, and escapism. . . . Fantastical television shows and movies, comic books, anything that diverts away from the confines of the modern world." But, she concedes, the old clothes do demand "endless repairs."[10]

The same yearnings have made The Container Store, with its seductively neat aisles of designer boxes, closet systems, office accessories, and drawer organizers, one of America's most glamorous retailers. Its "tidy, colorful aisles suggest that we can, at least for a time, triumph over the messy inevitable," observes business writer Kyle Stock. Crucial to the chain's appeal is its carefully edited abundance, including soothingly repetitive permutations of boxes, coat hangers, and kitchen gear that vary mostly by color, texture, and material. "In a world that is so stressful and busy, I think it's refreshing to enter an organized, clean, and refreshing space," explains

Leigh Atherton, a 27-year-old fan who says the store makes her "think I can become that organized."

The retailer deliberately cultivates a feeling of calm. "There's a Zen quality to having everything in its place," says Kip Tindell, the company's co-founder and chief executive.[11] But—critically—this metaphorical form of Zen indulges, rather than denies, material desire. There's nothing minimalist about the store design. The Container Store affirms the pleasures of stuff. The shelves are filled with aesthetically stimulating colors and patterns, and all sorts of goods you never knew you wanted. You don't have to relinquish anything to find peace, its merchandising suggests. You can, in fact, have a great time buying ingenious, adorable, tactile, or beautiful new things. The Container Store sells glamour for an age of abundance.

If the yearning for a calmer, more disciplined life informs the glamour of vintage clothing and The Container Store, the longing for opportunity infuses an even less likely object with promise. "Where I live in the Bay Area," writes the journalist Alexis Madrigal, "there's a certain glamour to Detroit." Detroit? To most people, the beautiful, prosperous, dynamic Bay Area seems far more glamorous than cold, rundown, and bankrupt Detroit. But the Bay Area is crowded, built-up, and expensive. Detroit appeals to the yearning, particularly among the young, for someplace cheap and open enough to allow people to take economic chances, following dreams that may not pay off—the kind of frontier California once represented.

The idea of Detroit is also alluring to those who'd like to reinvent the urban environment without the political resistance of activist residents and property owners. "Detroit," Madrigal observes, "is the place where Bay Area types imagine an urban tabula rasa, a place where enough has gone away that the problems of stuffing millions of people into a small region can be reimagined, redesigned, remade." But when he actually visits Detroit, the journalist finds that the emptiness that sounds promising in theory is depressing in person. "The number of abandoned buildings in Detroit—and the feeling they toss into the air—is truly unfathomable to someone raised on the west coast," he writes.[12] The city's glamour is an illusion that tells the truth not about Detroit but about Silicon Valley and San Francisco.

After several generations of pervasive glamour, we are savvy about many of its illusions. But that doesn't mean we're immune to its allure, or that

we really want to be. As the public has gotten more skeptical and media savvy, we've seen the growth of a wised-up glamour that follows designer Isaac Mizrahi's advice, quoted in chapter one, to "happily confront the manipulation" involved. Fergie's "Glamorous" video represents one version, revealing the frustrations of a pop star's life even as its imagery makes that life seem pretty great. Wised-up glamour admits the illusion, often employing a large dash of humor, while simultaneously indulging its pleasures. It's akin to the "utopian parody" that superhero comics have long used to let readers laugh at the medium's earnest ex-

Hot-stone massages have replaced fur coats as the glamorous symbols of feminine indulgence. *iStockphoto*

cesses while preserving its emotional satisfactions. Utopian parody protects audiences from losing sight of reality and, crucially, from fully exposing their vulnerabilities and longings: the truth revealed by the illusion. Not surprisingly, it often shows up in the glamour of groups, from drag queens to *Star Trek* fans, whose escapist pleasures are especially subject to mainstream mockery.[13] Wised-up glamour is affectionate and appreciative, not destructive. Its purpose is not to eliminate glamour but, by acknowledging its deceptions, to save it.

This double vision has now gone mainstream. Versions of it, some broader than others, animate such diverse movie franchises as the *Austin Powers* parodies (1997, 1999, 2002), the *Charlie's Angels* adventure romps (2000, 2003), and Quentin Tarantino's *Kill Bill* films (2003, 2004). It also increasingly shows up in advertising, as exemplified by Old Spice's wildly popular "The Man Your Man Could Smell Like" campaign. "We're not saying this body wash will make your man smell like a romantic millionaire jet fighter pilot, but we are insinuating it," declare the campaign's creators.[14] The Old Spice commercials spoof the romantic iconography of yachts, diamonds, and white horses—"You're on a boat with the man your man could smell like"—even as the camera stays focused on the buff, bare-chested Isaiah Mustafa, with his deep voice and preternatural poise. Like the Dos Equis beer ads featuring "the most interesting man in the world," the humor of the Old Spice campaign lets us enjoy glamour while puncturing its excesses.[15] And since Old Spice never promises to change anything more than your man's odor, the ads are technically truthful. Their hairsplitting modesty makes them all the more amusing.

Old Spice is a mass-market brand, and its commercials employ broad forms of both glamour and humor. The images are well-established clichés, and their absurdity in this context is obvious. While the ads might not be intelligible to someone from the 1930s, anyone likely to see the videos will know how to interpret them.

For an elite brand, however, wised-up glamour is trickier. Broad humor is too crass, and subtlety risks misinterpretation. Take the eighty-second online video for Dolce & Gabbana's The One perfume starring a "diva" played by Scarlett Johansson. As she adjusts her hair and makeup and poses for camera flashes, Johansson answers questions from an unheard interlocutor.

"Music inspires me. Art inspires me. But so does the wind."

"Ah, my favorite part of my body?" Head tilt. Shrug. "I like my lips. For kissing. And for words that start with the letter *M*."

The ad is not a send-up of perfume commercials. That would be too obvious. It is instead a deadpan parody of celebrity interviews, giving the audience a backstage pass and flattering viewers by assuming they're in the know about these ritualized exchanges.[16] Johansson is beautiful and flirtatious, and her hairstyle and eyeliner recall Marilyn Monroe and the young Sophia Loren. This sophisticated version of utopian parody works if you don't get the joke and enjoy it as straight glamour.

The problem arises when audiences recognize the silliness but miss the wink. "This ad stinks," declares the blogger Chris Greenhough, complaining about Johansson's "cheesy and smug" answers.[17] *AdWeek*'s Emma Bazilian writes that perfume ads "always seem to border on complete parody," but she doesn't realize that this video has knowingly crossed the border. "All perfume commercials, including this one, are, at their core, completely ridiculous," she writes. "But they're also a fantasy, an attempt to embody the idea of the scent, which in this case, seems to be a classic, luxurious sort of glamour."[18] She's close. But she misses the wised-up twenty-first-century reinvention: glamour for people who want their escape and transformation with a nod toward their media savvy.

Like glamour, humor depends on the audience. We're used to the idea that some people won't get a joke. But we tend to assume that the forms of glamour are universal, because throughout most of the twentieth century many were so easy to recognize. Different people might disagree about the relative merits of Grace Kelly, Marilyn Monroe, and Elizabeth Taylor, but a shared culture made it possible to see how each represented glamour. The same was true of airplanes, skyscrapers, and other markers of modernity and "the future." The cultural consensus behind the shared glamour has long since dissolved. Neither a single individual's response nor the mass market's is a reliable indicator of what is or isn't glamorous. The more fragmented the audience, the less predictable the response.

Idiosyncratic, subcultural, or unrecognized forms of glamour have always existed, of course. But today the marginal is often indistinguishable from the mainstream. Hence the Louis Vuitton "Core Values" ads or the deadpan Dolce & Gabbana parody, which aim at sophisticated elites by selling old luxuries with new forms of enchantment. Neither the new version of glamour nor the old is marginal, yet neither is fully mainstream. The documentary director Morgan Spurlock notes with wonder that the geeky Comic-Con now seems to offer something for everyone. "I mean now I could take my mom and she could find something there that she likes," he says. "They have [the musical TV show] 'Glee' there too, how does that happen? It's where any of the outsiders can go to find others like them but now maybe everyone is becoming an outsider. My mom, the outsider."[19]

When everyone is an outsider, the result is a proliferation of glamour whose meaning is often missed, dismissed, or (as in the Dolce & Gabbana video) misunderstood by critics who aren't part of the target audience. Old ladies shake their heads at young vintage lovers. Movie reviewers who would never belabor the essential absurdity of a screwball comedy or a

Fred and Ginger musical number make sure we know they understand that superheroes are ridiculous: "a gang of rowdy sociopaths with high muscle tone" existing only to justify "overblown, skull-assaulting action sequences."[20]

Meanwhile, the contemporary reincarnations of the old forms of glamour—the gold, diamonds, cognac, champagne, and fancy cars found in countless hip-hop videos—strike the economically secure as hopelessly crass.[21] "Asking why rappers always talk about their stuff is like asking why Milton is forever listing the attributes of heavenly armies. Because boasting is a formal condition of the epic form," observes the novelist Zadie Smith in a profile of rapper-turned-mogul Jay Z. The formal convention answers an emotional need: "Those taught that they deserve nothing rightly enjoy it when they succeed in terms the culture understands."[22] In the neighborhoods where hip-hop arose, luxuries that seem horribly obvious to critics represent distant ideals, just as they did to the moviegoers of the 1930s.

Jay Z's own aspirations were fueled by a visit to his sixth-grade teacher's home and, in particular, by the ice maker on her refrigerator. Push-button control, with its mysterious mechanism and effortless conversion of desire to reality, had been the epitome of futuristic kitchen glamour a few decades earlier—and for a boy from the projects it still was. "You push it and the ice and the water comes down. I was really amazed by that," he recalls. "I was like, I want one of those."[23] These luxuries, large and small, are bridges to displaced meaning. They represent a life of pleasure, but also of power and respect. If you see only the material, you miss the magic.

Jay Z in concert: "When you see me, see you!" The hip-hop mogul's own aspirations were fueled by the futuristic kitchen glamour of the automatic ice maker on his sixth-grade teacher's refrigerator. *Photofest*

In 2006, the novelist Salman Rushdie gave an interview to *Der Spiegel* in which he was asked about the causes of terrorism. After first challenging the idea that he qualified as a terrorism expert, Rushdie suggested several possibilities: "a misconceived sense of mission," a "herd mentality," the desire to become "a historic figure," an attraction to violence, and—a motivation that seemed to flabbergast his interviewer—*glamour.*

Q: Do you seriously mean that terrorism is glamorous?

A: Yes. Terror is glamour—not only, but also. I am firmly convinced that there's something like a fascination with death among suicide bombers. Many are influenced by the misdirected image of a kind of magic that is inherent in these insane acts. The suicide bomber's imagination leads him to believe in a brilliant act of heroism, when in fact he is simply blowing himself up pointlessly and taking other peoples' lives.[24]

To someone who thinks of glamour as a positive and trivial attribute of movie stars and designer dresses, the argument that terrorism is glamorous sounds bizarre. But it will surprise no one who has read the preceding chapters. Unlike his interviewer, Rushdie understands the deeper meaning of glamour as a form of enchantment and nonverbal rhetoric. (Note his references to fascination and magic.)

By arguing that glamour inspires terrorist acts, Rushdie reminds us that such acts spring not simply from anger or hatred but from imagination—and that glamour is not only pleasurable but persuasive. It is also persistent, continually emerging in new forms for new audiences in new circumstances. Jihadi terrorism combines two ancient forms of glamour, the martial and the religious, with the modern allure of media celebrity. It promises to fulfill a host of desires: for purity and meaning, union with God, historical significance, attention and fame, a sense of belonging, even (posthumous) riches and beautiful women. The jihadi's ultimate goal of a restored caliphate exemplifies the glamorous utopia, while the terrorist plot recalls the synchronization of heist movies, with a secret and intricate plan in which every team member is important and the goal is to outwit authorities and commit a crime. It's not hard to imagine how appealing all this might be to a bored, alienated, and impressionable person.[25]

As we've seen throughout this book, glamour can serve many purposes: individual and collective; personal, social, commercial, or political. The story of glamour is the story of human longing and its cultural manifestations. Like other forms of rhetoric and art, glamour can embody good ideas or bad ones. It can inspire life-enhancing actions or destructive ones. Its meaning and its effects depend on the audience. But one thing is certain: glamour is not trivial.

Even in its most apparently superficial and entertaining forms, glamour reveals inner truths. It exposes our vulnerabilities, to ourselves and perhaps to the world. We feel lonely, frustrated, and unappreciated; we long for fellowship, for meaningful work, for true love. We are social and biological creatures. We want to be looked at and admired, to be rich and powerful, to be painlessly heroic and effortlessly beautiful. We long to be sexually desired and recognized as special. Glamour defies demands for humility or modesty, self-denial or patient resignation. It is ambitious and self-involved. Above all, glamour reveals that we want to be something we are not. It demonstrates that we are not wholly content with life as it is. Glamour is pleasurable, but it is also disquieting.

Sophisticates often kid themselves that they're realists immune to its influence. "Truth is not found in dreaming," the historian Rosalind Williams lectures readers in *Dream Worlds,* her influential examination of intellectuals' reactions to nineteenth-century merchandising. Despite its penetrating critiques, the book is suffused with Williams's own utopian yearnings. She harbors a glamorous vision of a world of social harmony and individual happiness made possible by income equality and sumptuary laws. Vague in its details, that dream is as illusory and selective as any department store display.[26] One job of intellectuals is to puncture glamour by reminding us of what's hidden. But intellectuals are by no means exempt from glamour's effects. They simply have their own longings and hence their own versions of glamour, including in some cases the ideal of a life without meaningful illusions.

As Williams herself acknowledges, "Dream worlds of consumption may rely on fantasy, but popular preference for them is a social fact that cannot be wished away."[27] To understand glamour as no more than deception is to miss the psychological truths—and the real-world possibilities— it reveals. Although glamour's transformational promise may be destructive and false in some cases, it is positive and valid in others. Every unironic evocation of the American Dream is an exercise in glamour and, however illusory the dream may sometimes be, the country is better off for the inspiration.[28] When used as a guide rather than as an impossibly perfect goal in itself, glamour can point its audience toward a better, more satisfying life—as it did for James Boswell, Richard Neutra, Simon Doonan, Oprah Winfrey, and Michaela DePrince, or for the working-class housewives of 1930s England and the readers of 1950s *Ebony*. Twentieth-century modernity really did offer greater agency, efficiency, novelty, and stimulation. It really did provide alternatives to the "boredom of routine." But, of course, modern life also brought problems of its own. Once we got used to "the future," it no longer seemed so glamorous. It became real life, and new versions of glamour emerged, some more widely acknowledged than others.

In a culture marked by so much diversity, simply recognizing glamour can require a leap of empathetic imagination. We may appreciate the longings stirred by the New York skyline, a red-carpet moment, or a sports car on an open road, but a fuller theory of glamour allows us to expand beyond the obvious. It lets us understand what a little girl sees in a princess or a young man imagines in the Marines; why one busy mother dreams of an island kitchen and another of an island resort; the allure of the *Star Trek* bridge to its fans and Air Jordan shoes to theirs; the emotional resonance of wind turbines and of hip-hop bling; even the fervor of jihadi terrorists and of Barack Obama's 2008 campaign. While every object of glamour is in some way exotic to its audience, many audiences are even stranger to each other. Understanding glamour can never eliminate all that mystery, but it gives us a place to start.

The Power of Glamour: Michaela DePrince, once scorned as a "devil child" in her Sierra Leone orphanage, is now a professional ballerina like the dancer whose glamorous image inspired her. *Jordi Matas Photography*

ACKNOWLEDGMENTS

As someone attracted to the nitty-gritty details of commerce and culture, with more interest in the complexities of clothing fit than the latest runway fashion, I never expected to write anything, let alone a book, on glamour. Despite what you might infer from its title, my 2003 book *The Substance of Style* was about the rise and nature of aesthetic value in such previously unstylish realms as toilet brushes and business-hotel rooms. It had nothing to do with glamour.

A year after it came out, however, Joe Rosa, then the architecture and design curator at the San Francisco Museum of Modern Art, asked me to write the introductory essay for the catalogue accompanying an exhibit on glamour in fashion, industrial design, and architecture. Knowing next to nothing about glamour (including what Joe meant by the term), I agreed. The more I thought and read about the subject, and the more I contemplated glamorous objects, the more fascinated I became. Analyzing glamour appealed to my interest in artifice, in persuasion, in history, in beauty, and in commercial culture. My ideas have evolved a lot since that first essay (and the 2004 TED talk drawn from it), but I owe Joe and his SFMOMA colleagues Karen Levine and Greg Sandoval a big thanks for starting me on a fascinating journey. Thanks also to Chris Anderson of TED.

Before and after I embarked on the book, editors at a number of publications gave me the opportunity to develop glamour-related ideas in articles. I'm grateful to Meghan O'Rourke and Hanna Rosin at *Slate*, Claudia Payne at the *New York Times*, Rod Dreher at *Big Questions Online*, Gary Rosen and Ryan Sager at *The Wall Street Journal*, Phil Terzian at *The Weekly Standard*, Sarah Van Boven at *Allure*, and Ted Balaker and Nick Gillespie at Reason.tv. Robert Messenger, James Gibney, and James Bennet at *The Atlantic* deserve special thanks for indulging my interest in glamour, as do my wonderful current editors at *Bloomberg View*, Toby Harshaw and David Shipley.

Over the five years I worked on this book, many friends answered questions or sent me article links and other leads. With the growth of social media, their numbers have grown too great to track everyone by name. You all have my gratitude. I do want to particularly thank David B. Bernstein, Karlyn Bowman, Brian Chase, Christian Esquevin, Jacque Lynn Foltyn, Mike Godwin, Keating Holland, Grant McCracken, Adam Minter, Matt Novak, Charles Oliver, and Barry Strauss for their suggestions and help. I also enjoyed more formal research assistance from Bryan Castañeda, Dorian Electra, Crystal Hubbard, Herschel Nachlis, Paige Phelps, and Sara Dabney Tisdale.

I owe especially fervent research thanks to Autumn Whitefield-Madrano for retrieving the original *Mademoiselle* makeover articles from the New York Public Library and to Leslie Watkins for copying Lois Ardery's "Inarticulate Longings" article from the J. Walter Thompson archives at Duke. James Sanders, whose brilliant *Celluloid Skyline* is a model of integrating history, culture, and imagery, gave me important early encouragement, as did Michael Bierut, who introduced me to James. The book also benefited greatly from two resources that weren't available when I was researching my previous books: WorldCat.org, which provides a central hub for library catalogues, and Google Books, which identified, and in some cases unlocked, all sorts of hidden treasures. While I used many libraries in researching this book, I'm especially grateful to the Santa Monica Public Library for its magnificent, open-stacks collection of bound magazine volumes.

Liberty Fund, whose conferences constitute the major part of my formal postcollegiate education, supported a conference on luxury whose readings helped inform my thinking about glamour. Amity Shlaes persuaded me to enter my articles for the 2011 Bastiat Prize, the funds from which allowed me to rent a desert cabin as a writer's retreat while completing the manuscript. Before that, Bill and Karen Inman generously allowed me to use their vacation home for some valuable weeks of intense work. Joan Kron gave me moral support, access to her fantastic library, referral to many relevant articles from decades past, and many delightful nights of hospitality in her beautiful New York apartment.

In 2009 my friend Kate Coe and I started a group blog called *Deep Glamour*, allowing me to develop some of my own ideas, interview interesting people, and learn from my co-bloggers' posts. I want to thank all the *Deep Glamour* bloggers—Kate Coe, Randall Shinn, Jessica Barber, Doug Champion, Albina Colden, Ingrid Fetell, Christine Hall, Raquel Laneri, Paige Phelps, Kit Pollard, Diego Rodriquez, and Cosmo Wenman—as well as everyone who has shared thoughts in interviews, comments, or guest posts.

Another valuable adventure has been teaching a short seminar on glamour in the master's in branding program at the School of Visual Arts. Thanks to Debbie Millman for enticing me to join the faculty, to Katie Scott and J'aime Cohen for administrative support, and to my students, especially Brian Gaffney, a star in the 2011 class and my teaching assistant in 2012.

I benefited from comments on early chapter drafts from Ed Brenegar, Sue Inman, Sally Satel, Randall Shinn, and Sara Dabney Tisdale. Later in the process, Chuck Freund, Nancy Hass, Joan Kron, Howard Miller, Sarah Skwire, and Viviana Zelizer gave me valuable feedback. Deirdre McCloskey, Jonathan Rauch, and Bob Roe provided crucial insights into the strengths and weaknesses of my first complete draft. Leslie Watkins, who may very well be my ideal reader, commented on multiple versions of the completed manuscript.

Gathering the photos for the book was a monumental job. Tim Rogers and Saundra Groves of *D Magazine* helped me obtain the Metropolitan ad in the first chapter, while Laura Thomas at SHVO helped me with Rector Square. Lou D'Elia and Mike Salazar generously provided first-rate scans of the George Hurrell photos. Jeff Wendt was a huge help, both in his professional role at the Everett Collection (where his colleague Marci Brennan was also a delight) and as a friend retouching images from my own collection and the Library of Congress. Joan Kron, Kate Hahn, and Sally Satel helped me to decide which photos to keep.

Over the long course of its development, the book had many editors. Amber Qureshi brought it to Free Press, where it was successively nurtured by Hilary Redmon and Alessandra Bastagli. I also received comments on the manuscript from Daniella Wexler. Jon Karp eventually moved it to Simon & Schuster, with a much-appreciated commitment to publish it in the beautiful form you now see. As my primary final editor, Emily Graff offered enthusiastic and perceptive feedback, with a youthful perspective that was particularly valuable. I'm grateful to Marysue Rucci for her support and enthusiasm in bringing it to press, to Andrea DeWerd for her marketing savvy, to Peg Haller for copyediting and fact-checking that saved me from embarrassing errors, and to Nancy Singer for the beautiful design. Judy Kip, my go-to indexer since *The Future and Its Enemies*, did her usual excellent job. Jennifer George, Joy McCann, and Leslie Watkins supplemented my proofreading. Thanks to Jennifer Garza and especially Jessica Lawrence for publicity, and to my friend Susan Self for supplementing the S&S team's efforts.

My agent, Sarah Chalfant, has my eternal gratitude for her patience, persistence, and professionalism. She always believed in this project and was a cool head during many difficult moments.

My brilliant and beloved husband, Steven Postrel, was also enthusiastic from the start, and we had many fun and stimulating conversations sharing new examples and hammering out specific analytical points. He also read the manuscript countless times, providing tough, insightful criticism that, while not always well received, invariably turned out to be exactly right. I appreciate his willingness to spot contradictions and ask probing questions, despite the predictably unpleasant reaction, as much as I do his endless support and encouragement. He's the best.

In July 2007, barely a week after receiving the final signed contract for the book, I was diagnosed with what turned out to be HER2-positive breast cancer, a particularly aggressive form of the disease. Twenty years earlier, I would have had only a fifty-fifty chance of survival, given the details of my case. Today, I am officially cured. Although I underwent the traditional treatments of surgery, chemotherapy, and radiation, what made the crucial difference was the pathbreaking biologic drug Herceptin, first approved by the Food and Drug Administration in 1998.

The research that led to Herceptin was funded not by the federal government or a traditional cancer charity but by money from Ronald O. Perelman, in his role as chairman of Revlon, and by fundraising in the 1990s at a series of star-studded events called the Fire and Ice Balls. I am deeply grateful to the many people, only one of whom I know personally, responsible for bringing Herceptin to the world: to Dennis Slamon for his scientific vision; Lilly Tartikoff for her fund-raising energy; my oncologist, John Glaspy, for his persuasive eloquence; the researchers at Genentech for development and testing; and Perelman and Revlon for their financial contributions. In a very real way, I owe my life to the glamour of makeup and movie stars.

—*Virginia Postrel*
Los Angeles, May 2013

NOTES

ONE: THE MAGIC OF GLAMOUR

1. William Kremer, "Michaela DePrince: The War Orphan Who Became a Ballerina," *BBC News Magazine*, October 14, 2012, http://www.bbc.co.uk/news/magazine-19600296. Giannella Garrett, "Defying Gravity: Teen Ballerina Michaela DePrince," *Teen Vogue*, May 2012, http://www.teenvogue.com/my-life/profiles/2012-05/teen-ballerina-michaela-deprince. David Smith, "Sierra Leone War Orphan Returns to Africa en Pointe for Ballet Debut," *Guardian*, July 16, 2012, http://www.guardian.co.uk/stage/2012/jul/16/sierra-leone-ballet-michaela-deprince. Carley Petesch, "Michaela DePrince, Star Dancer Born into War, Grows Up to Inspire," Associated Press, July 11, 2012, http://www.huffingtonpost.com/2012/07/11/michaela-prince-star-danc_n_1665341.html. Nkepile Mabuse, "Michaela DePrince: From War Orphan to Teen Ballerina," African Voices, CNN, September 3, 2012, http://www.cnn.com/2012/08/29/world/africa/michaela-deprince-ballet-dancing/index.html?iid=article_sidebar.
2. Alicia Drake, *The Beautiful Fall: Fashion, Genius, and Glorious Excess in 1970s Paris* (New York: Back Bay Books, 2006) p. 2.
3. Robin Givhan, "Glamour, That Certain Something," *Washington Post*, February 17, 2008, p. M01, http://www.washingtonpost.com/wp-dyn/content/article/2008/02/15/AR2008021500837.html.
4. The word *style* has a different meaning in rhetorical studies. When I use it in this book, I mean it in the colloquial, fashion sense.
5. On science glamour and the "CSI effect," see Virginia Postrel, "Beautiful Minds," *Atlantic*, September 2007, pp. 140–41, http://www.theatlantic.com/doc/200709/csi.
6. Yiyun Li, "Passing Through," *New York Times Magazine*, September 25, 2005, p. 154, http://www.nytimes.com/2005/09/25/magazine/25lives.html.
7. Martin Wroe, "Prophet with a Beautiful Way Out of Consumerism," *Sunday Times*, December 21, 2003, section 5, http://www.thesundaytimes.co.uk/sto/news/article35245.ece.
8. David Hume, "Of Refinement in the Arts," in *Essays, Moral, Political, and Literary*, Eugene F. Miller, ed. (Indianapolis: Liberty Fund, 1987) p. 268, http://www.econlib.org/library/LFBooks/Hume/hmMPL25.html.
9. Stephen Gundle, *Glamour: A History* (New York: Oxford University Press, 2008). Carol Dyhouse, *Glamour: Women, History, Fashion* (London: Zed Books, 2010).
10. Stephen Gundle, *Glamour*, p. 385.
11. Virginia Postrel, "A Power to Persuade," *Weekly Standard*, March 29, 2010, pp. 30–32, http://www.weeklystandard.com/articles/power-persuade. In an online poll with 397 respondents, 251 deemed Hilton "not at all glamorous," while 89 said she was glamorous "to some people but not to me." Although unscientific, this result is enough to puncture the claim of indisputability. Virginia Postrel, "There's Something about Paris," March 2, 2012, *Deep Glamour*, http://www.deepglamour.net/deep_glamour/2010/03/is-paris-hilton-glamorous-brazilian-commercial.html and http://polldaddy.com/poll/2781486/?view=results.
12. Oxford English Dictionary Online, http://dictionary.oed.com.
13. Sir Walter Scott, "The Lay of the Last Minstrel," Canto Third, Section IX, http://www.theotherpages.org/poems

/canto03.html. *Journal of Walter Scott*, August 12, 1826, http://www.online-literature.com/walter_scott/journal
-of-scott/10/.

14. Charlotte Brontë, *Jane Eyre* (London: Penguin Classics, 2006) p. 249, http://www.literature.org/authors/bronte
-charlotte/jane-eyre/chapter-20.html.
15. Joseph Conrad, *Youth* (Middlesex: Penguin Books, 1975) pp. 29–30, 34–35.
16. *Webster's International Dictionary of the English Language* (Springfield, MA: G & C Merriam, 1902) p. 628.
17. Stephen Gundle, *Glamour*, pp. 18–50. Elizabeth Wilson, "A Note on Glamour," *Fashion Theory*, June/September
2007, pp. 95–108.
18. Robin Muir, *Norman Parkinson: Portraits in Fashion* (North Pomfret, VT: Trafalgar Square Publishing, 2004)
p. 11.
19. J. M. Barrie, *Peter Pan*, chapter 14, http://www.readprint.com/chapter-598/Peter-Pan-James-M-Barrie.
20. "Address of Mr. Butler of South Carolina," U.S. House of Representatives, 48th Congress, Second Session, Misc.
Doc. No. 28, "Memorial Addresses of the Life and Character of John H. Evins" (Washington: Government
Printing Office, 1885) p. 50, via Google Books.
21. Colonel James A. Moss, *Army Paperwork: A Practical Working Guide in Army Administration* (Menasha, WI:
George Banta Publishing Co., 1917) p. 21, via Google Books.
22. Samuel Hynes, *A War Imagined: The First World War and English Culture* (New York: Atheneum, 1991) p. 296.
23. D. H. Lawrence, Letter to Dollie Radford, June 29, 1916, *The Collected Letters of D. H. Lawrence*, vol. 1, Harry
T. Moore, ed. (London: Heinemann, 1962) p. 456. Lawrence spent a single night in a barracks before being
exempted from military service. In a letter to Amy Lowell, he described both the horror and glamour of the
experience, recalling ancient archetypes of martial glamour and camaraderie: "The whole thing is abhorrent to
me—even the camaraderie, that is so glamorous—the Achilles and Patroclus business. The spirit, the pure spirit
of militarism is sheer death to a nature that is at all constructive or social-creative. . . . How Aldington will stand
it I don't know. But I can tell that the glamour is getting hold of him: the 'now we're all men together' business,
the kind of love that was between Achilles and Patroclus. And if once that lays hold of a man, then farewell to
that man forever, as an independent or constructive soul." D. H. Lawrence, Letter to Amy Lowell, August 23,
1916, *The Letters of D. H. Lawrence: Volume: 2 June 1913–October 1916*, George J. Zytaruk and James T. Boulton,
ed. (Cambridge: Cambridge University Press, 2002) p. 644.
24. Frederick Palmer, "The Children Pay," *Collier's*, November 12, 1921, p. 23.
25. Brett Arends, "Tesla Motors: IPO Fueled by Glamour," WSJ.com, June 15, 2010, http://online.wsj.com/article
/SB10001424052748704009804575309142582894892.html.
26. This point was made explicitly on the project's website, which featured a soundtrack of city noises and photos of traffic, garbage, and graffiti. After the bursting of the real-estate bubble in 2008, neither condo project
did well. Initially, only 72 of Rector Square's 304 units sold and its developer settled a fraud suit involving
the building's reserve fund. Although more popular and less controversial, the Metropolitan initially sold only
about half its available units, later putting some up for auction. Sara Polsky, "Rector Square's Unsold Units Find
Only One Taker at Auction," *Curbed New York*, November 17, 2010, http://ny.curbed.com/archives/2010/11
/17/rector_squares_unsold_units_find_only_one_taker_at_auction.php. Sara Polsky, "Developer Loses Battery
Park City Hell Building Fund Suit," *Curbed New York*, May 27, 2011, http://ny.curbed.com/archives/2011/05/27
/developer_loses_battery_park_city_hell_building_fund_suit.php. Jake Mooney, "In Battery Park City, Resold,
Renovated, and Ready for Sale," *New York Times*, May 3, 2012, http://www.nytimes.com/2012/05/06/realestate
/battery-park-city-a-new-lease-on-life-for-condo.html?_r=2&partner=rss&emc=rss&. See also http://ny.curbed
.com/tags/rector-square. Steve Brown, "July Auction Scheduled for 35 Downtown Dallas Condos at the Metropolitan," *Dallas Morning News*, June 29, 2010, http://www.dallasnews.com/business/headlines/20100628-July
-auction-scheduled-for-35-downtown-6612.ece. "Metropolitan Condo Auction in Dallas," *Fort Worth Forum*,
http://www.fortwortharchitecture.com/forum/index.php?showtopic=4191.
27. Alain de Botton, *The Art of Travel* (London: Penguin Books, 2002) pp. 8–9.
28. This discussion draws on Virginia Postrel, "The Perils of Obama," TheAtlantic.com, April 3, 2008, http://
www.theatlantic.com/magazine/archive/2008/04/the-peril-of-obama/6778/?single_page=true, and Virginia Postrel,

"Obama's Glamour Can't Fix His Charisma Deficit," *Bloomberg View*, August 4, 2011, http://www.bloomberg.com/news/2011-08-05/obama-s-glamour-can-t-fix-his-charisma-deficit-virginia-postrel.html.

29. "Obama Practices Looking-Off-into-Future Pose," *Onion*, May 28, 2008, p. 1, http://www.theonion.com/content/news/obama_practices_looking_off_into.

30. Ben Wallace-Wells, "Destiny's Child," *Rolling Stone Commemorative Edition*, p. 14, originally published February 22, 2007, http://www.rollingstone.com/politics/story/13390609/campaign_08_the_radical_roots_of_barack_obama.

31. Howard Kurtz, "Obama? So Handsome, and Probably Delicious," *Washington Post*, October 30, 2006, p. C1, http://www.washingtonpost.com/wp-dyn/content/article/2006/10/29/AR2006102900916.html.

32. Barack Obama, *The Audacity of Hope: Thoughts on Reclaiming the American Dream* (New York: Vintage Books, 2006) p. 49.

33. Matt Negrin, "In Memoriam: The Old Obama, Who Wanted to Bring People Together," ABC News, May 23, 2012, http://abcnews.go.com/Politics/OTUS/memoriam-obama-wanted-bring-people/story?id=16407876&fb_ref=.T707NdQNMvM.like&fb_source=home_multiline#.UNZm5onjk5-. One interesting indicator of the change in enthusiasm was the difference in merchandise sales on the website CafePress, which lets the public upload designs for such items as T-shirts and coffee mugs. In the first six months of 2008, CafePress's sales of campaign-related items were 86 percent pro-Obama. In the first six months of 2012, by contrast, anti-Obama merchandise accounted for 55 percent of sales, with pro-Obama items only 45 percent—even though the president went on to win a solid reelection victory. Heather Mills, "CafePress Pro vs. Anti-Obama Merchandise Sales in 2008 and Today," press release, July 19, 2012.

34. Jim Lewis, "Face Forward," *W*, April 2012, p. 139.

35. Alice T. Friedman, *American Glamour and the Evolution of Modern Architecture* (New Haven: Yale University Press, 2010) p. 7.

36. On décor, see Virginia Postrel, "Glamorous Places: Tuscany or Paris," *Deep Glamour*, March 9, 2009, http://www.deepglamour.net/deep_glamour/2009/03/look-at-all-these-tuscan-makeovers-on-hgtv-heres-the-parisian-competition.html. *Under the Tuscan Sun* was on the *New York Times* paperback bestseller list for 144 weeks, making its last appearance on March 7, 2004. *Eat, Pray, Love* was on the list for 222 weeks, making its last appearance on May 29, 2011. Greg Cowles, *New York Times Book Review*, e-mail to the author, December 24, 2012.

37. Institute of International Education, "Open Doors Data: U.S. Study Abroad: Leading Destinations," http://www.iie.org/Research-and-Publications/Open-Doors/Data/US-Study-Abroad/Leading-Destinations. (As of May 2013, the latest data were for 2011.)

38. Jane Wilkie, *Confessions of an Ex–Fan Magazine Writer* (Garden City, NY: Doubleday, 1981) p. v.

39. Jay Lindsay, "JFK Moon Mission Tape Reveals Inner Doubts about Space Program," *Huffington Post*, May 25, 2011, http://www.huffingtonpost.com/2011/05/25/jfk-moon-mission_n_866715.html. Kennedy made the comment in a September 18, 1963, conversation with NASA administrator James Webb.

40. Manolo the Shoeblogger, "DG Q&A: The Manolo," *Deep Glamour*, October 29, 2008, http://www.deepglamour.net/deep_glamour/2008/10/dg-qa-manolo-the-shoeblogger.html.

41. On the space program: Guy Gugliotta, "NASA Chief to Oust 20," *Washington Post*, June 1, 2005, p. A1, http://www.washingtonpost.com/wp-dyn/content/article/2005/06/10/AR2005061001911.html. On engineering: Alex Mayhew-Smith, "How to Tackle the U.K. Skills Shortfall," *Electronic News*, October 2, 2000, p. 24, and Stephanie Gordon, "Pace Seeking 200 Staff," *Electronics Times*, July 10, 2000, p. 1. On high-energy particle physics: David Dickson, "New Machine Sparks Rivalries at CERN," *Science*, June 16, 1989, p. 1,257. On cruises: Harry Basch, "Traveling in Style," *Los Angeles Times Magazine*, March 20, 1988, Section 2, p. 38. On department stores: Suzanne Slesin, "Thespian Doings in Style," *New York Times*, April 10, 1990, p. B-5, http://www.nytimes.com/1990/04/10/style/thespian-doings-in-style.html, and *HFD*, September 21, 1992, p. 10. On air travel: Virginia Postrel, "Up, Up, and Away," *Atlantic*, January/February 2007, pp. 159–61, http://www.theatlantic.com/magazine/archive/2007/01/up-up-and-away/5547/.

42. "Glamour by Hurrell," *U.S. Camera*, January 1942, p. 25.

43. Isaac Mizrahi, "All the Things We Like as Human Beings Are Either Immoral, Illegal, or Fattening," *Harper's Bazaar*, March 2003, p. 236.

Icon THE AVIATOR

1. An earlier version of this discussion appeared as Virginia Postrel, "High in the Sunlit Silence," *Reason Online*, December 22, 2004, http://www.reason.com/news/show/32861.html.
2. Robert Wohl, *A Passion for Wings: Aviation and the Western Imagination 1908–1918* (New Haven: Yale University Press, 1994) p. 282.
3. Philip D. Caine, *Eagles of the RAF* (Washington, DC: National Defense University Press, 1991) p. 148. David Keen, education officer, Royal Air Force Museum, interview with the author, December 2004.
4. Gladys M. Cripps, "To C.A.L.," in *The Spirit of St. Louis: One Hundred Poems*, Charles Vale, ed. (New York: George H. Doran Co., 1927) p. 73.
5. Elizabeth Sampson, "The American Eagle," in *The Spirit of St. Louis*, p. 210.
6. Robert Wohl, *The Spectacle of Flight: Aviation and the Western Imagination, 1920–1950* (New Haven: Yale University Press, 2005) pp. 25–26.
7. On Earhart's image making, see Kristen Lubben and Erin Barnett, eds., *Amelia Earhart: Image and Icon* (New York: International Center of Photography, 2007).
8. J. Todd Moye, *Freedom Flyers: The Tuskegee Airmen of World War II* (New York: Oxford University Press, 2010) p. 40.
9. Robert Wohl, *The Spectacle of Flight*, p. 65.
10. Local academics have sought unsuccessfully to have the street renamed for the physicist and Nobel laureate Enrico Fermi, who fled Fascist Italy for Chicago. Deirdre McCloskey, e-mail to the author, August 1, 2012. "Naming Wrongs: Rename Balbo Drive," *Chicago Tribune*, June 27, 2011, http://articles.chicagotribune.com /2011-06-27/news/ct-edit-balbo-20110627_1_wrongs-balbo-drive-fascists.
11. Robert Wohl, *The Spectacle of Flight*, p. 5.
12. Scott W. Palmer, interview with the author, December 8, 2004. Scott W. Palmer, *Dictatorship of the Air: Aviation Culture and the Fate of Modern Russia* (New York: Cambridge University Press, 2006) pp. 144–52.
13. The movie's official English title is the less glamorous *Sky Fighters*.

Icon SMOKING

1. Judy Law, "One Polite Smoker Takes on the Zealots," *Newsweek*, May 2, 2005, p. 15.
2. Elizabeth Wilson, *Bohemians: The Glamorous Outcasts* (New Brunswick, NJ: Rutgers University Press, 2000) p. 37.
3. Ayn Rand, *Atlas Shrugged* (New York: Signet, 1957) p. 65.
4. Simon Mills, "Ban Club," *Tatler*, March 2008, pp. 125–26.
5. Katie Roiphe, "On 'Mad Men,' the Allure of Messy Lives," *New York Times*, August 1, 2010, Sunday Styles, p. 1, http://www.nytimes.com/2010/08/01/fashion/01Cultural.html.
6. Tamara Abraham, "Facing the Muse: 'Nervous' Lady Gaga Does Nicola Formichetti Proud in Modelling Debut on Thierry Mugler Catwalk," *Mail Online*, March 3, 2011, http://www.dailymail.co.uk/femail/article-1362369 /Lady-Gaga-does-stylist-Nicola-Formichetti-proud-Thierry-Mugler-catwalk.html.
7. Jess Cartner-Morley, "Kate Moss Smokes on the Catwalk and Steals the Show at Louis Vuitton," *Guardian*, March 9, 2011, http://www.guardian.co.uk/lifeandstyle/2011/mar/09/kate-moss-smokes-catwalk/print. Euan Ferguson, "Why Is Smoking Back in Fashion?" *Observer*, April 3, 2011, http://www.guardian.co.uk/society/2011 /apr/03/smoking-health/print.

TWO: INARTICULATE LONGINGS

1. John Berger, *Ways of Seeing* (London: Penguin Books, 1972) pp. 129–48. "Ways of Seeing (final episode—advertising) ¼," video uploaded March 9, 2008, http://www.youtube.com/watch?v=mmgGT3th_oI.

2. Kanye West and Jay Z, "Murder to Excellence," 2011.

3. Gladys M. Cripps, "To C.A.L.," in *The Spirit of St. Louis: One Hundred Poems*, Charles Vale, ed. (New York: George H. Doran Co., 1927) p. 73.

4. Naomi Wolf, "The Power of Angelina," *Harper's Bazaar*, July 2009, pp. 40–44, http://www.harpersbazaar.com /magazine/cover/angelina-jolie-essay-0709?click=pp.

5. Margaret Farrand Thorp, *America at the Movies* (New Haven: Yale University Press, 1939) p. 65.

6. Valerie Steele, "Fashion," in *Glamour: Fashion, Industrial Design, Architecture*, Joseph Rosa, ed. (San Francisco and New Haven: San Francisco Museum of Modern Art/Yale University Press, 2004) p. 42.

7. Harriet Quick, "Glamour Amour," *British Vogue*, November 2004, p. 102.

8. Emily Eakin, "Jackie's Closet," *Slate*, May 10, 2001, http://www.slate.com/id/105810.

9. Manohla Dargis, "Glamour Lives in Chinese Films," *New York Times*, December 5, 2004, Section 2, p. 1, http:// www.nytimes.com/2004/12/05/movies/05darg.html?ex=1226845203&ei=1&en=956c91a37a85c0c5.

10. Margaret Farrand Thorp, *America at the Movies*, pp. 5–6.

11. For a discussion of this topic not limited to glamour, see Virginia Postrel, "The Truth about Beauty," *Atlantic*, March 2007, pp. 125–27, http://www.theatlantic.com/magazine/archive/2007/03/the-truth-about-beauty/5620/.

12. Annette Kuhn, *An Everyday Magic: Cinema and Cultural Memory* (London: I. B. Tauris, 2002) pp. 231–32.

13. Boyé Lafayette De Mente, *The Japanese Have a Word for It: The Complete Guide to Japanese Thought and Culture* (Chicago: Passport Books, 1997) pp. 30–31. Karen Kelsky, *Women on the Verge: Japanese Women, Western Dreams* (Durham, NC: Duke University Press, 2001) p. 26. Thanks also to Sean Kinsell.

14. Lois Ardery, "She Wants It but She Doesn't Know It—Yet!" *J. Walter Thompson News Bulletin*, December 1924, pp. 18–21.

15. The dream of Gil Pender, the protagonist of Woody Allen's film *Midnight in Paris* (2011).

16. How this glamour plays out in posters, postcards, and other memorabilia is interestingly developed by Christopher Pinney, "Notes on the Epidemiology of Allure," in David Blamey and Robert D'Souza, eds., *Living Pictures: Perspectives on the Film Poster in India* (London: Open Editions, 2005) pp. 45–54, http://www.christopherpinney. com/Text_in_pdf/LivingPictures.pdf.

17. Brian Chase, interview with the author, July 4, 2006, quoted in Virginia Postrel, "Superhero Worship," *Atlantic*, October 2006, p. 142, http://www.theatlantic.com/doc/200610/postrel-superhero.

18. Rebecca Sullivan, *Visual Habits: Nuns, Feminism, and American Postwar Popular Culture* (Toronto: University of Toronto Press, 2005) pp. 61, 220. See also Rebecca Sullivan, "Nuns: Images, Icons and Identity," presented at Sisters Online, June 19, 2004.

19. Mary Gordon, "Women of God," *Atlantic*, January 2002, pp. 57–91, http://www.theatlantic.com/doc/200201 /gordon.

20. John Berger, *Ways of Seeing*, p. 133.

21. Kevin Curran, "Why I Love *Star Trek*, Essay #4: Kevin Curran," *Treknobabble*, January 21, 2010, http://www .treknobabble.net/2010/01/why-i-love-star-trek-essay-4-kevin.html.

22. Flint Mitchell, response to *Star Trek* Fan Survey, January 9, 2011. During the first three months of 2011, I conducted an online survey of *Star Trek* fans, receiving 1,444 completed surveys. The conclusions here are drawn from those survey results. A copy of the full survey may be found at http://vpostrel.com/Star_Trek_Fans_survey.pdf.

23. Anonymous, response to *Star Trek* Fan Survey, January 9, 2011.

24. Grant McCracken, *Culture and Consumption* (Bloomington, IN: Indiana University Press, 1988) p. 106.

25. Meghan Daum, *Life Would Be Perfect If I Lived in That House* (New York: Alfred A. Knopf, 2010) p. 47. The real-estate blog ICouldBeHappyHere.com picks up the same theme.

26. Grant McCracken, *Culture and Consumption*, p. 109.

27. Joan Kron, interview with the author, April 5, 2012.

28. Juliet McMains, *Glamour Addiction: Inside the American Ballroom Dance Industry* (Middletown, CT: Wesleyan University Press, 2006) pp. xvi–xvii.

29. Colin Campbell, *The Romantic Ethic and the Spirit of Modern Consumerism* (Oxford: Basil Blackwell, 1987) pp. 78, 84, 205.

30. Joanna Jeffreys, fashion manager at Harvey Nichols, quoted in Sarah Harris, "Does Your Wardrobe Match Your Life?" *British Vogue*, November 2007, p. 168.

31. Colin Campbell, *The Romantic Ethic and the Spirit of Modern Consumerism*, pp. 86–87.

32. Jens Beckert, "The Transcending Power of Goods: Imaginative Value in the Economy," Max Planck Institute for the Study of Societies, MPIfG Discussion Paper 10/4, April 2010, p. 16, http://www.mpifg.de/pu/mpifg_dp/dp10-4.pdf.

33. Simon Doonan, *Beautiful People: My Family and Other Glamorous Varmints* (New York: Simon & Schuster, 2005) pp. 6, 11, 15–16.

Icon THE PRINCESS

1. Jenna Goudreau, "Disney Princess Tops List of the 20 Best-Selling Entertainment Products," *Forbes*, September 17, 2012, http://www.forbes.com/sites/jennagoudreau/2012/09/17/disney-princess-tops-list-of-the-20-best-selling-entertainment-products/.

2. Andy Mooney, then-president and now chairman of Disney Consumer Products, quoted in Peggy Orenstein, "What's Wrong with Cinderella?" *New York Times Magazine*, December 24, 2006, http://www.nytimes.com/2006/12/24/magazine/24princess.t.html.

3. Google search for "Every little girl dreams of being a princess" with quotation marks, December 28, 2012.

4. American Gas Association ad, *Saturday Evening Post*, April 15, 1944, p. 75.

5. "Princesse Marie de Bourbon of Spain Tells How She Cares for Her Flower-like Skin," *Vogue,* March 1925, Emergence of Advertising On-Line Project, John W. Hartman Center for Sales, Advertising & Marketing History, Duke University Rare Book, Manuscript, and Special Collections Library, http://library.duke.edu/digital collections/eaa.P0193/pg.1/.

6. "The Wedding Veil of the Princess Rospigliosi's Great Grandmother," *Good Housekeeping,* May 1925, Emergence of Advertising On-Line Project, John W. Hartman Center for Sales, Advertising & Marketing History, Duke University Rare Book, Manuscript, and Special Collections Library, http://library.duke.edu/digitalcollections/eaa_L0081/. By the time this particular ad ran, the princess was dead. "Milestones," *Time*, November 17, 1924, http://www.time.com/time/magazine/article/0,9171,719425,00.html. "Americans Who Marry Italians," *New York Times*, May 5, 1907, p. C3.

7. Tina Brown, *The Diana Chronicles* (New York: Doubleday, 2007) pp. 75, 163.

8. Alexandra Shulman, "A Piece of Kate," *British Vogue*, April 2007, p. 242.

9. Michael Chabon, *The Amazing Adventures of Kavalier & Clay* (New York: Picador, 2000) p. 77.

10. Daniel Lin, e-mail to the author, September 1, 2011. Lin's daughter moved from playing princess at three years old, to incorporating superhero elements (magic spells, laser beams, Spider-Man web shooters) in her princess identities at five years old, to re-creating her own version of Batgirl and learning all about Marvel superheroes and villains at six. "Now," writes Lin, "whenever we have playtime, we each pick an Avenger and run around defending ourselves from villains (played by her stuffed animals)." Sarah Skwire, e-mail to the author, October 5, 2011: "Last night my 6 year old informed me, 'I'm not really so much into princesses anymore. Now I'm more into superheroes!'"

11. Marina DelVecchio, "The Disney Princess Fallacy," *Marinagraphy*, November 29, 2010, http://marinagraphy.com/princess-prophecy/.

12. Sasha Brown-Worsham, "Enough with the Princess Hate!" *The Stir*, October 31, 2010, http://thestir.cafemom.com/toddler/111733/enough_with_the_princess_hate.

13. A. O. Scott, "The Darker Side of the Story," *New York Times*, May 31, 2012, http://movies.nytimes.com/2012/06/01/movies/snow-white-and-the-huntsman-with-kristen-stewart.html.

14. S, comment on Lynn Harris, "Raising Girls in Princess Culture: Does It Really Affect Girls' Gender Roles?" Babble.com, October 27, 2010, http://www.babble.com/kid/child-development/defending-princess-dressup-parties-girls-gender-roles/.

Icon WIND TURBINES

1. Felicia Morton, e-mail to the author, November 5, 2010.
2. Sandra Santos, Etsy conversation with the author, November 2, 2010.
3. "MSNBC | Lean Forward," video uploaded October 27, 2010, http://www.youtube.com/watch?v=4CQAcewckXo.
4. Thomas Dolby, "Windfarm," *Official Thomas Dolby Blog*, October 17, 2010, http://blog.thomasdolby.com/?p=1245.
5. Al Gore, *Earth in the Balance: Ecology and the Human Spirit* (Boston: Houghton Mifflin, 1992) p. 274.
6. Tom Zeller Jr., "For Those Near, the Miserable Hum of Clean Energy," *New York Times*, October 5, 2010, http://www.nytimes.com/2010/10/06/business/energy-environment/06noise.html. Catherine Fahy, "Art as Political Statement: Lou Guarnaccia Publicly Protests the Proposed Nantucket Sound Wind Farm—by Altering a Painting," *Inquirer and Mirror*, http://www.ack.net/965iminthisissuestory.html. "An Artist's Nightmare" (image), http://www.windstop.org/towerphotos.html. Justin Good, "The Aesthetics of Wind Energy," *Human Ecology Review*, 2006, pp. 76–89, http://www.humanecologyreview.org/pastissues/her131/good.pdf.

THREE: DREAMS OF FLIGHT AND TRANSFORMATION AND ESCAPE

1. Michael Chabon, *The Amazing Adventures of Kavalier & Clay*, pp. 6–7. The character's specific glamorous dreams include "transmuting himself into a major American novelist, or a famous smart person, like Clifton Fadiman, or perhaps into a heroic doctor; or developing through practice and sheer force of will, the mental powers that would give him a preternatural control over the hearts and minds of men. . . . But like most natives of Brooklyn, Sammy considered himself a realist, and in general his escape plans centered around the attainment of fabulous sums of money."
2. "The Longing for Transcendence," *Manolo's Shoe Blog*, January 27, 2011, http://shoeblogs.com/2011/01/27/the-longing-for-transcendence/.
3. Art Eddy, "The Top 10 Air Jordans of All Time: A RETROspective," March 31, 2010, *The Bachelor Guy*, http://www.thebachelorguy.com/the-top-10-air-jordans-of-all-time-a-retrospective.html. Eddy was married in a pair of Air Jordan XIs.
4. Darcy Kuronen, "An Interview with Ralph Lauren," in Museum of Fine Arts, Boston, *Speed, Style, and Beauty: Cars from the Ralph Lauren Collection* (Boston: MFA Publications, 2005) p. xi.
5. The 1931 film *Possessed* has a completely different story from the 1947 movie by the same name, which also starred Joan Crawford. Interestingly, the 1920 play on which the 1931 movie was based, titled *The Mirage*, takes a less positive view. The hometown boyfriend is the protagonist, who comes to New York only to find that the woman he nursed a love for has changed irrevocably. The script has been lost but a review records that "the man from Erie cannot marry the girl who went to New York because in the big city she yielded to the blandishments of vice and became the mistress of a rich rogue." Another reviewer criticized the play for perpetrating "the mid-Victorians' assumptions" and condemning as a fallen woman a "soul whom degradation could not corrupt." Heywood Broun, "On the New York Stage," *Collier's*, October 30, 1920, p. 19. Ludwig Lewisohn, "Trade-Goods," *Nation*, October 20, 1920, p. 458.
6. Yi-Fu Tuan, *Escapism* (Baltimore: The Johns Hopkins University Press, 1998) pp. xiii, 6.
7. Gregory Benford, *The Wonderful Future That Never Was: Flying Cars, Mail Delivery by Parachute, and Other Predictions from the Past* (New York: Hearst, 2010) p. 13.
8. Sally Alexander, "Becoming a Woman in London in the 1920s and '30s," in *Becoming a Woman and Other Essays in 19th and 20th Century Feminist History* (New York: New York University Press, 1995) p. 205.
9. Jacqueline Trescott, "The Publishing World's Black Light," *Washington Post*, August 9, 2005, p. C-1. http://www.washingtonpost.com/wpdyn/content/article/2005/08/08/AR2005080801692.html.
10. E. Franklin Frazier, *Black Bourgeoisie* (New York: The Free Press, 1957) p. 174.
11. Jacqueline Trescott, "The Publishing World's Black Light."
12. Margaret Farrand Thorp, *America at the Movies*, p. 129.

13. Adam Nichols, "Black Stars Rise to Top at Box Office," *New York Daily News*, January 30, 2005, http://www.nydailynews.com/archives/news/black-stars-rise-top-box-office-article-1.584025.

14. In December 2012, Denzel Washington topped the list when the Harris Poll conducted its annual survey asking Americans to name their favorite movie star. He had been in the top ten in all but three years since the survey began in 1994. The Harris Poll, "Denzel Washington Flies to Number One and Is America's Favorite Movie Star," press release, January 23, 2013, http://www.harrisinteractive.com/NewsRoom/HarrisPolls/tabid/447/mid/1508/articleId/1141/ctl/ReadCustom%20Default/Default.aspx. Virginia Postrel, "Why You Want to Escape with Denzel Washington," *Bloomberg View*, February 21, 2013, http://www.bloomberg.com/news/2013-02-21/why-you-want-to-escape-with-denzel-washington.html.

15. Susie Boyt, "The Fabric of My Life," *Financial Times*, September 26, 2008, http://www.ft.com/cms/s/2/25e71d44-8b59-11dd-b634-0000779fd18c.html?nclick_check=1. Angus "Andrea" Grieve-Smith, commenting as grvsmith on Virginia Postrel, "Terror Is Glamour," Deep Glamour, September 16, 2008, http://www.deepglamour.net/deep_glamour/2011/05/terror-is-glamour-reposted.html #comment-6a00e553bc52568834010534a95fc1970b. Grieve-Smith has a related blog post at http://transblog.grieve-smith.com/?p=8.

16. Nella Larsen, *Quicksand and Passing*, Deborah E. McDowell, ed. (New Brunswick, NJ: Rutgers University Press, 1986) pp. 56–57.

17. Judith Brown, *Glamour in Six Dimensions: Modernism and the Radiance of Form* (Ithaca, NY: Cornell University Press, 2009) p. 140.

18. Andy Warhol, *The Philosophy of Andy Warhol: (From A to B and Back Again)* (San Diego, CA: Harcourt, 1975) p. 55.

19. Bob Colacello, *Holy Terror: Andy Warhol Close Up* (New York: HarperCollins, 1990) p. 88.

20. Anne C. Heller, *Ayn Rand and the World She Made* (New York: Anchor Books, 2009) p. 306.

21. Caitlin Flanagan, "The Glory of Oprah," *Atlantic*, December 2011, pp. 106–18, http://www.theatlantic.com/magazine/archive/2011/12/the-glory-of-oprah/8725/. "Mary Tyler Moore Surprise," video uploaded March 7, 2011, http://www.youtube.com/watch?v=oPd77roTra4.

22. Alicia Drake, *The Beautiful Fall*, pp. 227–28. Bertrand du Vignaud, "Interview with Karl Lagerfeld" (translated by Alicia Drake), in *Collection Lagerfeld* (catalog of sales held at Monaco, April 28-29, 2000) (New York and Monaco: Christie's, 2000) p. 17.

23. Alicia Drake, *The Beautiful Fall*, p. 228.

24. Karl Lagerfeld, "Introduction," in *Collection Lagerfeld*, p. 15.

25. Adam Smith, *The Theory of Moral Sentiments* (Indianapolis, IN: Liberty Fund, 1982) p. 181.

Icon THE GOLDEN STATE

1. KD Kurutz and Gary F. Kurutz, *California Calls You: The Art of Promoting the Golden State 1870 to 1940* (Sausalito, CA: Windgate Press, 2000) pp. 7, 11.

2. Thomas S. Hines, *Richard Neutra: And the Search for Modern Architecture* (New York: Rizzoli, 2005) p. 44.

3. Thomas S. Hines, *Richard Neutra: And the Search for Modern Architecture*, p. 99.

4. Katy Perry, "California Gurls," 2010.

5. Samihah Azim, "The 'Glamour' of Silicon Valley and Technology," Forbes.com, July 12, 2012, http://www.forbes.com/sites/women2/2012/07/12/the-glamour-of-silicon-valley-and-technology/.

6. Joel Splotchy, "California," *Joel on Software*, October 5, 2007, http://www.joelonsoftware.com/items/2007/10/05.html.

7. Phil McNamara, "The California—for China, Russia and beyond," *Car*, July 2008, pp. 22–23.

8. Chris Dannen, "Why Does Tesla Get All the Love? It's Selling California, Not Cars," FastCompany.com, March 27, 2009, http://www.fastcompany.com/blog/chris-dannen/techwatch/tesla-selling-cars-or-california. Some Tesla photos were obviously not taken on the PCH, because they have wind turbines in the background.

9. YouTube user CTSV4MEE, "K-Swiss 'Awesome Day' commercial," video uploaded March 17, 2010, http://www.youtube.com/watch?v=QrfL6LNzqA0.

Icon THE MAKEOVER

1. Eddie Senz, "Make the Most of Yourself," *Mademoiselle*, January 1937, p. 25. "Let's Make Up," *Mademoiselle*, December 1936, p. 54.
2. Diane Gardner, interview with the author, September 6, 2012.
3. *Extreme Makeover*, "Karen & Sandra," first aired May 14, 2003.
4. Barbara Phillips, "Cinderella," *Mademoiselle*, November 1936, pp. 22–24, 56–57, 60.
5. Elizabeth A. Ford and Deborah C. Mitchell, *The Makeover in Movies: Before and After in Hollywood Films, 1941–2002* (Jefferson, NC: McFarland & Co., 2004) p. 131.
6. Meg Cabot, *The Princess Diaries* (New York: HarperCollins, 2002) p. 115.
7. *The Twilight Zone*, "Number 12 Looks Just Like You," first aired January 24, 1964.
8. *What Not to Wear*, "Wear Are They Now: Emily," http://tlc.howstuffworks.com/tv/what-not-to-wear/videos/wear-are-they-now-emily.htm.

FOUR: THE ART THAT CONCEALS ART

1. Annette Sharp et al., "Fashion Confidential: Our Runway Review of 2010," *Daily Telegraph*, January 1, 2011, p. 24 (Blake Lively). Aaron Gill, "The Showgirl," *W*, July 2004, p. 106 (Catherine Zeta-Jones). Glynis Traill-Nash, "Style Icons out of the Closet," *Sydney Sun Herald*, October 7, 2007, Section S, p. 10 (Cary Grant). Ian Parker, "Somebody Has to Be in Control," *New Yorker*, April 14, 2008, p. 40, http://www.newyorker.com/reporting/2008/04/14/080414fa_fact_parker (George Clooney).
2. Rachel Dodes, "Dress Me, Kate! Modern Modesty à la Middleton," *Wall Street Journal*, February 16, 2011, p. D2, http://online.wsj.com/article/SB10001424052748704409004576146563072035774.html.
3. Noria Morales, "What I Want Now!" *Lucky*, July 2007, p. 47.
4. Vanessa Thorpe, "Snapshot of a Golden Era," *Observer*, April 24, 2005, Observer Escape Pages, p. 10, http://www.guardian.co.uk/travel/2005/apr/24/italy.observerescapesection1.
5. Robin Givhan, "Glamour, That Certain Something," *Washington Post*, February 17, 2008, p. M01, http://www.washingtonpost.com/wp-dyn/content/article/2008/02/15/AR2008021500837.html.
6. Baldassare Castiglione, *The Book of the Courtier,* Charles S. Singleton, trans. (Garden City, NY: Anchor, 1959) p. 43.
7. Diego Rodriguez, "Buff, Wax, Seal: Surface Integrity," *Deep Glamour*, September 8, 2008, http://www.deepglamour.net/deep_glamour/2008/09/lambo----what-d.html.
8. William Hazlitt, A. R. Waller, and Arnold Glover, eds., "On Beauty," February 4, 1816, in *The Collected Works of William Hazlitt: The Round Table. Characters of Shakespear's Plays. A Letter to William Gifford, Esq.* Volume 1 of *The Collected Works of William Hazlitt*, (London: J. R. Dent, 1902) p. 68.
9. Cameron Silver with Rebecca DiLiberto, *Decades: A Century of Fashion* (London: Bloomsbury, 2012) p. 9.
10. "Glamour by Hurrell," *U.S. Camera*, January 1942, p. 25.
11. Pamela Clarke Keogh, *Audrey Style* (New York: HarperCollins, 1999) p. 61.
12. John Cork and Bruce Scivally, *James Bond: The Legacy* (New York: Harry N. Abrams, 2002) p. 36.
13. Sarah Bradford, *Princess Grace* (New York: Stein & Day, 1984) pp. 46–47.
14. Graham McCann, *Cary Grant: A Class Apart* (London: Fourth Estate, 1996) pp. 150–51.
15. Juliet McMains, *Glamour Addiction: Inside the American Ballroom Dance Industry* (Middletown, CT: Wesleyan University Press, 2006) p. 79.
16. Nick Carson, "If It Looks Over-Designed, It's Under-Designed," http://ncarson.files.wordpress.com/2007/01/ten4-jonathanive.pdf.
17. Adam Tschorn, "Killer Suits," *Los Angeles Times*, November 16, 2008, p. P4. The Daniel Craig versions of Bond have largely eliminated the character's grace and mystery, destroying his glamour. Virginia Postrel, "James Bond without the Glamour," *Deep Glamour*, November 22, 2008, http://www.deepglamour.net/deep_glamour/2008/11/james-bond-without-the-glamour.html.

18. Retouching artist James Sharp did much of the work on Hurrell's photos at MGM. Mark A. Vieira, *Hurrell's Hollywood Portraits: The Chapman Collection* (New York: Harry N. Abrams, 1997) p. 51.

19. Kay and Digby Diehl, *Life: Remembering Grace* (New York: Time Inc. Home Entertainment Books, 2007) p. 20.

20. Kay and Digby Diehl, *Life: Remembering Grace*, p. 18. Bob Adelman, e-mail to the author, April 5, 2011.

21. Andy Warhol, *The Philosophy of Andy Warhol (From A to B and Back Again)* p. 62. To create his society portraits, Warhol first heavily manipulated the forty-inch-square negatives he made from Polaroids. Bob Colacello writes, "What Andy did to the negative was more like plastic surgery, though the end result was magical: beasts turned into beauties. He simply took scissors and snipped out double chins, bumps in noses, bags under eyes, the shadows of pimples, the blackness of beards. His most elderly clients were left, like Marilyn, like Elvis, with eyes, nostrils, lips, and jawlines. 'God,' I said, as I watched him attack a whole neck and scissor away seventy years of wrinkles, 'is that how you do it?'" Bob Colacello, *Holy Terror: Andy Warhol Close Up*, pp. 88–89.

22. Michael Casey, *Che's Afterlife: The Legacy of an Image* (New York: Vintage Books, 2009) p. 124.

23. Julius Shulman, *Architecture and Its Photography*, Peter Gössel, ed. (Köln: Taschen, 2001) p. 18. Virginia Postrel, "The Iconographer," *Atlantic*, November 2006, pp. 136–39, http://www.theatlantic.com/magazine/archive/2006 /11/the-iconographer/5288/.

24. Richard J. Neutra, "The Photographer and the Architect," in Julius Shulman, *Photographing Architecture and Interiors* (Glendale, CA: Balcony Press, 2000) pp. vii, ix. Donald Albrecht, *Designing Dreams: Modern Architecture in the Movies* (Santa Monica, CA: Hennessey & Ingalls, 1986) p. 86.

25. "Glamorized Houses," *Life*, April 11, 1949, pp. 146–48.

26. Talya Minsberg, "What the U.S. Can—and Can't—Learn from Israel's Ban on Ultra-Thin Models," The Atlantic.com, May 9, 2012, http://www.theatlantic.com/international/archive/2012/05/what-the-us-can-and -cant-learn-from-israels-ban-on-ultra-thin-models/256891/. Jessica Siegel, "The Lash Stand: Will New Attitudes and Regulatory Oversight Hit Delete on Some Photo Retouching in Print Ads?" *Adweek*, May 29, 2012, http://www.adweek.com/news/press/lash-stand-140785.

27. Jessica Coen, "Why You Must See Unretouched Images, and Why You Must See Them Repeatedly," *Jezebel*, August 23, 2010, http://jezebel.com/5619903/why-you-must-see-unretouched-images-and-why-you-must-see -them-repeatedly. An archive of the site's articles on retouching is at http://jezebel.com/photoshopofhorrors. The Photoshop Disasters website chronicles mostly inept retouching: http://www.psdisasters.com/.

28. Jonathan K. Nelson and Richard J. Zeckhauser, *The Patron's Payoff: Conspicuous Commissions in Italian Renaissance Art* (Princeton, NJ: Princeton University Press, 2008) p. 99. Alessandro Tirana's portrait of Caterina de' Medici has since been lost.

29. Anne Hollander, "Fashion Art," in Aperture Foundation, *The Idealizing Vision: The Art of Fashion Photography* (New York: Aperture, 1991) p. 41.

30. Virginia Postrel, "DG Q&A: Interiors Stylist Adam Fortner," *Deep Glamour*, February 9, 2011, http://www .deepglamour.net/deep_glamour/2011/02/dg-qa-interiors-stylist-adam-fortner.html.

31. Sarah Skwire, "Déshabille," *Manolo's Shoe Blog*, March 30, 2011, http://shoeblogs.com/2011/03/30/deshabille/.

32. Lorraine Daston and Peter Galison, *Objectivity* (New York: Zone Books, 2007) pp. 55–113. The Albinus quotation appears on pp. 73–74.

33. Anne Hollander, *Moving Pictures* (Cambridge, MA: Harvard University Press, 1991) p. 213.

34. Tom Parrette, "Mad Men Gives Sixties a Branded Makeover," *AdRants*, September 24, 2009, http://www.adrants .com/2009/09/mad-men-gives-sixties-a-branded-makeover.php.

35. In 2011, the company made the metaphorical connection explicit with a new series of ads where the beer alone transports someone from an otherwise stressful setting—a crowded airplane, for example—to the beach. This "Find Your Beach" campaign was developed to offset the perception of some literal-minded consumers that Corona is a summertime beer to be drunk at the beach. Andrew Meyer, group creative director at Cramer-Krasselt, interview with the author's School of Visual Arts Branding MPS class, May 11, 2011. Meyer also confessed that one of Corona's signature glamorous tropes—showing actors only from behind as they face the ocean—came about originally to save money on talent fees.

36. Margaret Farrand Thorp, *America at the Movies* (New Haven: Yale University Press, 1939) p. 72.

37. Sharon Waxman, "The Lost Art of Saying Thank You; The Oscar Acceptance Speech: Off and Running at the Mouth," *Washington Post*, March 21, 1999, p. G-1, http://www.washingtonpost.com/wp-srv/style/movies/oscars /speeches.htm.

38. Tom Zimmerman, *Light and Illusion: The Hollywood Portraits of Ray Jones*, John Jones, ed. (Glendale, CA: Balcony Press, 1998) p. 29.

39. Ronald L. Davis, *The Glamour Factory: Inside Hollywood's Big Studio System* (Dallas, TX: Southern Methodist University Press, 1993) p. 214. Virginia Postrel, "Leaning Boards: Behind-the-Scenes Support for Classic Hollywood Costumes," *Deep Glamour*, July 2, 2011, http://www.deepglamour.net/deep_glamour/2011/07/leaning -boards-behind-the-scenes-support-for-classic-hollywood-costumes.html.

40. Simone de Beauvoir, *The Second Sex*, H.M. Parshley, trans. (New York: Vintage Books, 1989) p. 536.

41. Mary Shelley, *Frankenstein: Or the Modern Prometheus*, Maurice Hindle, ed. (London: Penguin, 2003) pp. 58–59.

42. According to its founder, the group had about 75,000 members and Facebook shut it down, claiming it violated a prohibition on "hateful groups." Mike Stout, founder, e-mail to the author, November 30, 2009.

43. "Smoking Is Very Glamorous," Victoria & Albert Museum collection, http://collections.vam.ac.uk/item/O76205 /poster-smoking-is-very-glamorous/.

44. *Saturday Night Live*, Season 4, Episode 6, first aired December 16, 1978, transcript http://snltranscripts.jt.org/78 /78iupdate.phtml.

Icon WIRELESSNESS

1. Loewy's most enduring designs were in fact not industrial but graphic, including logos for Lucky Strikes and Exxon.

2. Paola Antonelli, interview with the author, December 27, 2010.

3. Robin Ford, e-mail to the author, December 30, 2010. Ford originally made this remark in a lecture to visual media students.

4. Adam Fortner, interview with the author, January 4, 2011.

5. David Hall, interview with the author, April 2005, quoted in Virginia Postrel, "Let's Make Some Magic, with No Strings Attached," *New York Times*, May 4, 2005, http://www.nytimes.com/2005/05/04/technology/techspecial /04postrel.html.

6. Chris Taylor, "What Apple Hopes You Didn't Notice about iPad 2," CNN.com, March 3, 2011, http://www.cnn .com/2011/TECH/gaming.gadgets/03/03/missing.from.ipad2.taylor/index.html.

Icon THE SUPERHERO

1. Paul Levitz, *75 Years of DC Comics: The Art of Modern Mythmaking* (Los Angeles: Taschen, 2011) p. 692.

2. Robert Biswas-Diener, "Positive Psychology of Peter Parker," in *The Psychology of Superheroes: An Unauthorized Exploration*, Robin S. Rosenberg, with Jennifer Canzoneri, ed. (Dallas, TX: Benbella Books, 2008) p. 67.

3. Geoffrey O'Brien, "Nick Fury's Dream," in *Give Our Regards to the Atomsmashers: Writers on Comics*, Sean Howe, ed. (New York: Pantheon, 2004) p. 123.

4. Geoffrey O'Brien, "Nick Fury's Dream," p. 127.

5. Gerard Jones, *Men of Tomorrow: Geeks, Gangsters, and the Birth of the Comic Book* (New York: Basic Books, 2004) pp. 143, 145.

FIVE: LEAVE SOMETHING TO THE IMAGINATION

1. This was the slogan of a long-running advertising campaign, featuring celebrities in Foster Grant sunglasses, which ran through the 1960s and into the 1970s.

2. Once, in a crowded and not especially brightly lit terminal at the Los Angeles airport, my attention was caught by

the anomalous sight of a woman in dark sunglasses. It was Julia Louis-Dreyfus, then at the height of her fame as a star of *Seinfeld*. The sunglasses made her stand out in the crowd, but they also kept other travelers at a distance.

3. Lorenz Eitner, "The Open Window and the Storm-Tossed Boat: An Essay in the Iconography of Romanticism," *Art Bulletin*, December 1955, p. 286.

4. Carolina Herrera, "Age of Elegance," *New York*, August 25–September 1, 2003, p. 75.

5. Ben Brantley, "Whatever Happened to Mystery?" *New York Times*, July 16, 2010, Sunday Styles p. 1, http://www.nytimes.com/2010/07/18/fashion/18mystery.html.

6. Brian McCollum, "Where Have All the Rock Stars Gone?" *Journal News*, November 9, 2007, http://www.lohud.com/article/20071110/ENTERTAINMENT/711100311/Where-all-rock-stars-gone-. (This article originally appeared in the *Detroit Free Press*.)

7. Norman Zierold, *Garbo* (New York: Stein and Day, 1969) p. 91.

8. Alexandra Shulman, "A Piece of Kate," *British Vogue*, April 2007, p. 240. The quotation, which compresses observations in the article, is from the subhead.

9. Interviewed in the documentary *Kate! The Making of an Icon*, 2010.

10. Ralph Lauren, *Ralph Lauren* (New York: Rizzoli, 2007) p. 215.

11. Woody Allen, Cannes press conference, in Kendis Gibson, "Woody Allen Explores Fantasy World with 'Midnight in Paris,'" CBS News video uploaded May 19, 2011, http://www.youtube.com/watch?v=UwgBHBail04&feature=fvsr. In the film, however, Gil is never disillusioned. The Paris of the 1920s that he and the audience experience is exactly as he imagined. All the famous characters are caricatures: a bombastic Hemingway, a scatterbrained, depressive Zelda and love-smitten Scott Fitzgerald, a rhinoceros-obsessed Dalí, a misogynist Picasso, an encouraging, no-nonsense Gertrude Stein.

12. Geneviève Verseau, *Une Histoire de Paravent* (Paris: Somogy, 2005) jacket copy.

13. Carolyne Roehm interviewed by Deb Schwartz, "A Classical Touch," *Wall Street Journal*, December 10, 2010, p. W11, http://online.wsj.com/article/SB10001424052748704679204575646873628519124.html.

14. George Hurrell, text by Whitney Stine, *The Hurrell Style: 50 Years of Photographing Hollywood* (New York: John Day Co., 1976) p. 206. This quotation originally appeared in a 1976 gallery catalogue.

15. "Glamour by Hurrell," *U.S. Camera*, January 1942, p. 25.

16. Barbara Leaming, *Mrs. Kennedy: The Missing History of the Kennedy Years* (London: Weidenfeld & Nicolson, 2001) pp. 1–2.

17. Even when not wearing the funeral veil, Kennedy looks veiled in all of Warhol's images because of the effects of the silk screen.

18. Virginia Postrel, "Hearing Jackie (and Where to See Her Smoking)," *Deep Glamour*, February 2, 2011, http://www.deepglamour.net/deep_glamour/2011/02/hearing-jackie-kennedy-onassis-recordings-interview-smoking.html. When recordings of interviews Kennedy did with historian Arthur Schlesinger Jr. a few months after her husband's assassination were released in 2011, press reports focused on her most negative comments, portraying her as a mean-spirited gossip prone to what one critic termed her "determined triviality." Paula Marantz Cohen, "Mean Girl," *Smart Set*, October 5, 2011, http://www.thesmartset.com/article/article10051101.aspx. Janny Scott, "In Tapes, Candid Talk by Young Kennedy Widow," *New York Times*, September 11, 2011, http://www.nytimes.com/2011/09/12/us/12jackie.html?pagewanted=all. Susan Cheever, "Jackie's Enduring Mystique," *Newsweek*, September 17, 2011, http://www.thedailybeast.com/newsweek/2011/09/17/jackie-kennedy-tapes-show-us-what-we-lost.html.

19. Wayne Koestenbaum, *Jackie Under My Skin: Interpreting an Icon* (New York: Farrar, Straus and Giroux, 1995) p. 43.

20. Joe Klein, "Starting Over: Can Obama Revive His Agenda?" *Time*, February 1, 2010, pp. 28–29, http://www.time.com/time/politics/article/0,8599,1955401,00.html. Jess Cartner-Morley, "Kate Moss Smokes on the Catwalk and Steals the Show at Louis Vuitton," http://www.guardian.co.uk/lifeandstyle/2011/mar/09/kate-moss-smokes-catwalk/print. Jeff Greenwald, *Future Perfect: How* Star Trek *Conquered Planet Earth* (New York: Viking, 1998) p. 109, comparing James Bond and Spock. Also, Jeff Greenwald, "Obama Is Spock: It's Quite Logical," *Salon*, May 7, 2009, http://www.salon.com/ent/feature/2009/05/07/obama_spock.

21. Ruth Barton, *Hedy Lamarr: The Most Beautiful Woman in Film* (Lexington, KY: University of Kentucky Press, 2010) p. 6.

22. George Hurrell, text by Whitney Stine, *The Hurrell Style: 50 Years of Photographing Hollywood*, p. 139.

23. Oscar Wilde, *The Picture of Dorian Gray* (New York: Barnes & Noble Classics, 2003) p. 6.

24. Valerie Steele, "Édouard Manet: *Nana*," in *Impressionism, Fashion, and Modernity*, Gloria Groom, ed. (Chicago: The Art Institute of Chicago, 2013) pp. 126–129. Steele quotes Campus.

25. Jenny Fellowman, "Once upon a Midnight Dreary," *Elle*, September 2005, p. 174.

26. Donald Spoto, *Falling in Love Again: Marlene Dietrich* (Boston: Little, Brown, 1985) p. 1.

27. Phil Taylor, "Michael Jordan at 50," *Sports Illustrated*, February 18, 2013, p. 39.

28. Melissa Maerz, "The Mind Behind 'Mad Men,'" *Rolling Stone*, June 25, 2009, http://www.rollingstone.com /culture/news/the-mind-behind-mad-men-20090617. Mark Gardner, one of the creative directors who developed the show's opening sequence, describes the challenge as showing that "there are actually two stories: the one that you see, but also the real story that you only get glimpses of." Cara McKenney, Steve Fuller, and Mark Gardner, interview, "Mad Men (2007)," *Art of the Title*, September 19, 2011, http://www.artofthetitle .com/title/mad-men/.

29. Larissa Juliet Taylor, *The Virgin Warrior: The Life and Death of Joan of Arc* (New Haven: Yale University Press, 2009) pp. 176, xix.

30. Ann W. Astell, *Joan of Arc and Spiritual Authorship* (Notre Dame, IN: University of Notre Dame Press, 2003) p. 185.

31. Jill R. Chancey, "Diana Doubled: The Fairytale Princess and the Photographer," *NWSA Journal*, Summer 1999, p. 172. In an endnote on p. 174, Chancey suggests that the revisionism could be permanent: "Given self-censorship on the Internet and the lack of archived back issues of tabloids, one wonders if the entire photographic record of the transgressive, scandalous Diana will one day be impossible to retrieve."

32. Brassaï, *Paris de nuit*, quoted in wall captions for "Night Vision: Photography after Dark," Metropolitan Museum of Art, April 26–September 18, 2011.

33. Suzy Menkes, "A Lensmen Always in Vogue," *International Herald Tribune*, September 30, 2008, http://www. nytimes.com/2008/09/30/style/30iht-rpatrick.4.16591932.html.

34. "Instant Glamour," *WSJ Magazine*, May 26, 2011, http://online.wsj.com/article/SB10001424052748703730804576321451188401400.html. "The Jewelry Guide," *Lucky*, June 2004, pp. 129–50. Suzanne Hamlin, "Shopping List: Getting Ready for Sleet and Slush," *New York Times*, November 8, 2002, http://www.nytimes.com/2002/11 /08/travel/shopping-list-getting-ready-for-sleet-and-slush.html.

35. William Shakespeare, *Antony and Cleopatra*, Act II, Scene 2, ll. 237–240.

36. James Fox, "The Riddle of Kate Moss," *Vanity Fair*, December 2012, p. 217.

37. Donald Spoto, *Falling in Love Again*, p. 41.

38. Candace Bushnell, "Love at First Sight," *Elle Decor*, September 2005, p. 134.

39. Jun'ichirō Tanizaki, *In Praise of Shadows* (Stony Creek, CT: Leete's Island Books, 1977) pp. 13–14.

40. David Brin, *The Transparent Society: Will Technology Force Us to Choose between Privacy and Freedom?* (New York: Basic Books, 1998).

41. Gustave Flaubert, *Madam Bovary*, Paul De Man, ed. (London: W. W. Norton, 1965) p. 41.

42. Joan DeJean, *The Essence of Style: How the French Invented High Fashion, Fine Food, Chic Cafés, Style, Sophistication, and Glamour* (New York: Free Press, 2005) p. 265.

43. Richard Saul Wurman, *Access Paris* (New York: Collins Reference, 2008) p. 218.

44. Quoted by antique broker Michael Andrew Wilson at http://www.mawparis.com/.

45. Sheila Johnston, "G'day to you Queen Bess," *Sunday Telegraph*, September 28, 1998, http://www.cate-blanchett .com/press/2010/12/the-sunday-telegraph-uk-september-20-1998/. Spelling has been Americanized.

46. Miranda Sawyer, "I Love Work but Life Is More Important," *Glamour UK*, August 2003, p. 60.

47. John Lahr, "Disappearing Act," *New Yorker*, February 12, 2007, pp. 38–45.

48. *Star Trek*, "Amok Time," first broadcast September 15, 1967.

49. Andreas Prater, *Venus at Her Mirror: Velázquez and the Art of Nude Painting*, Ishbel Flett, trans. (Munich: Prestel, 2002) pp. 24–25.

50. Edward Snow, "Theorizing the Male Gaze: Some Problems," *Representations*, Winter 1989, pp. 34–35.

51. Prater notes that the same pink ribbons show up explicitly symbolizing marriage in Veronese's *Mars and Venus United by Love*. Andreas Prater, *Venus at Her Mirror*, pp. 38, 40.

52. In this capacity, it recalls a modern-day South Korean custom: "Couples place a wedding portrait, almost three feet tall, of themselves in their bedroom above the bed. One anthropologist suggests the portrait is placed there as a reminder of the bride's beauty before she enters into a life of hard work and self-sacrifice. In addition, the portrait is a kind of romantic totem and object of worship. The beautiful couple blesses the couple's sexual relations even as in real life their beauty begins to fade." Cele C. Otnes and Elizabeth H. Pleck, *Cinderella Dreams: The Allure of the Lavish Wedding* (Berkeley: University of California Press, 2003) p. 212.

Icon THE WINDOW

1. Matteo Pericoli, *The City out My Window: 63 Views on New York* (New York: Simon & Schuster, 2009) p. 14.

2. Lorenz Eitner, "The Open Window and the Storm-Tossed Boat: An Essay in the Iconography of Romanticism," *The Art Bulletin*, December 1955, p. 286. Eitner focuses on Northern European artists, but an extreme version of the open window as a symbol of frustrated longing was particularly popular among the British Pre-Raphaelites: the Lady of Shalott, an Arthurian figure depicted in a popular poem by Alfred, Lord Tennyson. Imprisoned in an island tower, the lady is under a curse that forbids her from looking directly out her window. She perceives the comings and goings of the outside world only as reflections in a mirror, weaving what she sees into a tapestry. Lonely, she grows "half-sick of shadows" and, seeing one day the reflection of Sir Lancelot, she abandons her loom and looks out the window. The mirror cracks from side to side, she leaves the tower, finds a boat, lies down in it, and, dying, floats toward Camelot.

3. Paul Goldberger, "When Modernism Kissed the Land of Golden Dreams," *New York Times*, December 10, 1989, Section 2, p. 42. In a tribute to Shulman's idealizing lens, commentary on the photo often describes the women as models or dressed in the height of style ("elegantly dressed," wrote Goldberger). In truth, they were neither. The girlfriends of two architects who worked for Koenig, they were wearing ordinary, comfortable summer dresses. Julius Shulman, interview with the author, August 3, 2006.

Icon SHANGHAI

1. The film had three working titles: *Black Irish, Take This Woman*, and a variant on the final version, *The Girl from Shanghai*. Orson Welles and Peter Bogdanovich, *This Is Orson Welles* (New York: Da Capo Press, 1998) p. 401.

2. Lynn Pan, *Shanghai Style: Art and Design between the Wars* (South San Francisco, CA: Long River Press, 2008) p. 127. The story, titled "Country Scenes," was originally published in the February 1935 issue of *Art and Literature Pictorial*.

3. For an extensive discussion of Francophile intellectuals in Shanghai, see Leo Ou-fan Lee, *Shanghai Modern: The Flowering of a New Urban Culture in China, 1930–1945* (Cambridge, MA: Harvard University Press, 1999).

4. Pan Ling, *In Search of Old Shanghai* (Hong Kong: Joint Publishing Co., 1982) p. 58. Pan is better known under the English version of her name.

5. Dany Chen, "A Curator's Notes—Women in Shanghai, Part 1," *Asian Art Museum Blog*, April 29, 2010, http://www.asianart.org/blog/index.php/2010/04/29/a-curators-notes-women-in-shanghai-part-1/.

6. Tina Kanagaratnam, interview with the author, May 6, 2010.

7. Michelle Garnaut, interview with the author, May 5, 2010.

8. http://www.peninsula.com/Shanghai/en/default.aspx. When the hotel opened in 2010, the site headline read, "Glamous Reborn on the Bund," a significant failure of grace.

9. Daniel Brook, "Head of the Dragon: The Rise of the New Shanghai," *Design Observer*, February 18, 2013, http://places.designobserver.com/feature/the-rise-of-new-shanghai/37674/.

10. China boosters often cite the skyline, "supersize buildings sprouting in Shanghai," as evidence of its prosperity and success. Thomas L. Friedman, "China: Scapegoat or Sputnik," *New York Times,* November 10, 2006, http://www.nytimes.com/2006/11/10/opinion/10friedman.html. (See also Thomas L. Friedman, "A Biblical Seven

Years," *New York Times*, August 27, 2008, http://www.nytimes.com/2008/08/27/opinion/27friedman.html.) But as Daniel Brook and many others have noted, the glamorous Pudong skyline is not what it seems. Writes journalist Richard McGregor, the former China bureau chief for the *Financial Times*, "The image this view conveyed— that Shanghai had returned to its entrepreneurial heyday—was far from reality. Unlike southern China and the Yangtze delta region, where Deng's policies had bred a risk-taking, private economy, Shanghai was developed as a socialist showcase. Few visitors admiring the skyscrapers realized that most of them had been built by city government companies. Far from being the free-wheeling market place that many visitors believed, Shanghai represented the Party's ideal, a kind of Singapore-on-steroids, a combination of commercial prosperity and state control." Richard McGregor, *The Party: The Secret World of China's Communist Rulers* (New York: HarperCollins, 2010) pp. 150–51.

SIX: FROM A MUSE OF FIRE TO THE GLEAM OF A THOUSAND LIGHTS

1. William Goldman, *The Princess Bride: S. Morgenstern's Classic Tale of True Love and High Adventure* (New York: Ballantine, 1973) pp. 37–39, 50.
2. *Modern* is a term that has several quite different meanings. In the following discussion contrasting premodern and modern cultures, *modern* is used in a loose version of the way historians apply the term, suggesting the end of feudalism, the rise of large-scale commercial cities, and, importantly for the history of glamour, the development of significant markets for consumer goods, including widely circulated printed works of art and literature. Eighteenth-century London or Paris would be considered modern in this sense. The cities of Renaissance Italy and Edo-period Japan, while not modern in some important respects, also share some modern characteristics. The term as used here is not restricted to the industrial economies, political liberalism, technological progress, or aesthetic modernism of the nineteenth and twentieth centuries; the relation of glamour to this latter sense of the modern will be discussed in the next chapter.
3. Stephen Gundle, *Glamour: A History* (Oxford: Oxford University Press, 2008) pp. 6–7. Although Gundle distinguishes glamour from monarchial magnificence, he confuses the distinction by emphasizing Napoleon's court as a site of glamour. See Virginia Postrel, "A Power to Persuade," *Weekly Standard*, March 29, 2010, pp. 30–32, http://www.weeklystandard.com/articles/power-persuade.
4. John Berger, *Ways of Seeing* (London: Penguin Books, 1972) pp. 129-148. "Ways of Seeing (final episode—advertising) ¼," video uploaded March 9, 2008, http://www.youtube.com/watch?v=mmgGT3th_oI.
5. Cecilia Segawa Seigle, *Yoshiwara: The Glittering World of the Japanese Courtesan* (Honolulu, HI: University of Hawai'i Press, 1993) p. 63. The poem is Seigle's translation.
6. Sarah-Grace Heller, *Fashion in Medieval France* (Cambridge: D. S. Brewer, 2007) p. 62.
7. Sarah-Grace Heller, *Fashion in Medieval France*, pp. 130, 135.
8. Sarah-Grace Heller, *Fashion in Medieval France*, p. 128.
9. William Shakespeare, *Henry V*, Act 4, Scene 3, ll. 44–62. "O for a Muse of fire," is the play's opening line.
10. Timothy Verdon, *Mary in Western Art* (New York: Hudson Hills Press, 2005) pp. 211, 213.
11. Andrew Shanks, *Faith in Honesty: The Essential Nature of Theology* (Burlington, VT: Ashgate, 2005) p. 155.
12. Eliza Griswold, "The Believers," *New Republic*, June 4, 2007, p. 33, http://www.tnr.com/article/the-believers. On suicide bombers, see Chris Hedges, "Snapshot of Despair; The Deathly Glamour of Martyrdom," *New York Times*, October 29, 2000, http://www.nytimes.com/2000/10/29/weekinreview/the-world-snapshot-of-despair-the-deathly-glamour-of-martyrdom.html.
13. Christopher Coker, *The Warrior Ethos: Military Culture and the War on Terror* (London: Routledge, 2007) p. 27.
14. Bernard Knox, "Introduction," in Homer, *The Iliad*, Robert Fagles, trans. (New York: Penguin, 1990) p. 63.
15. We know that Alexander lived from 356 to 323 BC, but the dates of Homer and the Trojan War are far less certain. Here I follow Bernard Knox, who writes that "the most likely date for the composition of the Iliad is the fifty years running from 725 to 675 B.C. That is also the time to which the earliest examples of Greek alphabetic writing can be dated." The Trojan War probably occurred around 1200 BC. The exact dates are not important to the argument here, only the fact that Alexander lived many centuries after Homer—at least as many as separate

us from Shakespeare—and many more after the events from which Homer's epic was derived. Bernard Knox, "Introduction," in Homer, *The Iliad*, Robert Fagles, trans., p. 19.

16. Andrew Stewart, *Faces of Power: Alexander's Image and Hellenistic Politics* (Berkeley: University of California Press, 1993) pp. 73–75, 80–82. Plutarch, "Life of Alexander the Great," in *The Complete Collection of Plutarch's Lives*, John Dryden, trans. (Cambridge, MA: Charles River Editors) Kindle Edition, Kindle locations 27,007–28,286.

17. Andrew Stewart, *Faces of Power*, p. 84. Stewart writes that "*pothos* was both traditional in Greek thought as a motivation for unusual and irresistible desires and ambitions, and current in the inner circles of Alexander's court as an explanation for his own extraordinary lust to do things hitherto unattempted, 'in competition with himself in default of any other rival.'" In a different context, *pothos* was conventionally depicted on grave reliefs, where mourners would be shown looking upward with "melting" gazes, similar to those often used for Alexander, expressing their *pothos* for the departed. Andrew Stewart, *Faces of Power*, p. 118.

18. Christopher Coker, *The Warrior Ethos*, p. 32.

19. Aristotle, *Poetics*, S. H. Butcher, trans., Public Domain Books. Kindle Edition, Kindle Locations 333–337.

20. Bettany Hughes, *Helen of Troy: Goddess, Princess, Whore* (London: Pimlico, 2006) p. 309. Hughes notes that, unlike Aphrodite, Helen is rarely nude in classical art.

21. Robert Emmet Meagher, *The Meaning of Helen: In Search of an Ancient Icon* (Wauconda, IL: Bolchazy-Carducci Publishers, 1995) p. 23.

22. Homer, *The Iliad*, Robert Fagles, trans., Book III, ll. 190–191, pp. 133–34.

23. Bettany Hughes, *Helen of Troy*, p. 116.

24. Herodotus offers a naturalistic version of this story, in which Paris and Helen are shipwrecked off Egypt and the Pharoah (Proteus, here a mortal) expels Paris and protects Helen. Asked to return Helen, the Trojans say they don't have her, but the Greeks don't believe them, discovering the truth only after Troy falls. Herodotus writes, "Had Helen really been in Troy, she would have been handed over to the Greeks with or without Paris' consent; for I cannot believe that either Priam or any other kinsman of his was mad enough to be willing to risk his own and his children's lives and the safety of the city, simply to let Paris continue to live with Helen." Herodotus, *The Histories*, Aubrey de Selincourt, trans. (London: Penguin, 2003) pp. 137–41.

25. Jack Lindsay, *Helen of Troy: Woman and Goddess* (London: Constable, 1974) p. 149.

26. Bettany Hughes, *Helen of Troy*, p. 309.

27. Page duBois, "Sappho and Helen," in *Reading Sappho: Contemporary Approaches*, Ellen Greene, ed. (Berkeley: University of California Press, 1996) pp. 79–88.

28. Isocrates, *The Classic Works of Isocrates: Helen of Troy and 7 Other Works*, J. H. Freese, trans. (Cambridge, MA: Charles River Editors) Kindle Edition, Kindle locations 331, 362.

29. Homer, *The Iliad*, Robert Fagles, trans., Book IXX, ll. 386–87, p. 499. The word used is "*rigidanē*, a creature that chills and makes one shudder." Jack Lindsay, *Helen of Troy*, p. 30.

30. The translation "terrible beauty" appropriately recalls the Yeats refrain, "a terrible beauty is born," about the death of Irish nationalists who will be remembered "wherever green is worn." W. B. Yeats, "Easter, 1916," in *The Collected Poems of W. B. Yeats*, revised second edition, Richard J. Finneran, ed. (New York: Scribner Paperback Poetry, 1996) pp. 180–82.

31. Bernard Knox, "Introduction," in Homer, *The Iliad*, trans. Robert Fagles, p. 65.

32. Homer, *The Iliad*, Robert Fagles, trans., Book VI, ll. 424–26, p. 207.

33. Theodore Dreiser, *Sister Carrie* (New York: New American Library, 1961) pp. 113, 290.

34. Theodore Dreiser, *Sister Carrie*, p. 8.

35. Gustave Flaubert, *Madame Bovary*, Paul De Man, ed. (London: W. W. Norton, 1965) p. 41.

36. Eugen Weber, *France: Fin de Siècle* (Cambridge, MA: Harvard University Press, 1986) p. 52.

37. James Boswell, *Boswell's London Journal 1762–1763*, Frederick A. Pottle, ed. (New York: McGraw-Hill, 2004) p. 44.

38. James Boswell, *Boswell's London Journal*, p. 68.

39. Tobias Smollett, *The Expedition of Humphry Clinker*, Lewis M. Knapp, ed. (London: Oxford University Press, 1966) p. 88. Emphasis in the original.

40. Cecilia Sagawa Seigle, *Yoshiwara*, pp. 58–59. Seigle writes, "In theory, all clients of this pleasure quarter were classless and treated equally by Yoshiwara staff. The single criterion for preferential treatment was money. As a symbol of the quarter's 'egalitarianism,' all visitors' swords—whether the pair of long and short swords worn by the samurai class or the one short sword worn by the privileged among the merchants—were surrendered upon entering a Yoshiwara establishment and returned only on departure." Also Nishiyama Matsunosuke, *Edo Culture: Daily Life and Diversions in Urban Japan, 1600–1868*, Gerald Groemer, trans. and ed. (Honolulu, HI: University of Hawai'i Press, 1997) p. 45.

41. Howard Hibbett, *The Floating World in Japanese Fiction* (Boston: Tuttle Publishing, [1959] 2001) p. vii.

42. Joseph Addison, *The Spectator*, no. 131, July 31, 1711.

43. Eugen Weber, *France: Fin de Siècle*, p. 52.

44. David McCullough, *The Greater Journey: Americans in Paris* (New York: Simon & Schuster, 2011) p. 54.

45. James Boswell, *Boswell's London Journal*, p. 69.

46. Eugen Weber, *France: Fin de Siècle*, p. 159.

47. John Brewer, *The Pleasures of the Imagination: English Culture in the Eighteenth Century* (New York: Farrar, Straus and Giroux, 1997) p. 334.

48. Nishiyama Matsunosuke, *Edo Culture*, pp. 212–16.

49. Howard Hibbett, *The Floating World in Japanese Fiction* (Boston: Tuttle Publishing, 2001) p. 24.

50. Alexandre Privat d'Anglemont, cited in Elizabeth Wilson, *Bohemians: The Glamorous Outcasts* (New Brunswick, NJ: Rutgers University Press, 2000) p. 33.

51. Lady Duff Gordon ("Lucile"), *Discretions and Indiscretions* (New York: Frederick A. Stokes Co., 1932) p. 78. Like a Hollywood studio chief, Lucile gave her mannequins alluring new names, turning Susie into Gamela and Constance into Hebe, and gave them makeovers and deportment lessons. In her memoir, she recounts their marriages to millionaires.

52. Michael B. Miller, *Bon Marché: Bourgeois Culture and the Department Store, 1869–1920* (Princeton, NJ: Princeton University Press, 1981) p. 167.

53. Émile Zola, *The Ladies' Paradise*, introduction by Kristin Ross (Berkeley: University of California Press, 1992) pp. 98, 374.

54. Elaine S. Abelson, *When Ladies Go A-Thieving* (New York: Oxford University Press, 1989) pp. 76–83. Abelson quotes *Dry Goods Reporter*, February 16, 1901, p. 15.

55. Michael B. Miller, *Bon Marché*, p. 211. Jean-Martin Charcot was a neurologist known for his work on hypnotism. Jean Eugène Robert-Houdin was the nineteenth-century illusionist from whom Harry Houdini, born Ehrich Weiss, took his name.

56. Rosalind H. Williams, *Dream Worlds: Mass Consumption in Late Nineteenth-Century France* (Berkeley: University of California Press, 1982) p. 103.

57. Theodore Dreiser, *Sister Carrie*, pp. 289–90.

58. David McCullough, *The Greater Journey*, pp. 55–56. McCullough writes that Emma Willard, who traveled to Paris in the fall of 1830, "was appalled to learn that more than a third of the children in Paris were born out of wedlock. During a visit to the Hospice des Enfants-Trouvés, the Hospital for Foundlings, seeing the numbers of babies ranged in rows of cribs, she was heartstricken, exactly as Abigail Adams had been on a similar tour long before. Like Abigail Adams, Mrs. Willard was touched by the devotion shown by the nuns to the care of the infants, but felt there had to be something dreadfully amiss about a society in which so many babies were abandoned."

59. Elaine S. Abelson, *When Ladies Go A-Thieving*, pp. 173–96.

60. Erik Larson, *The Devil in the White City: Murder, Magic, and Madness at the Fair That Changed America* (New York: Vintage Books, 2003) p. 62.

61. Theodore Dreiser, *Sister Carrie*, pp. 273–74.

62. "The Immorality of Shop-Windows," *Atlantic Monthly*, December 1910, p. 853.

63. Émile Zola, *The Ladies' Paradise*, p. 72. By spending beyond her means, Madame de Boves causes her hardworking husband financial agonies, which are mirrored by those of Zola's protagonist Denise, whose brother is constantly hitting her up for money to fund his love affairs.

64. James Boswell, *Boswell's London Journal*, pp. 68–69.

Icon THE HORSEMAN

1. John Steinbeck, _The Red Pony_ (New York: Penguin, 1994) p. 13.
2. Baldassare Castiglione, _The Book of the Courtier_, Charles S. Singleton, trans. (Garden City, NY: Anchor, 1959) p. 45.
3. Alfred Noyes, "The Highwayman," ll. 1–6, http://www.potw.org/archive/potw85.html.
4. Randy Roberts and James S. Olson, _John Wayne: American_ (New York: Free Press, 1995) p. 135.
5. Donna Landry, _Noble Brutes: How Eastern Horses Transformed English Culture_, pp. 53–54, 66–77. John Baskett, _The Horse in Art_ (New Haven: Yale University Press, 2006) p. 25.
6. Burton Rascoe, "Opie Read and Zane Grey," _Saturday Review of Literature_, November 11, 1939, p. 8.
7. Buck Rainey, _The Reel Cowboy_ (Jefferson, NC: McFarland & Co., 1996) p. 10.
8. Buck Rainey, _The Reel Cowboy_, pp. 8–11. Rainey lists twenty-six unrealistic elements "accepted without thought" in B movies from the mid-1920s on, most of which involve some form of artificial grace, beginning with "clean, unlingering, unsuffering deaths."
9. Carl Werner, _Bringing Up the Boy: A Message to Fathers and Mothers from a Boy of Yesterday concerning the Men of To-morrow_ (New York: Dodd, Mead & Co., 1913) p. 71. Mrs. O. F. Walton, _A Peep behind the Scenes_ (Boston: Ira Bradley & Co., 1885) pp. 66–69. Via Google Books.
10. Hamlin Garland, _Boy Life on the Prairie_ (New York: Harper & Brothers, 1899) pp. 216–17. Via Google Books.

Icon THE GIBSON GIRL

1. Perriton Maxwell, "Charles Dana Gibson: Creator of American Social Types," _Pearson's Magazine_, February 1908, p. 187.
2. Simpson, Crawford & Simpson ad for "'Gibson' Picture Pillow Tops," _New York Times_, April 14, 1901, part 2, p. 15. Fairfax Downey, _Portrait of an Era as Drawn by C. D. Gibson_ (New York: Charles Scribner's Sons, 1936) p. 201.
3. H. I. Brock, "Evolution of the Gibson Girl," _New York Times Magazine_, December 2, 1934, p. SM10.
4. Sara Crowquill, "In London with Charles Dana Gibson," _National Magazine_, May 1898, p. 100.
5. J. M. Bulloch, "Charles Dana Gibson," _The Studio_, June 8, 1896, p. 77.
6. Caroline Ticknor, "The Steel-Engraving Lady and the Gibson Girl," _Atlantic Monthly_, July 1901, pp. 105–108.
7. "Three Typical Women," _New York Times_, June 29, 1901, Saturday Review of Books and Art, http://select.nytimes.com/gst/abstract.html?res=F40C15F7345C12738DDDA00A94DE405B818CF1D3.
8. Charlotte J. Rich, _Transcending the New Woman: Multiethnic Narratives in the Progressive Era_ (Columbia, MO: University of Missouri Press, 2009) p. 27. Leigh Summers, _Bound to Please: A History of the Victorian Corset_ (Oxford: Berg, 2001) p. 44.
9. Lois W. Banner, _American Beauty_ (New York: Alfred A. Knopf, 1983) p. 169.
10. Quoted in Lois W. Banner, _American Beauty_, p. 165.
11. Charlotte Perkins Gilman, _Women and Economics: A Study of the Economic Relation between Men and Women as a Factor in Social Evolution_ (Boston: Small, Maynard & Co., 1898) pp. 148–49. Via Google Books.

SEVEN: THE WORLD OF TOMORROW

1. Mellissa Huber, "Industry and Academia: NY Fashion Week Fall 2012, Norma Kamali Presentation," _Worn Through_, February 16, 2012, http://www.wornthrough.com/2012/02/16/industry-and-academia-ny-fashion-week-fall-2012-norma-kamali-presentation/. My thanks to Mellissa Huber for sending me the full text of Kamali's introduction.
2. For a detailed discussion of how exiled New Yorkers reimagined their city for the screen, see James Sanders, _Celluloid Skyline: New York and the Movies_ (New York: Alfred A. Knopf, 2003) pp. 44–60.
3. The makeover concept helped to turn around the struggling _Mademoiselle_. "The Press: Success in Fashions," _Time_, April 15, 1940, http://www.time.com/time/subscriber/article/0,33009,789757-1,00.html. In June 1939, the British weekly _Picture Post_ gave a charlady a makeover, briefly turning her into a "glamour girl" before she

washed off the makeup and went home. Carol Dyhouse, *Glamour: Women, History, Feminism* (London: Zed Books, 2010) p. 43. *Glamour*'s first makeover, of a woman who worked in Paramount's publicity department, ran in 1939. "Hello, Hello," *Glamour*, January 2003, p. 99.

4. "Dark Glasses Are New Fad for Wear on City Streets," *Life*, May 30, 1938, pp. 31–33. See also the Foster Grant Collection, Syracuse University, http://library.syr.edu/digital/guides/f/foster_grant.htm.

5. Michael Johnson, "Modernity in America," http://architecture.factoidz.com/streamlined-design-modernity-in -america/.

6. A Google Books ngram analysis of English-language books published from 1800 to 2000 shows use of the word *glamour* peaking in 1932 and the much less popular spelling *glamor* peaking in the early 1940s. http://books .google.com/ngrams/. Use of the word is indicative but not the same as the prevalence of the phenomenon.

7. Dennita Sewell, Phoenix Museum of Art, interview with the author, May 12, 2007.

8. Morris Dickstein, *Dancing in the Dark: A Cultural History of the Great Depression* (New York: W. W. Norton, 2009) p. 367.

9. Linda M. Scott, *Fresh Lipstick: Redressing Feminism and Fashion* (New York: Palgrave, 2002) pp. 275–76.

10. J. P. Mayer, *British Cinemas and Their Audiences: Sociological Studies* (London: Dennis Dobson Ltd., 1948) p. 85. The desire to travel comes up repeatedly in these responses.

11. The market for patent medicines, formerly the mainstay of American magazine advertising, collapsed around this time. Competition from aspirin, which offered more than a placebo effect, combined with federal regulation to wipe out much of the industry. Charles Goodrum and Helen Dalrymple, *Advertising in America: The First 200 Years* (New York: Harry N. Abrams, 1990) p. 35.

12. The thirties gave birth to such magazines as *Life* (1936), *Mademoiselle* (1935), and *Glamour* (1939) in the United States; *Woman's Own* (1932), *Woman* (1937), and *Picture Post* (1938) in the United Kingdom, and *Marie Claire* (1937) in France. The period also saw the growth of "pulp" genre-fiction magazines and movie fan magazines.

13. Kathleen Ash quoted in Fiona Hackney, "'They Opened Up a Whole New World': Narrative, Text and Image in British Women's Magazines in the 1930s," *Working Papers on Design* (2007), http://www.herts.ac.uk/artdes1 /research/papers/wpdesign/wpdvol2/vol2.html.

14. The lingerie collection is notable not only because the show is risqué but also because such lingerie is another of Lucile's legacies. When she expanded to new quarters in 1894, the designer writes, "I was particularly anxious to have a department for beautiful underclothes, as I hated the thought of my creations worn over the ugly nun's veiling or linen-cum-Swiss embroidery which was all that the really virtuous woman of those days permitted herself. With the arrogance which success was beginning to give me I vowed to change all that, and made plans for the day of chiffons and laces, of boudoir caps and transparent nightdresses. I was so sorry for the poor husbands, who had to see their wives looking so unattractive at night after taking off the romantic dresses I had created. So I started making underclothes as delicate as cobwebs and as beautifully tinted as flowers, and half the women in London flocked to see them, though they had not the courage to buy them at first." Lady Duff Gordon ("Lucile"), *Discretions and Indiscretions* (New York: Frederick A. Stokes Co., 1932) pp. 41–42.

15. Howard Gutner, *Gowns by Adrian: The MGM Years 1928–1941* (New York: Harry N. Abrams, 2001) p. 22.

16. Lynn Pan, *Shanghai Style: Art and Design Between the Wars* (South San Francisco, CA: Long River Press, 2008) pp. 247–53. Ruan Lingyu is often described as the Chinese Garbo. Pan notes that "between the 1980s and 1990s (and even into the 2000s) furniture like the kind seen in the movies . . . filled whole warehouses in Shanghai, sourced from prewar houses that were demolished in the frenzy of urban renewal that overtook the city during those decades."

17. Robert Sklar, *Movie-Made America: A Cultural History of American Movies* (New York: Vintage Books, 1994) pp. 222–27.

18. Howard Gutner, *Gowns by Adrian*, p. 9.

19. Colin McGinn, *The Power of Movies: How Screen and Mind Interact* (New York: Pantheon, 2005) p. 18.

20. Jackie Stacey, *Star Gazing: Hollywood Cinema and Female Spectatorship* (London: Routledge, 1994) p. 67.

21. Gregory Benford, *The Wonderful Future That Never Was* (New York: Hearst Books, 2010) p. 21.

22. Many "movie stills," including the iconic shots of Gilda and of Holly Golightly at breakfast, are not actually shots

that appeared on screen but rather staged publicity photos. Marilyn Monroe's skirt flying up in *The Seven-Year Itch* is probably the most famous example; the scene in the film is much less revealing.

23. Tom Zimmerman, *Light and Illusion: The Hollywood Portraits of Ray Jones*, John Jones, ed. (Glendale, CA: Balcony Press, 1998) p. 8.

24. General Electric Hotpoint Automatic Electric Range ad, *Ladies' Home Journal*, September 1929, p. 133. A Google Books ngram analysis shows use of the word *modern* peaking in 1932.

25. In such a hypothetical case it would be easier to maintain that sense of glamour through repeated, rather than one-time, exposure to its object—another reason commercial goods and media images are conducive to glamour. My high-school class included a boy who dreamed of being a game-show host, a role he clearly found glamorous in a way completely mystifying to the rest of us. He probably wasn't the only person in the world to entertain this notion of glamour, but even if he had been, he could enjoy experiencing it every weekday.

26. The idea of the "dream city" is explored in James Sanders, *Celluloid Skyline*.

27. Lynn Pan, *Shanghai Style*, pp. 12–13.

28. Richard Hudnut *Poudre de Début* ad, *Harper's Bazaar*, July 1929, unnumbered page between pp. 112 and 113.

29. Although invented in 1915, Maybelline mascara didn't take off until five-and-dime stores started to carry it in 1932, making it accessible to the working girls who read fan magazines and emulated the makeup of actresses. Linda M. Scott, *Fresh Lipstick*, pp. 202–205.

30. Maria DiBattista, *Fast-Talking Dames* (New Haven: Yale University Press, 2001) pp. x, xii, 11.

31. A Google Books ngram analysis shows the phrase *modern woman* peaking in 1929.

32. Heon Stevenson, *American Automobile Advertising, 1930–1980: An Illustrated History* (Jefferson, NC: McFarland & Co., 2008) p. C4. Zephyr was also the name of a streamlined train, a streamlined radio console, and a streamlined electric clock.

33. Jeffrey L. Meikle, *Twentieth Century Limited: Industrial Design in America, 1925–1939* (Philadelphia, PA: Temple University Press, 1979) p. 164.

34. Joan Kron, interview with the author, April 5, 2012.

35. Norman Bel Geddes, *Horizons* (Boston: Little, Brown & Co., 1932) p. 24.

36. Vicki Goldberg, *Margaret Bourke-White: A Biography* (New York: Harper & Row, 1986) p. 104. Dwight Macdonald was at that time a Trotskyite contemptuous of *Fortune*'s viewpoint.

37. Edna Robb Webster, "This Daring Camera Girl Scales Skyscrapers for Art," *American Magazine*, November 1930, pp. 66–69.

38. Vicki Goldberg, *Margaret Bourke-White*, p. 130.

39. Vicki Goldberg, *Margaret Bourke-White*, pp. 114, 127–29. Later in her career, Bourke-White did do photography that focused on individuals, including her 1937 book with Erskine Caldwell on the Depression-era South, *You Have Seen Their Faces*.

40. Edna Robb Webster, "This Daring Camera Girl Scales Skyscrapers for Art," p. 66.

41. Warren I. Susman, "The People's Fair: Cultural Contradictions of a Consumer Society," in *Dawn of a New Era: The New York World's Fair, 1939/40*, Helen A. Harrison, ed. (New York: New York University Press, 1980) p. 22. Countering fears that advances in technology would lead to unemployment was a major theme in *The Middleton Family at the New York World's Fair*, a film produced by Westinghouse, http://archive.org/details/middleton _family_worlds_fair_1939.

42. Bennett Lincoln, "Is Man Doomed by the Machine Age?" *Modern Mechanix*, March 1931, pp. 50–55, http://blog. modernmechanix.com/2010/11/08/is-man-doomed-by-the-machine-age/.

43. *Superman: The Mechanical Monsters*, directed by Dave Fleisher, 1941, http://archive.org/details/superman_the_ mechanical_monsters. At the end of 1942, comic books made up more than 30 percent of the periodicals mailed to military bases, an indicator of their popularity among adults. At the time, *Superman* sold more than a million copies an issue. Gerard Jones, *Men of Tomorrow: Geeks, Gangsters, and the Birth of the Comic Book* (New York: Basic Books, 2004) p. 213.

44. Otto Julius Bierbaum, *Ein empfindsame Reis im Automobil* (1903), cited in Wolfgang Sachs, *For the Love of the Automobile: Looking Back into the History of Our Desires*, Don Reneau, trans. (Berkeley: University of California Press, 1992) p. 95.

45. Mike Rugel, "Ford Blues," *Uncensored History of the Blues*, March 30, 2011, http://uncensoredhistoryoftheblues. purplebeech.com/2011/03/show-52-ford-blues.html. Rugel notes that "Ford movement" is a play on the phrase "Elgin movement," a watch slogan that showed up in many songs of the era. Cars held a special allure for African Americans, for whom private automobiles provided an escape from the indignities of segregated trains, buses, and streetcars. Warren Brown, "For Automobile Writer, Cars Have Long Been Synonymous with Freedom," *Washington Post*, October 11, 2011, http://www.washingtonpost.com/business/for-automobile-writer-cars-have -long-been-synonymous-with-freedom/2011/10/11/gIQAfq15jL_story.html.

46. On "radioman," see E. L. Doctorow, *World's Fair* (New York: Plume, 1985) p. 220.

47. Princess Bibesco, "The Aura of New York," *Harper's Bazaar*, January 15, 1934, p. 88.

48. The New York Public Library, "The Age of Power and Wonder" digital gallery, http://digitalgallery.nypl.org/ nypldigital/dgkeysearchresult.cfm?parent_id=113558&word=.

49. Olga Scowen quoted in Annette Kuhn, *An Everyday Magic: Cinema and Cultural Memory* (London: I.B. Tauris, 2002) pp. 120–21.

50. US Census Bureau, Sixteenth Census of the United States—1940, Housing: General Characteristics, Table 6: "State of Repair and Plumbing Equipment for All Dwelling Units, by Occupancy and Tenure, for the United States, by Regions, Urban and Rural: 1940." Table 6c shows that 55 percent of homes of white Americans had private baths and private flush toilets, compared to only 17 percent of homes of nonwhites.

51. Cecil B. DeMille, *The Autobiography of Cecil B. DeMille,* Donald Hayne, ed. (Englewood Cliffs, NJ: Prentice-Hall, 1959) pp. 210–11.

52. Richard Griffith and Arthur Mayer, *The Movies* (New York: Simon & Schuster, 1970) p. 125.

53. Gilbert Whalen, the president of the 1939 New York World's Fair, quoted in Helen A. Harrison, ed., *Dawn of a New Era*, p. 34.

54. Quoted in Helen A. Harrison, ed., *Dawn of a New Era*, p. 12.

55. Sidney and Beatrice Webb, *Soviet Communism: A New Civilisation?* (New York: Charles Scribner's Sons, 1936) p. 661.

56. Wolfgang Sachs, *For the Love of the Automobile*, pp. 51–55.

57. John M. Jordan, *Machine-Age Ideology: Social Engineering and American Liberalism, 1911–1939* (Chapel Hill, NC: University of North Carolina Press, 1994) p. 66.

58. Steven Heller, *Iron Fists: Branding the 20th-Century Totalitarian State* (New York: Phaidon, 2008) pp. 112–13.

59. Steven Heller, *Iron Fists*, p. 138.

60. Quoted in Helen A. Harrison, ed., *Dawn of a New Era*, p. 4.

61. Quoted in Joseph P. Cusker, "The World of Tomorrow: Science, Culture, and Community at the New York World's Fair," in Helen A. Harrison, ed., *Dawn of a New Era*, p. 15.

62. Jeffrey L. Meikle, *Twentieth Century Limited*, p. 197.

63. Helen A. Harrison, ed., *Dawn of a New Era*, p. 2.

64. Christopher Innes, *Designing Modern America: Broadway to Main Street* (New Haven: Yale University Press, 2005) pp. 130–43. Innes provides an unusually detailed description of the Futurama, as well as the insight that the simulated flight would have been most visitors' first such experience.

65. E. L. Doctorow, *World's Fair*, pp. 252–53.

66. "A Captain of the Ocean Air," *Life*, June 18, 1956, pp. 123–30. A standard American bathtub is five feet long from the outside, with less than four feet of interior space.

67. Eddie Rickenbacker, "Introducing the Air Age," *Life*, June 18, 1956, p. 2. By contrast, at least 80 percent of today's Americans have flown, http://www.nationalatlas.gov/transportation.html. This figure appears to be based on a 1999 Gallup survey, the most recent in which the polling firm asked the question, where 83 percent of respondents said they had flown on a commercial airliner. Alyssa Brown, e-mail to the author, May 9, 2012.

68. "A Captain of the Ocean Air," *Life*, June 18, 1956, p. 130.

69. Grant McCracken, "When Cars Could Fly," in *Culture and Consumption II: Markets, Meaning and Brand Management* (Bloomington, IN: Indiana University Press, 2005) pp. 53–90. The first quotation is from p. 84, and a sentence has been omitted between the two quoted. The second quotation is from p. 80.

70. For British audiences, Bond's escapades in America were as glamorous and exotic as his trips to other locales, a perspective discussed in Simon Winder, *The Man Who Saved Britain: A Personal Journey into the Disturbing World*

of James Bond (London: Picador, 2006) pp. 112–13. Because Jet Age glamour meant different things in different national contexts, I am confining my discussion to the United States.

71. In recent years, the glamorous, globe-trotting secret agent has been reincarnated as a woman in such TV shows as *Alias* and *Covert Affairs*.

72. Sandra Tsing Loh, *Depth Takes a Holiday: Essays from Lesser Los Angeles* (New York: Riverhead Books, 1996) p. 71.

73. "Come to the U.N." ad, *Time*, April 8, 1966, p. 116.

74. Sally Bedell Smith, *Grace and Power: The Private World of the Kennedy White House* (New York: Random House, 2004) p. 135.

75. C. David Heymann, *A Woman Named Jackie* (New York: Lyle Stuart, 1989) pp. 388–93.

76. It is, of course, hard to know for sure, since Kennedy's death forestalled the reelection campaign in which such issues might have arisen.

77. C. David Heymann, *A Woman Named Jackie*, p. 220. Peters is best known as the founder and longtime editor of *The Washington Monthly*.

78. She was number two in 1961, after Eleanor Roosevelt, who died the following year and thus no longer qualified for consideration. Frank Newport, David W. Moore, and Lydia Saad, "Most Admired Men and Women: 1948–1998," Gallup News Service, December 13, 1999, http://www.gallup.com/poll/3415/most-admired-men -women-19481998.aspx. The June 1961 survey was the only one during the Kennedy years to ask specifically about attitudes toward Jacqueline Kennedy. Sixteen percent of respondents said they did not know and six percent had a "mixed" impression. My thanks to Karlyn Bowman of the American Enterprise Institute for her research on polls during this period.

79. The architect Morris Lapidus explicitly drew on his audience's movie memories when designing Miami Beach hotels in the 1950s, creating interiors that would give guests experiences they associated with movie glamour. Alice T. Friedman, "The Luxury of Lapidus," *Harvard Design Magazine*, Summer 2000, pp. 39–47, http://www. nyc-architecture.com/ARCH/ARCH-Lapidus.htm.

80. Virginia Postrel, "Up, Up, and Away," *Atlantic*, January/February 2007, pp. 159–61, http://www.theatlantic.com /magazine/archive/2007/01/up-up-and-away/5547/.

Icon THE SUNTAN

1. Graham McCann, *Cary Grant: A Class Apart* (London: Fourth Estate, 1996) pp. 57–58.

2. Kerry Segrave, *Suntanning in 20th Century America*, (Jefferson, NC: McFarland & Co., 2005) pp. 3–11. Segrave writes that the Chanel story appears to originate with a 1971 *Mademoiselle* article. His book emphasizes the medical claims for tanning's health benefits, which are important to its popularity but not to its glamour.

3. "Back to Sunburn with the Mode," *Vogue*, July 20, 1929, p. 76.

4. Stehli Silks, "Now Copper-toned Shoulders Greet the Evening," *Vogue*, March 2, 1929, unnumbered four-color page between pp. 16 and 17. In the twenties, *suntan* and *sunburn* were still synonyms.

5. "Back to Sunburn with the Mode," *Vogue*, July 20, 1929, p. 94.

6. Carola de Peyster Kip, "Irradiated Beauty," *Harper's Bazaar*, July 1935, pp. 66–67, 97.

7. John Weightman, "The Solar Revolution," *Encounter*, December 1970, p. 9, http://www.unz.org/Pub/Encounter -1970dec-00009.

8. John Weightman, "The Solar Revolution," pp. 12, 14.

9. Agnès Poirier, "Happy Birthday, Brigitte Bardot," *Guardian*, September 21, 2009, http://www.guardian.co.uk /film/2009/sep/22/brigitte-bardot-french-cinema.

10. Nina G. Jablonski, "From Bardot to Beckham: The Decline of Celebrity Tanning," *Skin Cancer Foundation Journal*, January 2010, pp. 42–44, http://www.skincancer.org/prevention/tanning/from-bardot-to-beckham-the -decline-of-celebrity-tanning.

Icon THE STRIDING WOMAN

1. Deirdre Bird, Helen Caldwell, and Mark DeFanti, "A Fragrance to Empower Women: The History of 'Charlie,'"

15th Conference on Historical Analysis & Research in Marketing, May 20, 2011, http://faculty.quinnipiac.edu/CHARM/CHARM%20proceedings/CHARM%20article%20archive%20pdf%20format/Volume%2015%202011/A%20fragrance%20to%20empower%20Women.pdf. "Perfume," *Ad Age Encyclopedia*, September 15, 2003, http://adage.com/article/adage-encyclopedia/perfume/98816/.

2. A 1976 television commercial showed her driving up to a club in a Rolls-Royce wearing a gold-colored satin jumpsuit and signing in as Charlie, using the scent's logo. The men in the commercial, including her date, are decidedly subordinate. Revlon "'Charlie'" Ad with Shelley Hack & Bobby Short, uploaded by ohbutyes, March 16, 2009, http://youtu.be/9Sn8H42FZcI.

3. Susan Joy, "Stretch Pants, Vertically Speaking," *New York Times*, October 13, 2010, p. E11, http://www.nytimes.com/2010/10/14/fashion/14PANTS.html.

4. Christina Binkley, "The Return of the Charlie Girl," WSJ.com, March 4, 2010, http://blogs.wsj.com/juggle/2010/03/04/the-return-of-the-charlie-girl/.

5. Deirdre Bird, Helen Caldwell, and Mark DeFanti, "A Fragrance to Empower Women."

6. This discussion draws on an examination of every issue of *Vogue* and *Harper's Bazaar* from 1920, 1925, 1929, 1934, 1939, 1949, 1954, 1959, 1964, 1969, and 1974, along with a few samples from other years and other titles. For practical reasons, the survey was limited to US publications, although images of striding women do appear internationally in the period. I am grateful to the Santa Monica Public Library for maintaining bound volumes of these magazines.

7. *Vogue*, September 1, 1928, p. 106.

8. Duro Gloss, "'Gray Day' Coats for Men and Women," *Vogue*, October 29, 1929, p. 16h.

9. "Long Strides across Paris," *Harper's Bazaar*, October 1935, pp. 104–105.

10. Vertes, "The Skyscrapers," *Harper's Bazaar*, July 1937, p. 70.

11. *Collier's*, July 30, 1938.

12. Munkacsi and Norman Parkinson also continued to portray striding women in photographs reminiscent of their prewar work.

13. Simone de Beauvoir, *The Second Sex* (New York: Vintage Books, 1989) p. 536.

14. "The Jaipur Look for Summer," *Vogue*, June 1964, pp. 68–69.

15. Nancy White, "What Do I Remember?" in Nancy White and John Esten, *Style in Motion: Munkacsi Photographs '20s, '30s, '40s* (New York: Clarkson N. Potter, 1979) p. 15. Unfortunately, *Harper's Bazaar* did not maintain archives of his work and most of Munkacsi's original photos and negatives have been lost. Only the magazine spreads remain.

16. Richard Avedon, "Munkacsi," *Harper's Bazaar*, June 1964, pp. 64–68.

17. "The Wilder Shores of Chic," *Harper's Bazaar*, August 1964, pp. 67–77. "Paris: A Time for Decision," *Harper's Bazaar*, September 1964, pp. 195–212. "The Dress with Nine Lives," *Harper's Bazaar*, September 1964, pp. 266–67. "Swinging in the Rain," *Harper's Bazaar*, October 1964, pp. 186–93. "What's Happening: Courrèges," *Harper's Bazaar*, April 1965, pp. 180–81.

EIGHT: THE USES OF ENCHANTMENT

1. Theron said that making the ad "was incredibly glamorous and fantastic." Kate Shapland, "Charlize Theron in the new Dior J'Adore Ad Campaign," Telegraph.co.uk, September 5, 2011, http://fashion.telegraph.co.uk/beauty/news-features/TMG8741135/Charlize-Theron-in-the-new-Dior-JAdore-ad-campaign.html. "British Airways Advert 2011: To Fly. To Serve. (HD)," video uploaded October 9, 2011, http://youtu.be/XozHLoqwp_4.

2. There is also a tradition of the martial-arts heroine in Chinese cinema.

3. "Fergie: Glamorous ft. Ludacris," video uploaded June 16, 2009, http://youtu.be/q0SyUgw98tE.

4. Some audiences did find the sitcom portraits of idealized family life—from *Father Knows Best* to *The Brady Bunch*—glamorous. "I remember daydreaming about walking into Mr. Brady's den and asking for fatherly advice. What a guy! . . . I wanted to join the Brady family so badly that I was often unbearable in my judgement of my own home life," writes blogger Jason Loper. Jason Loper, "Design Remembrance: *The Brady Bunch House*," *Apartment Therapy*, July 13, 2011, http://www.apartmenttherapy.com/design-remembrance-the-brady-b-151256. The movie *Pleasantville* (1998) plays with this idea.

5. Mark Mather, "U.S. Children in Single-Mother Families," *Population Research Bureau Data Brief*, May 2010, http://www.prb.org/Publications/PolicyBriefs/singlemotherfamilies.aspx. James R. Wetzel, "American Families: 75 Years of Change," *Monthly Labor Review*, March 1990, pp. 4–13, http://www.bls.gov/mlr/1990/03/art1full .pdf. In real life, Fergie's parents divorced when she was a teenager, but she and her father remain close. Clare O'Connor, "Fergie's Fortune: Inside the Pop Diva's Power Portfolio," *Forbes Life*, May 7, 2012, http://www.forbes .com/sites/clareoconnor/2012/05/07/fergies-fortune-inside-the-pop-divas-power-portfolio/.

6. The longings and illusions of actual backpacking, culturally oriented travelers are interestingly discussed in Andrew Causey, *Hard Bargaining in Sumatra: Western Travelers and Toba Bataks in the Marketplace of Souvenirs* (Honolulu: University of Hawai'i Press, 2003).

7. Rachael Hammon, "Blogger of the Month December: Solanah of Vixen Vintage," *The Paraders*, December 6, 2012, http://blog.theparaders.com/2012/12/blogger-of-month-december-solanah-of.html.

8. Virginia Postrel, "Vintage Week: DG Q&A with Vixen Vintage Blogger Solanah Cornell," *Deep Glamour*, March 21, 2012, http://www.deepglamour.net/deep_glamour/2013/03/vintage-week-dg-qa-with-vixen-vintage -blogger-solanah-cornell.html. Solanah Cornell, e-mail to the author, March 21, 2013.

9. For an overview of the motivations of vintage buyers, see Virginia Postrel, "Vintage Week: DG Q&A with Liza D. of Better Dresses Vintage," *Deep Glamour*, March 18, 2013, http://www.deepglamour.net/deep_glamour/2013 /03/vintage-week-dg-qa-with-liza-d-of-better-dresses-vintage.html.

10. Virginia Postrel, "Vintage Week: DG Q&A with Vixen Vintage Blogger Solanah Cornell." Rachael Hammon, "Blogger of the Month December: Solanah of Vixen Vintage."

11. Kyle Stock, "As It Preps for an IPO, the Container Store Cleans Up," *Bloomberg Businessweek*, June 7, 2013, http://www.businessweek.com/articles/2013-06-07/as-it-preps-for-an-ipo-thecontainer-store-cleans-up. Leigh Atherton, e-mail to the author, June 19, 2013, and https://twitter.com/Leigh_Atherton, June 17, 2013. "How the Container Store Turns Order into Profits," Bloomberg TV, February 15, 2013, http://www.bloomberg.com /video/what-is-thecontainer-store-really-selling-h6Rru9g5SuGE0WIFTy98nw.html. This discussion draws on Virginia Postrel, "Container Store Sells Zen and Glamour in a Box," Bloomberg View, July 2, 2013, http://www. bloomberg.com/news/2013-07-02/container-store-sells-zen-and-glamour-in-a-box.html.

12. Alexis Madrigal, "Detroit's Gleaming Start-up Tower," TheAtlantic.com, September 23, 2012, http://www. theatlantic.com/technology/archive/2012/09/detroits-gleaming-start-up-tower/262730/.

13. The movie *Galaxy Quest* (1999) offers a multilayered and much-loved utopian parody of *Star Trek*.

14. "Old Spice: The Man Your Man Could Smell Like," video uploaded February 4, 2010, http://youtu.be /owGykVbfgUE.

15. Preserving an element of genuine glamour also enables, even encourages, the countless grassroots parodies that further engage viewers.

16. *The One*, directed by Jean-Baptiste Mondino, ("Dolce & Gabbana The One with Scarlett Johansson" [new 1'20" uncut version]), video uploaded October 14, 2011, http://youtu.be/O_Lj58hsOO4. Confirming the ritual nature of the questions, in a May 24, 2012, Facebook discussion of the video, the entertainment journalist Kate Hahn wrote, "I confess, I have asked an actress, 'What part of your body do you love the most?'"

17. Chris Greenhough, "Scarlett Johansson's Dolce & Gabbana Ad Hits the Net [Video]," Inquisitr.com, October 24, 2011, http://www.inquisitr.com/153410/scarlett-johansson-dolce-gabbana-perfume-ad/#Wxh11ofMCbK44ZRs.99.

18. Emma Bazilian, "Dolce & Gabbana Scarlett Johansson's New Fragrance Spot Is Totally Ridiculous. So, Why Is It Sort of Wonderful?" AdWeek.com, October 21, 2011, http://www.adweek.com/news/advertising-branding /ad-day-dolce-gabbana-135986.

19. Geoff Boucher, "Morgan Spurlock's new Comic-Con documentary gives fans hope," LATimes.com, April 3, 2012, http://herocomplex.latimes.com/2012/04/03/morgan-spurlocks-new-comic-con-documentary-gives-fans-hope/.

20. Anthony Lane, "Double Lives," *New Yorker*, May 14, 2012, pp. 121–22, http://www.newyorker.com/arts/critics /cinema/2012/05/14/120514crci_cinema_lane#ixzz1w1zKpDVi. A. O. Scott, "Super Heroes, Super Battles, Super Egos," *New York Times*, May 3, 2012, http://www.nytimes.com/2012/05/04/movies/robert-downey-jr-in -the-avengers-directed-by-joss-whedon.html.

21. Johnnie L. Roberts, "The Rap of Luxury," *Newsweek*, September 1, 2002, http://www.thedailybeast.com

/newsweek/2002/09/01/the-rap-of-luxury.html. Jay Z, "Jay-Z on Cristal: 'Disrespect for the Culture of Hip-Hop,'" *Time*, November 18, 2010, http://www.time.com/time/arts/article/0,8599,2032217,00.html.

22. Zadie Smith, "The House That Hova Built," *T Magazine* (*New York Times*), September 6, 2012, p. 110, http://www.nytimes.com/2012/09/09/t-magazine/the-house-that-hova-built.html.

23. Bruce Upbin, "Jay Z, Buffett and Forbes on Success and Giving Back," *Forbes*, October 11, 2010, http://www.forbes.com/forbes/2010/1011/rich-list-10-omaha-warren-buffett-jay-z-steve-forbes-summit-interview_2.html.

24. Erich Follath, "Terror Is Glamour," *Der Spiegel*, August 28, 2006, http://www.spiegel.de/international/0,1518,433969,00.html.

25. Virginia Postrel, "Terror Is Glamour," *Deep Glamour*, May 2, 2011, http://www.deepglamour.net/deep_glamour/2011/05/terror-is-glamour-reposted.html.

26. Rosalind H. Williams, *Dream Worlds: Mass Consumption in Late Nineteenth-Century France* (Berkeley: University of California Press, 1982) pp. 103–106, 398. Except for a return to sumptuary laws, Williams's exact political program is vague. It consists mostly of yearnings for equality and "spiritual" rather than material goods.

27. Rosalind H. Williams, *Dream Worlds*, p. 176.

28. When the American Dream is elaborated into stories of struggle and triumph, turning the snapshot idea into narrative, it becomes romance.

INDEX

Page numbers followed by n and nn indicate notes. *Italicized* page numbers indicate illustrations and their captions and credits.

A

Achilles, martial glamour and, 145–47, *145*, 149

action heroines, and female glamour, 210

Adams, Abigail, 247n58

Addison, Joseph, 153, 154

African Americans

    actors, 62–63, 238n14

    automobiles and, 251n45

    Ebony and, 62

    Tuskegee Airmen, 25, *25*

airplane travel

    Jet Age glamour and, 193–99, *193*, *194*, *196*, *198*

    modernity and, 188–89, *210*

    see also aviator, as icon

akogare, 36

Air Jordan shoes, 58, 222

Alaïa shoes, 46

Albinus, Bernhard Siegfried, 90

Alexander, Sally, 61, 140

Alexander the Great, 101, 146–47, *146*, 245n15, 246n17

Allen, Woody, 111–12, 242n11

Amadas et Ydoine, 140

Amazing Adventures of Kavalier & Clay, The (Chabon), 51, 57, 237n1

Ambrosi, Alfredo Gauro, 26

American Cancer Society, 99

androgynous style, mystery and, 121, *121*

Antonelli, Paola, 102–3

Apple products

    effortlessness and, 83

    glamour of California and, 73

    wirelessness and, 103, 104

architecture, 18, 20, 71–72, *72*, 97, 122, 130, 133, 172. *See also* Shulman, Julius

Ardery, Lois, 36–37

Arens, Egmont, 182

Aristotle, 147

Arrian, 146

art deco, 122, 133, 172, *172*, 175–76, *176*, 182, *183*, *186*, *204*. *See also* streamlining

Astaire, Fred, 82–83, *82*

Atherton, Leigh, 215

Atlantic Monthly, 160, 168

automobiles, 2, *7*, 16, *19*, 45, *47*, 73, *73*, *78*, 167, *179*, *190*, 205
  escape and, 58
  Jet Age glamour and, 194
  modernity and, 182, 185–86, *185*, 251n45
autonomy, and glamour of standing out, 93–94
Avedon, Richard, 207
aviator, as icon, 24–27, *24*, *25*, *27*, *30*. *See also* airplane travel
Aviator, The (film), 27, *27*
Azim, Samihah, 73

B

Bacall, Lauren, *28*
Balbo, Italo, 26
Banner, Lois, 168
Bardot, Brigitte, 202
Basic Instinct (film), 29, *29*
Bassman, Lillian, 129, *129*
bathrooms, modernity and, *187*, 188
battle, glamour of. *See* martial glamour
"Beautiful People," 46–48, *48*, 125
  suntans and, 200, 202
  see also seductive female beauty
Beauvoir, Simone de, 97–98, 204
Beckert, Jens, 46
Bel Geddes, Norman, 183, 192
belonging
  desire for, 39–41, 94, 220
  to an elite, 37, 59
  see also fellowship
Benford, Gregory, 61, 177
Berendt, John, 129
Berger, John, 31–32, 39, 138
Berry, Halle, 62
Bibesco, Princess Elizabeth, 187
Binkley, Christina, 203

Bird, Deirdre, 203
Biswas-Diener, Robert, 106
Black Bourgeoisie (Frazier), 62
Blair, Lara (photographer), *213*
Blanchett, Cate, 124–25
Bloemker, Emily, 77
Bogart, Humphrey, *28*, 82
Bollywood, 37
Book of the Courtier (Castiglione), 162
Boswell, James, 152, 153, 154, 159, 160–61
Botticelli, Sandro, 90, *90*
Botton, Alain de, 15–16
Bourbon, Marie de, 49–50
Bourke-White, Margaret, *182*, 183–84, 250n39
Bowie, David, 121
Boy Life on the Prairie (Garland), 165
Brantley, Ben, 110
Brassaï, 119
Brazilian, Emma, 217
Brewer, John, 155
Brin, David, 122–23
British Vogue, 111
Brook, Daniel, 133, 245n10
Brown, Judith, 65
Brown, Tina, 50
Brown-Worsham, Sasha, 51
Bush, George W., 26
Bushnell, Candace, 121
Butow, David (photographer), *133*
Buttolph, Angela, 111
Butts, Cassandra, 17

C

Caldwell, Helen, 203
California, as icon, 71–74, *71*, *72*, *73*
California Calls You: The Art of Promoting the Golden State 1870 to 1940 (Kurutz and Kurutz), 71

California homes, "transfiguration" of, *73*, 87, *108*

Cameron, James, 93

Campbell, Colin, 44–46, 152

Campus, Eugène, 115

careers, glamour as influence on choice of, 7, 16, 67, 69

Cartner-Morley, Jess, 29

Case Study House No. 22 photograph, *108*, 130

Castiglione, Baldassare, 80, 162, 239n6, 248n2

Catch Me If You Can (film), 27

celebrities, 88, 99–100, 115, *151*, 217, 239n1. *See also* movie stars

celebrity, 6, 8, 59, 62, 64, 211, 220. *See also* fame

Chabon, Michael, 51, 57, 95, 237n1

Chancey, Jill R., 119, 243n31

Chanel, Coco, 200, 252n2

Chardin, Jean-Baptiste-Siméon, 91, *91*

charisma, distinguished from glamour, 116–19

Charlie (fragrance), 203, *203*, 252n2

Cheung, Maggie, *34*

Chicago, 26, 67, 150, 153, 159, *186*, 234n10

Chin, Walter (photographer), *210*

Christian Dior 2011 Spring Couture Collection, 58, *58*

circus performers, on horses, *164*, 165

Cleopatra, 120

Coen, Jessica, 87–88

Coker, Christopher, 146–47

Colacello, Bob, 66, 239n21

Collier's, 204

Comic-Con, 218

Conant, Howell, 85–86, *85*

condominiums, advertised with glamour, 14–15, *15*, 233n26. *See also* houses; real estate

Connery, Sean, 82

Conrad, Joseph, 10–11

Container Store, The, 214–15

convenience, modernity and, 187–89, *187*, *190*

convents, longing and, 38–39, *39*

Cornell, Solanah, 213–14, *213*

Corona beer, 93, 240n35

cosmetics, 7, 36, 85, 88, 110, 181, 250n29. *See also* makeover, as icon

cosmopolitan aura, 18, *18*

courtesans, 131, *131*, 138, *151*, 153, 159, 175

cowboys, 164–65, *164*, *165*, 248n8

Crawford, Grey (photographer), *6*, *45*

Crawford, Joan, 43, 49, 138, 175, *175*, 181, 182, 188, 237n5

Crowquill, Sara, 167

Cukor, George, *95*

Curran, Kevin, 40

D

Dargis, Manohla, 34

darkroom grace, 81–82, *81*, *82*, 85–90, *85*, *86*, *87*, *88*, *90*

Daston, Lorraine, 90

Daum, Meghan, 43

Davis, Benjamin O., *25*

"D.B. Blues" (song), 185–86

Dean, James, 18, 28

death
  charisma and, 118–19
  immortality and, 146, 149–50
  terrorism and, 220
  at young age, 24, 101

DeFanti, Mark, 203

DeJean, Joan, 123

DelVecchio, Marina, 51

Demarchelier, Patrick, 120

DeMille, Cecil B., 175, 188

DeMille, William, 175

Democracity, at New York World's Fair, 191

DePrince, Michaela, 3–4, *223*

Detroit, 215

Devil in the White City, The (Larson), 159

Diana, Princess of Wales, 50, *50*, 119, 243n31

DiBattista, Maria, 182

DiCaprio, Leonardo, 27, *27*

Dickstein, Morris, 173

Diehl, Kay and Digby, 85

Dietrich, Marlene, 115, 121, *121*, 131

Dinner at Eight (film), 184

Disney, 49, 195

"displaced meaning," 41–45, *44*, 48, 90, 144, 219

Doctorow, E. L., 192

Dolby, Thomas, 53

Dolce & Gabbana commercials, 217–18, 254n16

Doonan, Simon, 46–48, 125

Dos Equis beer commercials, 217

Dr. Faustus (Marlowe), 148, 150

Dr. Strangelove (film), 95

drag balls, 63–64

Drake, Alicia, 4, 68

Dream Worlds (Williams), 221

Dreiser, Theodore, 151–52, 154, 158–59, 160, 176

Duarte, Eva, 176

Duff-Gordon, Lady Lucy (Lucile), 156, 175, 247n51, 249n14

Duro Gloss coats, 204, *206*

E

Earhart, Amelia, 25, 33

Ebony magazine, 62, 222

Eddy, Art, 58

Edo, Japan, 150, 153, 155, 247n40

effortlessness, 79–80

eidolon, Helen of Troy as, 148

Eitner, Lorenz, 130, 244n2

Emerson, Ralph Waldo, 154

Endless Summer, The (film), 104, 195

entrepreneurship and startups, 73, 83, 104
  Shanghai and, 245n10

entropy, glamour's attempt to escape, 80–81, 98, 100

envy, Berger on glamour and, 31–32, 39

escape and transformation, *56*, 57–70, 58, *58*
  channeled into personal fulfillment, 67–70
  in Depression era, 171–74
  emotions and object of glamour, 57–60
  as heart of human culture, 60–61
  as hope and spark of real-world change, 61–65
  obscuring of difficulties, 69–70
  vulnerability and revelation, 66–67

Euripides, 148, 150

F

fame, 5, 63–64, 66, 141–42, *141*, 144, 146, 149–50, 211, 220. *See also* celebrity

family life, ideal of, 211–12, 253n4

fashion, 4, 34, 88–89, 91, 97–98, 100, 114–15, 140, 158, 173, 175, 178
  designers and, 22, 29, 68, 79, 106, 110, 156, 171, 209
  glamour misunderstood as, 7–8
  photographs, *2*, 5–6, 12, *20*, *58*, *64*, 89, *96*, *110*, 129, *129*, 133, *196*, 204–7, *210*
  runway shows, 29, 58, 109, 156, 175, 209
  transformation and, 38, 45–46, 58, 64

fascism, 25–26, 189–190, 234n10

fellowship, desire for, 39, 41, 59, 64, 94, 142, 152, 220. *See also* belonging

Feng Zikai, 132

Fergie (singer), 210–11, 216, 253n5

Ferrari, 73

Flaubert, Gustave, 98, 123, 152

Flight (film), 26–27

Flying Down to Rio (film), 188

Ford, Elizabeth A., 76

Ford, Robin, 103

Formichetti, Nicola, 29

Formula One racing, 84–85

Fortner, Adam, 89, 103

Fortune magazine, 172, 183
Foxx, Jamie, 62
Frankenstein (Shelley), 98–99
Frazier, E. Frank, 62
Friedman, Alice, 18, 252n79
Friedman, Thomas, 244n10
Frissell, Toni, 2, 5, 25, *25*, 212
furs, 20, *20*, 99, 131, *193*, 210, 215
Furman, Michael (photographer), *78*
Futurama, at World's Fair, 183, 191–93
future, modernity's glamour and, 178–186, *179*, *183*

G

Gable, Clark, 60, *175*
Galella, Ron, 86, *86*, 114
Galison, Peter, 90
Garbo, Greta, 22–23, 34, 100–101, *101*, 110
Gardner, Diane, 75
Garland, Hamlin, 165
Garnaut, Michelle, 133
Gay Divorcée, The (film), *82*, 212
Gehry, Frank, 122
General Motors. *See* Futurama, at World's Fair
Gervex, Henri, *151*
Gibson, Charles Dana, 141–42, *141*, 166, 174
Gibson Girl, as icon, 166–69, *166*, *167*, *169*
Gilman, Charlotte Perkins, 168–69
Gioventu fascista, 190
Givhan, Robin, 4, 79–80
"Glamorous" (song), 210–11, 216
glamour, *2*, 3–8, *5*, *6*, *7*
    familiarity, fragility, and loss of, 20–21
    as form of nonverbal rhetoric, 3–6, 10–11
    as illusion, 11–13
    as inspiration for life-changing action, 6–7, 46–48
    as interaction between object and audience, 12
    reality distortion aspect of, 21–23, *22*

revelation of emotional truths, 36–38, 221–22
    spelling of, 4, 249n6
    subjective nature of, 209–15
    subjective nature of, and similarity to humor, 17–20
    terrorism and, 220–21
    used as sales tool, 13–17
    utopian parody and wised-up glamour, 216–18
Glamour: A History (Gundle), 138, 245n3
Gleed, Edward C., *25*
Goldberg, Vicki, 183, 184
Goldberger, Paul, 130, 244n3
Golden State. *See* California, as icon
Goldman, William, 137
Goodbye, Shanghai (film), 176
Gordon, Mary, 38–39, 145
Gore, Al, 53
grace, 79–101
    autonomy and synchronization as types of, 93–95
    combination of detailed and ideal and, 90–92, *91*
    danger of disillusionment following real-world action, 95–98
    darkroom grace, 81–82, *81*, *82*, 85–90, *85*, *86*, *87*, *88*, *90*
    effortlessness and, 79–80
    horror and, 98–100
    theatrical grace, 81, 82–85, *82*, *83*
    timeless glamour and, 100–101
Graham, Billy, 118
Grant, Cary, *18*, 82, 178, 200
Green, Jonathan, 87
Greenhough, Chris, 217
Grey, Zane, 164
Griffith, Richard, 188
Guerero, Ed, 63
"Guerrillero Heroico" photograph, 86–87, *87*, 99, 241n42
Guevara, Che, 86–87, 99, 117
Gundlach, F. C. (photographer), *193*

Gundle, Stephen, 8, 138, 245n3
Gutner, Howard, 176

H

Hack, Shelley, 203, *203*, 252n2
Hall, David, 103–4
Hardworking Mother, The (Chardin), 91, *91*
Harlow, Jean, *81*, 85, *95*, 184
Harper's Bazaar, 6, 32, 173, 201, 204, 205, 207
Harrison, Helen A., 191
Haslam, Nicky, 29
Hathaway, Anne, *75*
Hazlitt, William, 80
Helen (Euripides), 148
Helen of Troy, 145, 147–150, *148*, 246nn24,30
Heller, Anne, 66
Heller, Sarah-Grace, 140
Heller, Steven, 190
Henry V (Shakespeare), 142–43, 144
Hepburn, Audrey, 39, *39*, 109, 128, *128*
Herodotus, 246n24
Herrera, Carolina, 110
Hibbett, Howard, 153, 156
Highwayman, The (Noyes), 162–63
Hilton, Paris, 8, 231n11
hip-hop, 32, 59, 219, *219*, 222
Hitler, Adolf, 190
Hollander, Anne, 89, 91
"Hollywood glamour," 4, *5*, 14, *18*, *22*, *28*, 33, 64, 81, *81*, *95*, 100, *101*, *113*, *121*, 171, *175*, *176*, 178, 209. *See also* Hurrell, George
Homer, 145–150, 245n15
horror, as flip side of glamour, 98–100
horseman, as icon, 162–65, *162*, *163*, *164*, *165*
Horst, Horst P., 64, *64*
hot-stone massages, 20, *216*
houses, glamour and, *6*, 42–43, *45*, 61, 72, *72*, 87, *108*, 151, 194, 235n25. *See also* condominiums;
real estate
Hughes, Bettany, 148, 149
Hume, David, 8
humor
audience and, 217–18
glamour's similarity to, 17–20
superheroes and, 106–7
Hurrell, George, *22*, 64, 81, *81*, 85, 86, 113, *113*, 114, 115–16, 120

I

I Spy (television program), 195
Ideal (Rand), 66
Iliad (Homer), 145–150, 245n15
In Praise of Shadows (Tanizaki), 122
In the Mood for Love (film), *34*
inarticulate longings, and what glamour does, 31–48
desire for significance, 38–41
displaced meaning and, 41–46
envy and, 31–32
idealization of romantic love, 35, 140
life-changing positive action and, 46–48
luxury and sex appeal and, 33–35
revelation of emotional truths, 36–38, 220–22
industrial design exhibition, 102–3, *102*
innovation and novelty, 22, 44, 181, 183, 187, 221, 222
interior design and furnishings, *6*, 7, 19, 42–43, *45*, 89, 103, *103*, 121, 160, 249n16, 252n79. *See also* art deco
International House of Pancakes, 196
internationalism, Jet Age glamour and, 195–96
intrigue, mystery and, 114–16
Iooss, Walter Jr. (photographer), *83*
Isocrates, 149
Italy, 20, 25–26
Ive, Jonathan, 83
"I've Got a Ford Movement in My Hips" (song), 186, 250n45

J

Jablonski, Nina G., 202
Jackson, Andrew, 118
James Bond character, 34, 84, 94, 195, 239n17
Jane Eyre (Brontë), 10, 12
Jay Z, 32, 109, 219, *219*
Jefferson, Blind Lemon, 185–86
Jeffreys, Joanna, 45–46
Jehan et Blonde, 140
Jezebel, antiretouching of photographs campaign of, 87–88
Joan of Arc, 118–19
Johansson, Scarlett, *208*, 209–10, 217
Johnson, John H., 62
Johnson, Michael, 172
Jolie, Angelina, *30*, 32–33, 42, 210, *211*, 212–13
Jones, Gerard, 107
Jordan, Dorothy, *22*
Jordan, John M., 190
Jordan, Michael, 58, *83*, 115
Joy, Susan, 203
Julia necklace, of Newsom, 122, *122*

K

kabuki "street knights," urban glamour and, 155–56
Kamali, Norma, 171, 178
Kanagaratnam, Tina, 132–33
Kaufmann House, in California, *72*
Kelly, Grace, *18*, 34, 82, 85–86, *85*
Kennedy, Jackie. *See* Onassis, Jacqueline Kennedy
Kennedy, John F., 16, 21, 101, 197
Knox, Bernard, 245n15
Koenig, Pierre, *108*, 130
Koestenbaum, Wayne, 114
Kohn, Robert, 191
Korda, Alberto, 86–87, *87*
Kron, Joan, 43, 182–83
K-Swiss, 74

Kuhn, Annette, 36, 187–88
Kurtz, Howard, 17
Kurutz, Gary F., 71
Kurutz, KD, 71

L

Ladies' Paradise, The (Zola), 157, 160, 247n63
Lady from Shanghai, The (film), 131, 244n1
Lady Gaga, 29, 84
Lagerfeld, Karl, 68–69
Lahr, John, 124
Lamarr, Hedy, 114
Lang, Fritz, 177
Lanval, 140
Lapidus, Morris, 252n79
laptop computers, at beach, 104
Larsen, Nella, 64–65, 159
Larson, Erik, 159
Launi, J. Christopher (photographer), *176*, *183*
Lauren, Ralph, 58, 111
Lawrence, D. H., 13, 39, 232n23
Leaming, Barbara, 113–14
"leaning boards," movie glamour and, *95*, 97
Leibovitz, Annie, *30*, *211*, 212
Lewis, Jim, 18
Li, Yiyun, 7
Life magazine, 87, 183, 193–94
life-changing, positive actions
    danger of disillusionment following, 95–98
    escape and transformation and, 61–65
    inspiration for, 6–7, 46–48
Lindbergh, Charles, 24, *24*
Lindsay, Jack, 148
Lingyu, Ruan, 176, 249n16
Lippi, Filippino, 143–44, *143*
lipstick, 79, 171, 180, 209. *See also* cosmetics
Loewy, Raymond, 102, *102*
Loh, Sandra Tsing, 195

Lombard, Carole, *113*, 178, 182

London & North Eastern Railway advertisement, 163, *163*

London, England, 15, 47, 118, 153–56, 161, 175

Loper, Jason, 253n4

Los Angeles, 72, *108*, 130. *See also* "Hollywood glamour"

Louis Vuitton advertisements, *211*, 212–13, 218

Louis-Dreyfus, Julia, 241n2

luxury, 4, 8, 21, 33–35, 38, 60, 157–61, 188, 219

M

MacArthur, Douglas, 109

Macdonald, Dwight, 183

Mad Men (television program), 29, 91–92, 116

Madam Bovary (Flaubert), 98, 123, 152

Mademoiselle, 75–76, 172

Madonna, 64

Madrigal, Alexis, 215

magazines, exposure to glamour and, 174–75, 249nn11,12

makeover, as icon, 75–77, *75*, 172

Manolo the Shoeblogger, 58

Marass, Reinfried (photographer), *19, 47, 123*

Marlowe, Christopher, 148, 150

marriage and divorce, 211–12

martial glamour

    illusions and subjective responses, *11*, 13–14, *13, 36*, 94, 99, 232n23

    masculine prowess and premodern glamour, 144, 145–47, *145, 146*, 149

    terrorism and, 220

    martyrdom, glamour of, 145

Mary Tyler Moore Show, The (television program), 67–68, *67*

masculine glamour, 13, 24, 28, 34, 144, 184–85, 162, 200

Matsunosuke, Nishiyama, 155

Mayer, Arthur, 188

McCain, John, 26

McCollum, Brian, 110

McCracken, Grant, 41–42, 194

McCullough, David, 248n58

McGinn, Colin, 177

McGregor, Richard, 244n10

McMains, Juliet, 43–44, 82

McQueen, Alexander, 121

McQueen, Steve, 109

Meagher, Robert Emmet, 147

Meikle, Jeffrey L., 191

Menin Road, The (Nash), 13

Menzel, Adolph von, 68, *68*

Metropolis (film), 177

Metropolitan condominium, Dallas, 14–15, *15*, 233n26

Meyer, Andrew, 240n35

Middleton, Kate, 51

Midnight in Paris (film), 39, 111–12, 242n11

military. *See* martial glamour

Miller, Michael B., 157

Mills, Simon, 29

mink coats. *See* furs

Mission Impossible (television program), 195

Mitchell, Deborah C., 76

Mizrahi, Isaac, *22*, 216

modeling and fashion shows, urban glamour and, 156

modern, use of term, 245n2

"modern, self-illusory hedonism," 44–46, *44*, 152

modern glamour, 171–199

    convenience and, *186*, 187–89, *187, 190*

    Depression-era escapism and longing, 171–74

    increase in audience size and, 174–78, 249nn1,12

    Jet Age and, 193–99, *193, 194, 196, 198*

    modernity and the future, 178–183, *179, 180*

    planning and control, 189–193, *190*

Modern Mechanix (magazine), 184

Modern Times (film), 184

Moleskine, *8*, 9, 37, 43

Monroe, Marilyn, 18, 177, 249–50n22

Moral, Jean, 204

"More Fashion Mileage per Dress" photograph, 129, *129*

Moss, Kate, 29, 50, 111, *114*, 121

movie stars, 4–5, 21, 27, 32–33, 36, 64, 70, 81, 93–94, 95, 98, 105, 109, 124, 163, 175–78, 200, 218. *See also* celebrities; "Hollywood glamour"

movies, exposure to glamour and, 175–78, *175*, *176*, 249–50n22, 252n79. *See also* "Hollywood glamour"

Moye, Todd, 25

Mr. and Mrs. Smith (film), 210

Mrs. Kennedy (Leaming), 113–14

Mu Shiying, 132

Mumford, Lewis, 190–91

Munkasci, Martin, 201, 205–7, *205*, 253n15

Mussolini, Benito, 25–26

Mustafa, Isaiah, 217

My Fair Lady (film), 77

mystery, 109–27

    charisma distinguished from glamour and, 116–19

    intrigue and, 114–16

    restraint and balance between the obvious and the hidden, 125–27, *126*

    shadow, sparkle, and complexity as forms of, 119–125, *121*, *122*

    as tool and essential element of glamour, 112–14

    translucence and, *111*, 112–13

N

Nash, Paul, 13

Negrin, Matt, 17

Neutra, Richard, 71, *72*

New York, 21, 43, 60, *61*, 105, *106*, 111, 129, 131, 138, 150, 153, 158, 172, *172*, 180, 187, *196*, 204–5, *205*, 222. *See also* World's Fair, New York

Newsom, Marc, 122, *122*

Newton, Helmut, 121

Nike. *See* Air Jordan shoes

North by Northwest (film), 80

Novalis, 110

Now, Voyager (film), 76

Noyes, Alfred, 162–63

nuns, as objects of glamour, 38–39, *39*

Nun's Story, The (film), 39, *39*

O

Obama, Barack, 16–17, *16*, 117, 233n33

O'Brien, Geoffrey, 106–7

Old Spice advertisements, 216–17

Olson, James S., 163–64

Onassis, Aristotle, 196, 197

Onassis, Jacqueline Kennedy, 34, 86, *86*, 109, 113–14, 196–98, 242n18, 252n78

Our Blushing Brides (film), 175

P

Palmer, Scott W., 26

Pan, Lynn, 132, 176, 180, 249n16

Pan American flight crew, profiled in *Life*, 193–94

Pantages Theater, *176*

Paris, France, 4, 20, 24–25, 37, 39, 45, 111–12, 119, 121, 123–24, 138, 150, 154–55, 157, 159, 172, 175, 193, 204, 245n2, 247n58

Paris Is Burning (documentary), 63–64

Parkinson, Norman, 12, *96*, *110*

perfume, 33, 121, 123, 131, 158, 193, 203, *203*, 209, 217–18

Peròn, Eva (Evita). *See* Duarte, Eva

Peròn, Juan, 176

Perry, Katy, *72*
Peter Pan (Barrie), 12
Peters, Charles, 197
Phillips, Barbara, 75–76
Picture of Dorian Gray, The (Wilde), 114
Pindar, 146
Pitt, Brad, 210
planning and control, modernity and, 189–193, *190*
Plato, 148
Plato's Atlantis collection, of A. McQueen, 121
Possessed (film), 59–60, 138, *175*, 181, 237n5
pothos, Alexander the Great and, 146, *146*, 245n17
Poudre de Début, 181
Powell, Adam Clayton Jr., *61*
"power to the weak," 155–56
Prater, Andreas, 125–26
premodern glamour, 137–50
    discontent and imagined transformation as precondition for, 139–140
    images of projection as precondition for, 141–44, *143*
    masculine martial prowess and, 142–43, 144, 145–47, *145*, *146*, 149
    religious devotion and, 143–45
    seductive female beauty and, 144, 147–150, *148*
    urban glamour and phase change from, 150–51
    use of term "modern," 245n2
Presley, Elvis, 18, 202, 240n21
Pretty Woman (film), 76
princess, as icon, 49–51, *49*, *50*, 236n10
Princess Bride, The (film), 137, 138
Princess Diaries, The (film), *75*
Princess Diaries, The (novel), 76–77
projection, as precondition for glamour, 141–44, *141*, *143*
promenades, urban glamour and, 158
Prpich, Marc (photographer), *103*
Pulp Fiction (film), 29
push-button control, glamour of, 94, 194, 219
Pygmalion (Shaw), 77

Q
qipao, *131*, 132
Queen Christina (film), 22–23, 60
Quicksand (Larsen), 64–65, 159
Quinn, Marc, 121

R
Radner, Gilda, 99–100
Rainey, Buck, 165, 248n8
Rand, Ayn, 28–29, 66–67
Rascoe, Burton, 164
real estate
    displaced meaning and, 42–43
    glamour used to sell, 14–15, 71
    see also condominiums; houses
Rector Square, New York, 15, *15*, 232n26
Red Pony, The (Steinbeck), 162
religion
    glamour and longing, 38–39, *39*
    premodern glamour and religious devotion, 143–45, *143*
    ritual and rejection of "glamour of evil," 22
    terrorism and, 220
Republic, The (Plato), 148
Revlon, 203, *203*, 229
Roberts, Randy, 163–64
Rockwell, Norman, *32*
Rodriguez, Diego, 80
Roehm, Carolyne, 112
Rogers, Ginger, 21, 82–83, *82*
Roiphe, Katie, 29
Rokeby Venus (Velázquez), 125–27, *126*, 244n52
romance
    American Dream and, 255n27
    glamour contrasted, 83–84
    idealization of romantic love, 35, 50, 140
Roosevelt, Eleanor, 117, 197, 252n78
Roosevelt, Franklin, 28, 182

Roosevelt, Franklin, Jr., 196

Rospigliosi, Princess Giambattista, 50

Rothstein, Arthur, *185*, 186

Roy, Rachel, 79

Rugel, Mike, 251n45

Rushdie, Salman, 220

S

Saint, The (television program), 195

Sample, Jessica (photographer), 17

Santos, Sandra, 52

Sappho, 149

Saturday Night Live routine, 99–100

Sawyer, Miranda, 124

science

    glamour of, 6–7

    grace and, 90–91

    modernity and, 179–81

Scott, Hazel, *61*

Scott, Sir Walter, 10

science fiction, 61, 177, 182. See also *Star Trek*

Second Sex, The (Beauvoir), 97–98, 204

secret agents, Jet Age glamour and, 195

seductive female beauty, premodern glamour and, 144, 147–150, *148*

Seed of Ambition (Gibson), *141*

Segrave, Kerry, 252n2

Seigle, Cecelia Sagawa, 247n40

Sewell, Dennita, 173

shadow, mystery and, 119–120, 122–25

Shakespeare, William, 120, 142–43, 144

Shall We Dansu? (film), 130

Shanghai, 131–33, *131, 133*, 175–76, 180, 244n10, 249n16

Shanghai Express (film), 131, *131*

Shanks, Andrew, 145

Shaw, George Bernard, 77

Shearer, Norma, 176

shoes, 4, 12, 45–46, 58, 61, 74, 79, 82, 91, *91*, 100, 113, 132, 180, 222

shopping, urban glamour and, 156–58, *157, 161*

Shulman, Julius, *59, 72*, 87, *88*, 100–101, *108*, 130, 172, 244n3

silence, mystery and, 110–11, 114

Silver, Cameron, 81

Sister Carrie (Dreiser), 151–52, 154, 158–59, *160*, 176

Skwire, Sarah, 89–90

Smith, Adam, 69–70, 138

Smith, Zadie, 219

smoking, 28–29, *28, 29*, 99

Snow, Edward, 126

Som, Peter, 115

Soviet propaganda posters, aviation and, 26

space program, glamour of, 21

sparkle, mystery and, 120–21, 122–25

spectacle, glamour's difference from, 84–85

Spencer, Lady Diana. *See* Diana, Princess of Wales

Spider-Man character, 106, *106*

Spoto, Donald, 115, 121, *121*

sprezzatura, and glamour's grace, 80, 82, 84, 89–90, 93, 162, 210

Spurlock, Morgan, 218

Stacey, Jackie, 177

Stalin, Josef, 190

Star Trek, 40–41, *40*, 42, 94, 125, 195

Steele, Valerie, 33, 35, 114–15

Steinbeck, John, 162

Stewart, Andrew, 246n17

still photographs, from movies, 177–78, 249–50n22

Stock, Kyle, 214

Stone, Sharon, 29, *29*

streamlining, *78*, 172, *179*, 182–83, *183*

striding woman, as icon, 203–7, *203, 204, 205, 206, 210*

Sullivan, Rebecca, 38

sunglasses, mystery and, 109–10, 112, *114*, 172, *210*, 241–42nn1,2

Sunset Blvd. (film), 100

suntan, as icon, 200–202, *200, 201*

superheroes
  as icons, 105–7, *105*, *106*, *107*, 172
  princess icon and, 51, 236n10
Superman (film), 81
Superman character, 105, *105*, 106, 107, *107*, 185, 250n43
synchronization, and glamour of fitting in, 93, 94–95

T

Tafelrunde, Die (Menzel), 68, *68*
Tanizaki, Jun'ichirō, 122
Taylor, Chris, 104
Taylor, Elizabeth, *48*
Taylor, Larissa Juliet, 118–19
Taylor, Phil, 115
Teague, Walter Dorwin, 189–190
technology, glamour and, 14, 26, 28, 52–54, 61, 73, 75, 103–5, 172, 179, 181, 183, 187, 190, 192, 250n41
terrorism, glamour and, 220–21
Tesla (automobiles), 14, 74
theater, urban glamour and, 154–56, *155*
theatrical grace, 81, 82–85, *82*, *83*
Theory of Moral Sentiments, The (Smith), 69–70
Thoren, Virginia (photographer), *20*
Thorp, Margaret Farrand, 33, 35, 62–63, 93
Thorpe, Vanessa, 79
Thurman, Uma, 29
Tindell, Kip, 215
To Catch a Thief (film), *18*
To Have and Have Not (film), 28
Top Hat (film), 188–89
"transfiguration," in photographs, 87, *88*, *108*
transistor radios, 103–4
translucence, 20, *111*, 112–13, 153
travel, sold with glamour, 15–16, *17*
"truth to desire," 91

"truth to nature," 90
Tuan, Yi-Fu, 60–61
Turpin, Dick (highwayman), 163, *163*
Tuskegee Airmen, 25, *25*
Twilight Zone episode, 77

U

Une soirée au Pré-Catelan (Gervex), *151*
United Nations headquarters, 196, *196*
urban glamour, 150–54, *151*
  disillusionment and, 158–161, 247n58
  fashion and shopping and, 156–58, *157*
  theater and, 154–56, *155*
USSR in Construction magazine, 190
"utopian parody" and glamour, 106–7, 216–18
utopias as forms of glamour, 98

V

Valèry, Paul, 152
Velázquez, Diego, 125–27, *126*, 244n52
Verdon, Timothy, 143
vintage clothing, 213–14, *213*
Virgin Warrior: The Life and Death of Joan of Arc, The (Taylor), 118–19
Vision of Saint Bernard, The (Lippi), 143–44, *143*
Vogue (magazine), 173, 201
"Vogue" (song), 64
von Furstenberg, Diane, 106
voyeurism, contrast to glamour, 128–29
Vreeland, Diana, 173, *205*

W

Wai, Tony Leung Chiu, *34*
Warhol, Andy, 66, 86, 107, *107*, 114, 240n21

Washington, Denzel, 62, 238n14
Waxman, Sharon, 93
Wayne, John, 163–64
Webb, Sidney and Beatrice, 189–190
Weber, Eugen, 155
Weightman, John, 201–2
Weiner, Matthew, 116
Weiss, Pierre, 24–25
Welles, Orson, 131
Westinghouse, *186*, 191, 250n41
Whalen, Grover, 191
What Not to Wear (television program), 77
Wilde, Oscar, 114
Wilder, Billy, 110
Wilkie, Jane, 21
Willard, Emma, 247n58
Williams, Rosalind H., 157–58, 221
Wilson, Cleo, 186, 251n45
Wilson, Darryl (interior designer), *6, 45*
Wilson, Elizabeth, 28
wind turbines, as icon, 52–54, *53*
"Windblown Jackie" photo, 86, *86*, 114
window, as icon, *108*, 128–130, *128*, *129*, 244nn2,3
Winfrey, Oprah, 67–68
Wintour, Anna, 109
wirelessness, as icon, 102–4, *102*, *103*
wised-up glamour, 216–18

Wohl, Robert, 24, 26
Wolf, Naomi, 32–33, 42, 147
Women, The (film), 187, 188
Wong, Anna May, 131, *131*
Working Girl (film), 76
workplace, desire for meritocratic, 40–41
World's Fair (Doctorow), 192
World's Fair, New York, *170*, 171, 172, 183, 190–93
Wroe, Martin, 7–8

X

X, Y, and Zee (film), *48*

Y

Yeats, W. B., 246n30
Youth (Conrad), 10–11

Z

Zimmerman, Tom, 178
Zola, Émile, 157, 160, 247n63

ABOUT THE AUTHOR

Virginia Postrel is a columnist for *Bloomberg View* and has been a regular contributor to *The Wall Street Journal, The Atlantic, The New York Times,* and *Forbes.* Formerly the editor of *Reason* magazine, she is the author of *The Substance of Style* and *The Future and Its Enemies.* She lives in Los Angeles. Visit her website at vpostrel.com.